KV-050-975

Literature of the 1950s

The Edinburgh History of Twentieth-Century Literature in Britain
General Editor: Randall Stevenson

Published:

Vol. 6 *Literature of the 1950s: Good, Brave Causes*
        Alice Ferrebe
Vol. 9 *Literature of the 1980s: After the Watershed*
        Joseph Brooker

Forthcoming:

Vol. 1 *Literature of the 1900s: The Great Edwardian Emporium*
        Jonathan Wild
Vol. 2 *Literature of the 1910s: Making and Breaking*
        Laura Marcus
Vol. 3 *Literature of the 1920s: Writers among the Ruins*
        Chris Baldick
Vol. 4 *Literature of the 1930s: Border Country*
        Rod Mengham
Vol. 5 *Literature of the 1940s: War, Postwar and 'Peace'*
        Gill Plain
Vol. 7 *Literature of the 1960s*: *Some Happenings*
        Rick Rylance
Vol. 8 *Literature of the 1970s: Things Fall Apart, Again*
        Simon Malpas
Vol. 10 *Literature of the 1990s*: *The Major Phase*
        Sean Mathews

Literature of the 1950s

Good, Brave Causes

Alice Ferrebe

EDINBURGH
University Press

For James, for making everything better

Edinburgh University Press Ltd
22 George Square, Edinburgh

www.euppublishing.com

Typeset in 10.5/13 Adobe Sabon
by Servis Filmsetting Ltd, Stockport, Cheshire, and
printed and bound in Great Britain by
CPI Group (UK) Ltd, Croydon, CR0 4YY

A CIP record for this book is available from the British Library

ISBN 978 0 7486 2771 4 (hardback)
ISBN 978 0 7486 3166 7 (webready PDF)
ISBN 978 0 7486 5531 1 (epub)
ISBN 978 0 7486 5530 4 (Amazon ebook)

Contents

Acknowledgements   vii

Illustrations   viii

General Editor's Preface   x

 1 Introduction: 'All this, and Everest too!'   1

I. The Voice of the Young

 2 The Metaphorical Utility of Youth   19
 3 First Writing: 1950s Fiction   39
 4 Angering Aunt Edna: 1950s Theatre   54

II. The Less Deceived

 5 Women, Children and Home   77
 6 The Sensation of Movement: Poetry in the 1950s   94
 7 Evil Men: Literature and Homosexuality   112

III. Postwar Settlements

 8 Coming Home: The Literature of Immigration   127
 9 Organic Communities: Regional Literature   145
10 The Scholarship Class: Literature and Social Mobility   163

IV. Other Uses of Literacy

11 Criticism Under Scrutiny   185
12 The Dedicated Man: Publishing, Media and Reviewing   192

13 Where East Meets West: Literature, the New Left and the
    Cold War   207
14 Conclusions: Decade Talk   223

Works Cited   226
Index   245

Acknowledgements

A huge thank you to Series Editor Randall Stevenson and Edinburgh University Press's Jackie Jones, for endless patience and cheer through my recently (rather overly) eventful life. Many thanks too to my colleagues at Liverpool John Moores University, for all their support, their suggestions, and a sabbatical in the course of writing this book.

My thanks to all those who allowed and aided me to use the images included here. I am grateful to Faber & Faber Ltd. for their permission to quote from so many of the key writers considered in this study.

Love and thanks to my family, for helping me through it all. And last but most, my love to Douglas, for making finishing nigh on impossible but even more worthwhile.

Illustrations

Figure 1   The Coronation of Queen Elizabeth II, 1953:
           scrambling for a view. Courtesy of Horst Koch.   4
Figure 2   Official guide to London's South Bank site, Festival of
           Britain, 1951. The heraldic star with Britannia's head
           was the Festival's ubiquitous logo. Photo: Alice Ferrebe. 13
Figure 3   South Bank Exhibition, London, Festival of Britain,
           1951. Courtesy of Horst Koch.   14
Figure 4   The first production of Ann Jellicoe's *The Sport of My
           Mad Mother*, at the Royal Court Theatre, London,
           on 25 February 1958. All of the cast appear in this
           scene, with Greta, played by Wendy Craig (centre),
           brandishing a gun. Courtesy of Mary Evans Picture
           Library/Roger Mayne.   27
Figure 5   Keith Waterhouse's contribution to the 'Beanstalk
           Generation' series, *Daily Mirror*, 15 September 1958.
           © Mirrorpix.   34
Figure 6   US Vice President Richard Nixon and Soviet Premier
           Nikita Khrushchev argue in a mock-up kitchen at
           the American National Exhibition in Moscow, 1959.
           Courtesy of the Press Association.   78
Figure 7   The 1950s housewife of the advertisers' dreams.
           Courtesy of the Advertising Archive.   79
Figure 8   West Indian immigrants arriving at Victoria Station,
           London, 1956. Courtesy of Haywood Magee / Hulton
           Archives / Getty Images.   131
Figure 9   The 1960 Pan paperback edition of Alan Sillitoe's
           novel *Saturday Night and Sunday Morning*, with
           its tie-in to the film of the same year. Courtesy of
           Palgrave Macmillan.   199

Figure 10   Graham Sutherland, 'Standing Forms II' (1952).
Sutherland's work was exhibited at the Festival of
Britain, but its mutant humanoid forms suggested a
much darker approach to the legacies and realities of
nation. Courtesy of the Graham Sutherland Estate/
Tate Images.   213

General Editor's Preface

One decade is covered by each of the ten volumes in the *Edinburgh History of Twentieth-Century Literature in Britain* series. Individual volumes may argue that theirs is *the* decade of the century. The series as a whole considers the twentieth century as *the* century of decades. All eras are changeful, but the pace of change has itself steadily accelerated throughout modern history, and never more swiftly than under the pressures of political crises and of new technologies and media in the twentieth century. Ideas, styles and outlooks came into dominance, and were then displaced, in more and more rapid succession, characterising ever-briefer periods, sharply separated from predecessors and successors.

Time-spans appropriate to literary or cultural history shortened correspondingly, and on account of not only change itself, but also its effect on perception. How distant, for example, that tranquil, sunlit, Edwardian decade already seemed, even ten years later, after the First World War, at the start of the Twenties. And how essential, too, to the self-definition of that restless decade, and later ones, that the years from 1900 to 1910 *should* seem tranquil and sunlit – as a convenient contrast, not necessarily based altogether firmly on ways the Edwardians may have thought of themselves. A need to secure the past in this way – for clarity and definition, in changeful times – encourages views of earlier decades almost as a hand of familiar, well-differentiated cards, dealt out, one by one, by prior times to the present one. These no longer offer pictures of kings and queens; King Edward VII, at the start of the century, and, briefly, George V, were the last monarchs to give their names to an age. Instead, the cards are marked all the more clearly by image and number, as 'the Twenties', 'the Thirties', 'the Forties' and so on. History itself often seems to join in the game, with so many epochal dates – 1918, 1929, 1939, 1968, 1979, 1989, 2001 – approximating to the end of decades.

By the end of the century, decade divisions had at any rate become a firmly established habit, even a necessity, for cultural understanding and analysis. They offer much virtue, and opportunity, to the present series. Concentration within firm temporal boundaries gives each volume further scope to range geographically – to explore the literary production and shifting mutual influences of nations, regions and minorities within a less and less surely 'United' Kingdom. Attention to film and broadcasting allows individual volumes to reflect another key aspect of literature's rapidly changing role throughout the century. In its early years, writing and publishing remained almost the only media for imagination but, by the end of the century, they were hugely challenged by competition from new technologies. Changes of this kind were accompanied by wide divergences in ways that the literary was conceived and studied. The shifting emphases of literary criticism, at various stages of the century, are also considered throughout the series.

Above all, though, the series' decade divisions promote productive, sharply focused literary-historical analysis. Ezra Pound's celebrated definition of literature, as 'news that stays news', helps emphasise the advantages. It is easy enough to work with the second part of Pound's equation: to explain the continuing appeal of literature from the past. It is harder to recover what made a literary work news in the first place, or, crucially for literary history, to establish just how it related *to* the news of its day – how it digested, evaded or sublimated pressures bearing on its author's imagination at the time. Concentration on individual decades facilitates attention to this 'news'. It helps recover the brisk, chill feel of the day, as authors stepped out to buy their morning newspapers – the immediate, actual climate of their time, as well as the tranquillity, sunshine or cloud ascribed to it in later commentary. Close concentration on individual periods can also renew attention to writing that did *not* stay news – to works that, significantly, pleased contemporary readers and reviewers, and might repay careful re-reading by later critics.

In its later years, critics of twentieth-century writing sometimes concentrated more on characterising than periodising the literature they surveyed, usually under the rubrics of modernism or postmodernism. No decade is an island, entire of itself, and volumes in the series consider, where appropriate, broader movements and influences of this kind, stretching beyond their allotted periods. Each volume also offers, of course, a fuller picture of the writing of its times than necessarily selective studies of modernism and postmodernism can provide. Modernism and postmodernism, moreover, are thoroughly specific in their historical origins and development, and the nature of each can be usefully illumined by the close, detailed analyses the series provides. Changeful, tumultuous and challenging, history in the twentieth century perhaps pressed harder and more variously on literary imagination than ever before, requiring a literary history correspondingly meticulous, flexible and multifocal. This is what the *Edinburgh History of Twentieth-Century Literature in Britain* provides.

The idea for the series originated with Jackie Jones in Edinburgh University Press, and all involved are grateful for her vision and guidance, and for support from the Press, at every stage throughout.

Randall Stevenson
University of Edinburgh

Chapter One

Introduction: 'All this, and Everest too!'

'What will the 1950s be called by future generations?' asked John Montgomery in 1965. 'Fabulous, frantic or frenetic? The Age of Recovery, the Atomic Age, the Age of Affluence, the Age of Hire Purchase, or the Age of Self-Service shops?' (11). None of his upbeat options quite matches the symbolism later ascribed to the central decade of the twentieth century in Britain's sense of itself. In popular memory, the 1950s function most frequently as a kind of nostalgic shorthand for national consensus, contentment and order (as mobilised by Margaret Thatcher, for example). Alternatively, they are cited as a negative example of the cultural stasis caused by affluence and apathy (by Left-leaners since). John Osborne looked back disparagingly on 'the fat and spineless fifties' as early as 1959 (Osborne 1994: 191). In a review for the *Spectator* in 1956, Kingsley Amis suggested that 'There is some ground for equanimity in looking forward to an era of minor literature' (69). His choice of wording cannot be coincidental in a year of dramatic literary and cultural debate centred upon his peer Osborne. Rather than looking forward in equanimity, Osborne chose another stance for his hero Jimmy Porter in the play *Look Back in Anger*, yet it is Jimmy's announcement that 'There aren't any good, brave causes left' that is most often quoted to encapsulate the decade's reputation for 'minor literature'.

Jimmy's notorious speech is a curious one. It is to be delivered, the stage directions state, '*In his familiar, semi-serious mood*' (Osborne 1989: 84). Within its own social and cultural context, Jimmy's humour hinges upon the irony of his statement. All sorts of good, brave causes were presenting themselves to the committed young man or woman: the Bomb, the Cold War, and the ethical negotiation of Britain's newly disintegrating Empire and its ingrained racial attitudes, to name but three. Looking back at the relatively settled domestic party politics of the 1950s has, however, tended to obscure the conflicts and change at work within the experiences of those living, and writing, through them. Though voting was a duty, over-emotional engagement in a mass Politics was understandably anathema to a society with so recent an experience of Fascism (and truths about the death camps still coming to harsh light). Yet the decade (and its literature) is crucial within British history for its emergent and increasingly complicated politics of difference: age, class, gender, racial, sexual, regional and national. This study spans a movement from a homogenous British identity (or its necessary non-contestation during the Second World War) towards far more complex understandings of identity, genealogy and belonging. In so doing, it contests the myths of the 1950s (the Movement and the Angry Young Men amongst them) while exploring and extending their symbolic resonance. Canonical texts (if such there are in such an under-valued period of writing) are read alongside more unfamiliar works to provide this fresh perspective.

All decades are, of course, transitional in a prosaic sense, but the 1950s was a time of genuine sea-change in British experience and atti-tudes. Literature, as a potential site of multiple voices and competing values, provides a uniquely privileged space to explore such transition. In *The Angry Decade* (1958) Kenneth Allsop offered the first sustained attempt at characterising the decade's cultural life. Rather than one of settled consensus, he professed the age to be:

> The most profuse and *excited* – in a neurotic and superficial sense – I have lived through. So many oddly arraigned forces are at work. There is, first, that enormous umbrella fact at which hardly anyone does more than sneak an occasional glance, and which it seems almost too brash to mention, the H-bomb . . . Leaving that out of it (and somehow we all seem to do exactly that) the central spectacle of our broken-winded economy is the extraordinar-ily stubborn effort that has been made in the Fifties to revive the meaningful panoply of the pre-war Establishment. We are, let it not be forgotten – and there seem to be few reasons to remember it – the New Elizabethans. (Allsop 1958: 31)

The New Elizabethans

In the 1945 General Election the Labour Party had won its first abso-lute majority in British history. Allsop attributes this to 'a spasm of nervous idealism' amidst an exhausted but relieved electorate (19), but to the party's slightly bemused politicians it seemed, at last, a mandate to legislate Socialism. To this end, they set about organising a British (Welfare) State underpinned by a triumphant ideal of collective respon-sibility, a British New Deal to end all avoidable injustices, inequalities and privations. This was informed by William Beveridge's vision of social insurance, Aneurin Bevan's of a National Health Service, and R. A. Butler's of (tripartite) universal education. Yet, as always in British politics, the mandate was not that simple. Voters had moved against the Conservative Party in memory of their inter-war record and in a new spirit of communality fostered by war-time conditions, and returned the Labour Party, again with a slim lead, in 1950. In 1951, Ernest Bevin relinquished his post as Foreign Secretary and almost immediately died, and Bevan and Harold Wilson resigned over the proposal to make a charge for National Health spectacles and teeth. Then Guy Burgess and Donald Maclean disappeared, and when Labour called another election in the hope of increasing their majority, the voters moved, moderately, back to the Right, responding to some skilful Conservative manipulation of their dissatisfaction with continued rationing and austerity following the outbreak in 1950 of the Korean War. Yet in recognition of the slender margin of their success, the Conservative government and its successors throughout the decade largely preserved the changes Labour had made, on a scale and in a direction that would never have been countenanced by the pre-war party. Britain, it seemed, had a new vision of itself, and of its role both at home and abroad.

The nation's new place in the world involved a complex renegotiation of allegiance: to Empire (or rather to a Commonwealth of relinquished imperial holdings), to the United States, long-standing ally and reconstruction bankroller, and to the states of Europe, both friends and ex-foes. Winston Churchill, Prime Minister again from 1951 to 1955, saw Britain at the triangulation point of Atlantic, Commonwealth and European relations; historian Peter Hennessy entitles a chapter dealing with this vision 'The Geometric Conceit' (Hennessy 2006: 178–311). Such enduring conceit was to lead Britain to withhold her signature from the 1957 Treaty of Rome, foundation document of the European Economic Community, later the European Union (EU). Churchill's grandiose vision of the nation found symbolic expression in the 1953 coronation of the twenty-five-year-old Elizabeth II (or I in Scotland), in an event he firmly hoped would trump the Labour-conceived celebration of the Festival of Britain in 1951. For sheer pomp, it undoubtedly did, and also for national participation, if television viewers constitute such. No less than 56 per cent (20.4 million people) of the adult population watched at least half an hour of the service, although the mass purchasing of the necessary sets had been sparked by coverage of King George VI's funeral the year before (Kynaston 2009: 299). Historian A. L. Rowse has suggested, with understated appreciation, 'It was a good thing, in the bleak and gloomy post war years, to have a radiant

Figure 1   The Coronation of Queen Elizabeth II, 1953: scrambling for a view.

young woman coming to the throne, against the background of elderly bald-pated generals and presidents on the international scene' (Ollard 2003: 426). On the day itself, 2 June, the *Daily Express* was less stinting in its joy, running with the headline 'All this, and Everest too!', as the news of New Zealander Edmund Hillary and Nepali–Indian Tenzing Norgay's reaching the summit was claimed as the achievement of the British expedition of which they were part.

Conekin, Mort and Waters have called the Coronation 'a Janus-faced event. Orchestrated against a background of elaborate tradition, it simultaneously strove to project a vision of the future' (Conekin et al. 1999: 1). Nigel Dennis's national satire *Cards of Identity* (1955) parodies what it presents as the new emptiness of such ceremony in the spoof conference paper 'The Case of the Co-Warden of the Badgeries', detailing a civic role now reduced from duties to protect real badgers to an annual charade:

> The stuffed, or token, boar-badger is inserted into a symbolic den and then eased out with your official emblem, a symbolical gold spade. In this way, there is no need actually to disturb any living badger: the whole ceremony is performed quietly in London . . . Once you start letting your symbolic acts overlap, each tends to deny the significance of the other. That's what's wrong with the Health Service, of course. One minute people think they're getting it free, the next that it is an intolerable burden. They don't know if they're giving or receiving. (Dennis 1999: 152)

Cynicism over the gap between rhetoric and reality widened as the decade went on. Lofty public commitments to welcome any and all of Her Majesty's overseas citizens were brought down to earth in 1958 by the first serious racial violence experienced within the United Kingdom. This occurred in Nottingham and in Notting Hill in west London, wreaked in the main by a majority of white rioters upon West Indian victims. (In fact, for all the ensuing moral panic over colonial migration, and despite its unprecedented levels during the 1950s, the net flow of migration was an outward one for a quarter-century after the war, as Britons continued to seek different lives in Australia and New Zealand in particular – Clarke 1996: 321.) By 3 February 1960, Prime Minister Harold Macmillan was using very different rhetoric regarding the colonies; the 'Winds of Change' speech in Cape Town abandoned high-souled imperialism for a straight-talking statement of the inevitability of African independence. Yet the moment that Britain's real, reduced standing in the world came home was, of course, on the decade's hinge, 1956, on the undeviating shores of the Suez Canal. The leader 'Escapers' Club' in *The Times* on 27 August tried to maintain an imperious bullishness towards Britain's escalating confrontation with Egypt's President Nasser.

> Doubtless [it ran] it is good to have a flourishing tourist trade, to win Test Matches, and be regaled by photographs of MISS DIANA DORS being pushed into a swimming pool. But nations do not live by circuses alone. The people, in their silent way, know this better than the critics. They still want Britain great. (9)

Other papers, and people, were more clear-sighted, and the eventual botched invasion in October, grubbily hatched up in secret with France and Israel and immediately and angrily rebuked by the Americans, proved them right. In *A State of England* (1963), journalist Anthony Hartley summed up the consequences of the nation's deeply improper national behaviour:

> The dream of moral leadership, with which we had fleetingly comforted ourselves, ended on the banks of the Sweetwater Canal, and we were left with the disagreeable thought that we too were not immune from outbursts of chauvinism or from politicians who judged the world by pre-1914 standards. (Hartley 1963: 20)

Anthony Eden, who had been Prime Minister since Churchill's retirement in 1955, was destroyed by the crisis, and resigned the following year when the pain of both political humiliation and an earlier botched bile duct operation became unbearable. The Suez invasion coincided closely with the brutal suppression of a popular uprising in Hungary by Soviet troops, also in October. And 1956 was also a year of upheaval in the enduring literary narrative for the decade, for as John Russell Taylor claimed in *Anger and After* (1962): 'The whole picture of writing in this country has undergone a transformation in the last six years or so, and the event which marks "then" off decisively from "now" is the first performance of *Look Back in Anger* on 8 May' (Taylor 1968: 11).

For those on the Left, the years after the war had seen a shift from upholding the Russian Revolution as inspiration, to a Russia and a Russian leader (Stalin died in 1953) as emblems of aggressive totalitarianism. More generally, the Cold War – a climate rather than a series of events – comprised both the obvious opposition of the military and diplomatic forces of East and West, and a psychological state of fear and suspicion. This sat uneasily with the easement brought by Welfare and affluence. Britain never reached the violent paranoia of McCarthyism in the US, where, as Richard Freeland has put it, the idea was beginning to take hold 'that any gain by communist forces, in whatever country, however remote and tiny, was a direct threat to American interests, to be opposed by the full force of American power' (Freeland 1972: 3). Yet the Cold War – the hostilities short of armed conflict that had existed between the USSR and the Western powers since the Second World War – had important effects during the 1950s, and on more than just a national mood. The 1957 Defence White Paper announced the end of National Service in 1962, and slashed substantial numbers of enlisted personnel, judging them largely useless in the face of the new military threat: the H-bomb. Britain's only possibility of keeping the peace, her powers now believed, was by maintaining a nuclear arsenal, and this they duly assembled.

Writing in 2009, historian Dominic Sandbrook noted that:

> The years from 1950 to 1959 work incredibly badly as a single narrative unit with a uniform cultural flavour. They begin with an exhausted Labour government, rationing at its peak, cities scarred by bomb damage and maps of the world still marked by swathes of pink. They end, however, with Supermac in Downing Street, Cliff Richard in the charts, televisions in the living rooms and union flags coming down across the globe. (Sandbrook 2009: 9)

The 1950s are irreparably split, genuinely transitional. The decade saw Britain shift from austerity to affluence (average earnings doubled between 1951 and 1961) and begin the process of deindustrialisation, moving from a reliance on manufacturing to a service-based economy (Marwick 1990: 114). There was a marked increase in wealth, but also a notable change in the use of that wealth. It was increasingly invested in consumer durables, themselves definitively finite and non-productive. These fundamental economic changes were wreathed in a new rhetoric of meritocratic classlessness, itself underpinned by the expansion of education that entitled all children to free secondary schooling. The particularly gifted academically were given scholarships to attend grammar schools, or even, on occasion, the private (fee-paying) schools, previously reserved exclusively for offspring of the upper echelons of the class hierarchy. Hennessy claims that it is 'difficult, perhaps, to appreciate the degree to which education before the late 1940s added to and even reinforced social inequality', but also notes how the new system maintained its own class hierarchy: 'by 1950 around 60% of the children of professionals and businessmen could expect to win grammar-school places compared with 10% of children from the 75% of the population who lived in working-class homes' (Hennessy 2006: 69, 76). The decade also saw a concomitant and significant increase in university education; the proportion of the 18 to 21 age group becoming full-time university students increased from 3.2 per cent in 1954 to 4.2 per cent by 1959 (77). More than three-quarters of students in England were receiving State grants, but they were mostly middle-class, and the majority of university entrants still came from direct-grant and public schools (Floud 1956: 122–3). Despite, or rather perhaps because of, this middle-class nature of the beneficiaries of this increased opportunity, Macmillan was able to announce with some resonance after victory at the polls in 1959 that 'this election has shown that the class war is obsolete' ('Conservative's Hat Trick' 1959: 6).

Affluence and Admass

Stefan Collini has recently identified a key concern from the mid-1950s onwards to be 'the embourgeoisment of the working class', which 'was not just a matter of increased prosperity, but a fundamental change of identity. It involved losing or repudiating the old self-consciously separate, fatalistic, working-class stance, and adopting broadly middle-class attitudes and ways of life' (Collini 2008: 271–2). This was certainly the case for numerous writers included in this study, many of them recipients of the scholarships and grants noted above. Yet we can set against this another anxiety that the working class was being beaten down, not up, under the barrage of a newly invigorated media and the burgeoning advertising industry, or 'Admass', to use J. B. Priestley's coinage (Priestley and Hawkes 1955). As Francis Williams ominously put it: 'Only rarely are these instruments of mass communication used to aid the international interchange of ideas and modes of thought. Their main purpose is to promote a commercialism which is concerned primarily to shape people to the pattern most conforming to the requirements of salesmanship' (Williams 1962: 35).

One new medium in particular served as portal for this perceivedly malign influence. In *The Fifties*, Peter Lewis suggests of (then exclusively BBC) television in 1950 that:

> The programmes themselves were . . . of a blandness that is hard to recapture. There was about them a strong flavour of evening classes run by a well-endowed Workers' Educational Institute: cookery lessons from the TV chef . . . ; gardening hints from the TV gardener . . . ; 'Music for You' – nothing too demandingly classical – conducted in a black tie and introduced with an ingratiating few words . . . ; and, for nursery tea, the dancing, or rather jerking, puppets, Muffin the Mule, Andy Pandy and the Flowerpot Men. (Lewis 1978: 208)

ITV began in 1954 (with that 'Independent' a euphemism for 'commercial'), initiating too a perceivable relaxation in the tone and style of BBC broadcasting. On 22 September 1955 at 8.12 pm, the first television commercial, for Gibbs SR toothpaste, ran in Britain, and was described in *The Manchester Guardian* by Bernard Levin the next day: 'A charming young lady brushed her teeth, while a charming young gentleman told us the benefits of the toothpaste with which she was doing it' (Levin 1955: 6). Frank Mort notes how

> The arrival of commercial television in Britain . . . brought to a head an already heated debate among public intellectuals about the creeping effects of consumerism. Television advertising was viewed by its opponents as ushering in an American culture of mediocrity, hidden costs and sinister methods of persuasion. (Mort 1999: 65)

Worst of all, it ushered them into a space crucial to the ideology of Britain's project of reconstruction: the home. The sheer number of official reports and commissions focused upon the family in the immediate postwar period is evidence of its psychological and institutional importance during the 1950s. 'Kitchen sink' realism, a term taken from art criticism of the 1940s describing John Bratby's work (an example of which graces the cover of this volume), was the definitive genre of the decade's writing. It was not just the relationships between its inhabitants, but the structure and site of the home itself that were causing anxiety. The 1957 Rent Act, initiated by Enoch Powell as part of a crusade to free up the market, allowed rents to rise steeply, and aggravated an already fraught situation of the overcrowding of immigrants in many English inner cities. Unscrupulous landlords like the notorious Peter Rachman created a series of almost instant ghettoes exploiting their new black tenants, which had implications beyond the violence of 1958. Andrew Marr claims 'The Brixton, Tottenham and Toxteth riots of the eighties can be traced back, in part, to the moral effects of early young-male migration and the housing practices of the fifties' (Marr 2009: 197). In other neighbourhoods, the situation was slightly more genteel, but none the less a long way from the gleaming domesticity of Admass. At the close of George Scott's 1956 autobiography, *Time and Place*, he confesses:

> The last few paragraphs of this book have been written on the top of the washing machine in the kitchen. A man and wife, their two children, plus two visiting relations, into a three-roomed flat will not go. There is no space remaining for the man to do his writing except in the kitchen where his head becomes swathed in damp nappies and the Ideal Boiler gives off sickening fumes. (Scott 1956: 220)

The Double Voice

Scott's insertion of his immediate situation into wider cultural discussions of the time is instructive of an emerging style of writing and thought during the decade. We have noted the dominance of realism in the literary legacy of the 1950s; David Lodge has defined the realist mode as 'the representation of experience in a manner which approximates closely to descriptions of similar experience in non-literary texts of the same culture' (Lodge 1977: 25). In *Success Stories: Literature and the Media in England, 1950–1959* (1988) Harry Ritchie rails against the tendency in 1950s literary criticism, and in criticism of 1950s writing since, to view literature as straightforwardly sociological, an unmediated record not just of the experience of the times, but also of the author's experience encapsulated in the protagonist. He argues that:

> Correlations between literary works and the society in which they are written and first read are surely more subtle and complex than this. Straightforward connections can certainly be traced in the fifties, but they concern social developments which affected literature directly – the relaxation of the obscenity laws, for example, or the importance of radio (especially the Third Programme) and then television [and, we might add, cinema] in advertising new writing. (Ritchie 1988: 210)

Yet there is no denying that an important impulse in 1950s literature is a sociological, even anthropological one, giving voice to members of society who are traditionally grossly under-represented: the teenager, for example, or the homosexual, or the immigrant. Rather than adopting the traditional position of detached observer, the key non-fictional text of the decade, Richard Hoggart's study of the working-class culture of his home, Hunslet, called *The Uses of Literacy* (1957), draws frequent attention to its own 'first-personness'. Himself a well-educated scholarship boy, Hoggart's emotional responses to the return to his roots are recorded in a profoundly literary way before being reasoned into wider cultural observations. Together with Raymond Williams's *Culture and Society: 1780–1950* (1958), which independently adopts a similar methodology, Hoggart's book is the foundation of our contemporary discipline of Cultural Studies, and an important influence on the consolidation of its contemporary, the New Left.

What is at stake in both literary and sociological writing of the 1950s is a fundamental debate over the best way to record experience. Despite a (justified) reputation for a broad cultural suspicion of experimental writing, realism – its methods and philosophies – is equally under debate during the decade. David Jones wrote in the preface to his long and strikingly modernist poem *The Anathemata* (1952) that 'It might not be a bad idea to remind ourselves here that the attitude of the artist is necessarily empirical rather than speculative. "Art is a virtue of the practical intelligence." All "artistic" problems are, as such, practical problems' (Jones 1952: 18). This faith in empiricism, and a muted revival of A. J. Ayer's 1936 tract *Language, Truth and Logic*, the bible of Logical Positivism, is particularly legible in the poetry of that much-debated grouping, 'the Movement', discussed in Chapter 6. It stands in an instructive opposition to the validation placed on authentic, often non-intellectual, feeling by Hoggart, Williams and numerous literary writers. Indeed, the self-contradicting, double-voiced quality of much 1950s writing, Hoggart's included, is explored in this study as the definitive symptom of a transitional decade, and polyvalent literature upheld as a particularly privileged site of this dual perspective.

A fairly recent interpretive turn in studies of the 1950s has been towards the decade's characterisation as the 'beginning of postmodernism'. 'The problem of personal identity,' wrote Nigel Dennis in 1958, 'the question: who am I? seems to arise only when there is an absence of established religion, of absolutely fixed points' (Dennis 1958: 43). English newspapers told a different story: 'Religion Ousts Marxism at Oxford' blared the *Sunday Times* in 1956, claiming '51% of men and 63% of women at Oxford regularly practise their religion' (10). Yet this sense of a disintegration in the surety of selfhood (along with the possibility of its realistic representation) is important in the literature we will go on to consider here. For agnostics and atheists, French existentialism, or a British interpretation of it, provided another approach to personal identity, Colin Wilson's self-styled 'religious existentialism' still another (Wilson 1956). The alleged lack of good, brave causes has been found akin to the sense of the 'end of history', or at least of a meaningful means of connecting with history. As John Brannigan sees it, this 'is the constitutive anxiety of the postwar generation, which Jimmy Porter was supposed to represent, a past with which they can find no sense of belonging or identification, a present that is vacuous and futile without meaningful connections to the past' (Brannigan 2003: 43). Such a sense is aggravated by the realisation of all culture as textual. During the 1950s, American anthropologist Clifford Geertz was undertaking fieldwork in South-East Asia. One of the resultant essays, 'Deep Play: Notes on the Balinese Cockfight', maintained that all art forms render:

> ordinary everyday experience comprehensible by presenting it in terms of acts and objects which have had their practical consequences removed and been reduced . . . to a level of sheer appearance, where the meaning can be more powerfully articulated and more exactly perceived. (Geertz 1973: 443)

Geertz's surname has become adjectival to indicate a particularly densely descriptive method of recording experience; *The Uses of Literacy* is a prime exemplar of Geertzian, or 'thick' description. A sense of the reduction of real life to its surfaces, aggravated by the sheen put on those surfaces by Admass, is important to 1950s thinking, deprived as it was of the rhetoric of freedom and play that will come in later postmodernist theorisation. This, perhaps, explains the decade's most favoured master-metaphor for the individual confronted by these new conditions – that of theatre. From (Lucky) Jim Dixon's repertoire of face pulling (Amis 1954) to Stephen Potter's funny / serious games of 'Upmanship' (Potter 1952), everyone in the 1950s, it seems, is acting a role. Little wonder, then, that it was a play, *Look Back in Anger*, that came to dominate the decade's literary historiography.

Don't Make Fun of the Fair

This first chapter will end with a trip to the 1951 Festival of Britain. This was intended as a (slightly belated) way of marking the century's mid-point, as well as the centenary of the Great Exhibition. It was also a celebration: of victory (though 'war-like achievements' were strictly excluded from display), of the beginning of recovery, and, of course, of Britain itself – 'a sort of national prestige advertisement' (Frayn 1963: 32). Gerald Barry, the Festival's Director General, famously suggested it would be 'A Tonic to the Nation', but, unlike the Coronation two years later, it was a deliberately modest pick-me-up, 'conceived in austerity and shaped by expediency' (334). At the end of the 1951 retrospective film *Brief City*, over shots of the lights of the Houses of Parliament and a dark, swirling Thames, *Observer* journalist Patrick O'Donovan states with a certain maudlin pride, 'At a time when nations were becoming assertive and more intolerant, here was a national exhibition that avoided these emotions, and tried to stay rational.'

It is Saturday, 8 September 1951, 10.12 a.m., and, in true British style, you're in a lengthy queue. The South Bank Exhibition doesn't open for another eighteen minutes. In your hand is your ticket, bought in advance for five shillings, and a copy of the site's official guidebook, priced 2s 6d. Both are emblazoned with the official logo, a heraldic star with Britannia's head looking, appropriately enough under the current government, to the left. Just after 10.30, you push through the turnstile and almost immediately there's 'a surprise, a sudden sense of space and leisured gaiety'. There's no soot, no smoke – everything is gleaming white, or blazing 'with bright nursery colours'. You've seen photographs of the new New Towns, of course, but you've never before *been* anywhere like this: it's so clean, so open, so *modern*. You start to wander, ignoring the signposts (their lettering scrupulously chosen by the Festival's Typography Panel) for now. Cheerful music plays on the loudspeakers. Different spaces and levels seem to flow together, 'like rooms opening one out of the other', and different views continually present themselves: of fountains, Richard Huw's ingenious water mobile, the sparkling river and the 'great stone drop curtain of familiar buildings' on the North Bank. There's the Royal Festival Hall (a malign critic has likened it to a giant chicken coop), Barbara Hepworth's unfamiliarly voluptuous sculptures, an ungainly and spiky radar grill atop an old brick tower, more fountains, cafés . . . There are two shapes in particular you've looked forward to seeing in this 'gigantic toy shop for adults' – the futuristic scallop shell of the Dome of Discovery, its hinged struts freeing it to sway gently in the breeze coming off the Thames, and the Skylon sculpture, conceived 'simply to hang upright in the air, and astonish'.

Eight and a half million people visited the South Bank Exhibition, with 158,365 coming on Saturday, 22 September alone, its busiest day (Montgomery 1965: 31). Few in the nation would have avoided experiencing the Festival on some level: at one of the rather ramshackle sequence of events across the nation, or even just in glimpsing its somewhat Gallic-looking logo in newspapers, or on the BBC's vast array of related programming. The Festival's inclusivity was debatable. Despite the more traditional (that is, working-class) fairground of the Battersea Pleasure Gardens down the river (entrance only 2s 6d, Far Tottering

Figure 2   Official guide to London's South Bank site, Festival of Britain, 1951. The heraldic star with Britannia's head was the Festival's ubiquitous logo.

Railway a favourite ride), Michael Frayn rightly identified that it was 'Middle-class Britain that was being fêted', land of what he called 'the Herbivores, or gentle ruminants, who look out from the lush pastures which are their natural station in life with eyes full of sorrow for less fortunate creatures, guiltily conscious of their advantages, though not

Figure 3   South Bank Exhibition, London, Festival of Britain, 1951.

usually ceasing to eat the grass' (Frayn 1963: 320). The Festival had its detractors – many of them, in fact, although they became fewer, or more muted, once the event began. Noël Coward, himself for a time on the Festival Council, wrote a song for the 1951 Lyric Revue, 'Don't Make Fun of the Fair':

> Take a nip from your brandy flask,
> Scream and caper and shout,
> Don't give anyone time to ask
> What the Hell it's about. (322)

Frayn casts Coward as a 'Carnivore', part of a rapacious ex-elite increasingly disgruntled at the shape the (Welfare) State had recently taken. Yet the symbolism of the Festival could be confusing, with the South Bank site a case in point. The modernist architecture had all that spindly futurism of Sputnik, which was to begin the Space Age proper on its launch in 1957, and the exhibits championed Britain's grip on the latest scientific developments – the Dome of Discovery featured a large mural of atomic science, all in those jolly primary colours. However, as Hewison puts it, 'The modernist architecture was a lightweight framework for yet another exploration of Deep England' (Hewison 1995: 59). Brian Aldiss called the South Bank 'a monument to the future' (Banham and Hillier 1976: 176), encapsulating its Janus-faced nature.

By the juxtaposition of exhibits within the Dome, nuclear science, it was suggested, was somehow sparked by the native curiosity of Sir Francis Drake, and in the Lion and Unicorn Pavilion the modern nation was rooted firmly in the soil, conjured by Edward Bawden's 'Country Life' mural. This was the future with a profoundly traditional structure – Humphrey Jennings's 1950 public information / promotional film *Family Portrait* cast the Festival as 'a kind of family reunion' – and much of the new British design showcased was focused upon the home, indicating it as the decade's privileged site of scientific advance (and economic recovery).

'For centuries,' intones Michael Goodliffe over Jennings's images of wharves and fields, 'the family has mixed poetry and prose together.' Literature played a crucial role in the Festival, in its packed programme of amateur productions and poetry readings across the country, and in the Lion and Unicorn Pavilion, built to celebrate the inimitable British character, with all its glories and whimsicalities. Laurie Lee had been selected to caption the pavilion's exhibit, and behind gigantic figures made of straw in the corn dolly technique by Fred Mizen of Great Bardfield, he placed the words, 'We are the Lion and the Unicorn, twin symbols of the Briton's character. As a Lion I give him solidity and strength. With the Unicorn he lets himself go' (Russell and Goodden 1976: 97). Realism and abandon: though it is the former pole that exerts the greater influence on writing during the 1950s, it is by no means an unfettered attraction. Catherine Jolivette reads in the Festival 'an account of the legacy of the British Isles articulated by means of a narrative that was teleological, inward-looking and peculiarly retrospective' (Jolivette 2009: 18). That account might have striven for a teleological empiricism of narrative, but the pavilion, for one, did not cooperate. Its final hurrah, a life-sized tableau of Tenniel's Alice going through the Looking Glass, itself confused the building's designers, Russell and Gooden: 'Alas, memory finds no answer to the question: why was Alice there at all?' (Russell and Goodden 1976: 99). She was there, of course, as evidence of whimsy (the Festival's promotional films reference Lewis Carroll and Edward Lear as often as they do Shakespeare), and as a link to a Golden Age – of childhood, and of the Great Exhibition, which had none of the financial, political or ethical constraints of 1951. At the planning stage, Director General Gerald Barry had resolved the Executive Committee's determination that 'One mistake we should *not* make, we should not fall into the error of supposing we were going to produce anything conclusive. In this skeptical age, the glorious assurance of the mid-Victorians would find no echo' (quoted Frayn 1963: 324). The Lion and the Unicorn themselves were made of straw so that they might slowly decompose as the show went on, and the South Bank's 'Brief City' itself was dismantled and demolished at the Festival's close, leaving behind nothing but a concert hall. No conclusion was reached; past, present and future, the nation was still up for debate.

I.

The Voice of the Young

Chapter Two

The Metaphorical Utility of Youth

Kenneth Tynan's declamatory review of John Osborne's *Look Back in Anger*, published in the *Observer* in 1956, was emblazoned with a heading as bold as the article's spirited rhetoric: 'The Voice of the Young' (Tynan 1956: 11). This title comprised a dual claim: Tynan's, that Jimmy Porter was a long-awaited authentic spokesman of 1950s youth, and his editor's, that Tynan was the same. These terms – 'the young', 'youth' – were already heavily freighted in the cultural symbolism of the decade. This section will examine youth as a nexus for aspiration and anxiety during the 1950s; a topic of extensive political debate, intense social scientific investigation, and frequent, fraught literary representation. John Davis has noted the 'metaphorical utility' within British culture of the category of youth 'in the ongoing project of the general and particular making sense of what was (and is) a seemingly rapidly and fundamentally changing social order' (Davis 1990: 86). During the 1950s, youth is utilised to symbolise the new, to celebrate, or more frequently, to fret over, perceivedly unprecedented experiences of affluence, consumerism, pervasive media and advertising industries, sexual freedom, immigration and Americanisation (with the latter equated in the public mind with mass culture). Apparently assuming the innate ability of adults to deal with these new forces, precocity is a key cultural issue: how old is old enough to respond to these influences safely? How might a young person best be aided to cope with new demands to be 'a mass reader, a mass viewer and listener, a mass motorist and purchaser of gadgets' (Fyvel 1963: 230)? The Albemarle Report, one of two controversial reports on education to issue from the decade, expressed a presiding perception of young people as unusually susceptible to the forces of the new: 'Adolescents are the litmus paper of society. Subject to continuous and considerable mental, emotional and physical changes, as yet unregulated by the formal demands in the daily life of the breadwinner or housewife, adolescents are unusually exposed to social change' (Ministry of Education 1960: 29).

Yet this 'metaphorical utility' of youth, in Davis's phrase, was also exercised culturally to explore the influence of the Old, and events of the past – of the War, the Bomb, the Welfare State, the state of industry and the education system, for example. Symbolic of both positive potential and potential problems, the representation of the young and their behaviour was a site of anxiety about national reconstruction and redefinition in the society of the 1950s. Erik H. Erikson's 1950 study *Childhood and Society* became a key sociological text, as it established the theoretical understanding of adolescence as characterised by a 'quest for identity' and a 'role moratorium', still the presiding narrative defining this life-stage in Western culture. It is impossible not to see a correlation between this sense of (active) quest and (static, shell-shocked) reassessment as indicative of the wider atmosphere of Britain during the decade as it endured a succession of overlapping aftermaths – postwar, post-Suez and (partially) post-imperial. Though responsibility and reaction to all of these powerful currents of social change were, of course, experienced across the age-range, it was young people or, rather, the spectacle created of them as cultural 'go-betweens', that formed a focus for anxiety. As Musgrove was to point out in the 1964 study *Youth and the Social Order*, 'the contemporary social order and adult social attitudes are based, if not upon hypocrisy, on gigantic myths concerning the needs and nature of the young' (Musgrove 1964: 157).

Significantly, Leo Colston, who at the age of twelve is the emotional centre of L. P. Hartley's 1953 novel *The Go-Between*, does not know the meaning of the word 'myth'. Staying for the summer of 1900 with Marcus Maudsley, a much wealthier classmate, and sweating heavily in an overly formal Norfolk jacket, he invents a story that his 'summer clothes' have been accidentally left at home. Marian, Marcus's elder sister, buys Leo an outfit, and prompts him gently: '"Those clothes you had at home were a myth, weren't they?" she said. "A myth?" I echoed. "I mean you didn't really have them?" I nodded, happy to have been found out, delighting in the shared secret' (Hartley 1961: 46). In fact, Leo's school life is febrile with myth and superstitious ritual. He is fascinated by the zodiac, replacing his real name, Lionel (rejected as 'rather a *fancy* name', 44), with his birth sign, Leo; and his diary contains a blood-penned curse upon schoolmates Jenkins and Strode, who almost immediately slip and fall from the institution's roof. For Leo, the mythic is both powerfully occult, and as innocuous or 'made up' as the summer clothes story – the retrospective narrator remarks wryly of 'the traditional terms of schoolboy experience; so fantastic in some ways, so matter of fact in others' (18). Such anxious and ambiguous thinking characterises the treatment of the state of adolescence more generally. The narrator says of his twelve-year-old self that 'I wanted to think of myself as a man' (10), and his Edwardian, middle-class, fatherless upbringing has encouraged this. Leo is clad by his mother in constrictive, miniature versions of a lower middle-class fantasy of adult life at Brandham Hall. To the adults who live there he is used as a messenger, charged with sexual and social information without the experience to understand the messages with which he is burdened. Marian and Lord Trimingham, her war-hero suitor, Leo tells us, 'thought of me in terms of another person' (231); he is a means of access only, a go-between.

Trimingham's experience of the Boer War has left him with a scar that 'pulled the eye down, exposing a tract of glistening red under-lid, and the mouth up' (61), the stiff upper lip of a stricken aristocracy. Standing in a love rivalry with this peer of the realm is Ted Burgess, a farmer, who is, in Leo's potently astrological imagination, an ebullient Water-Carrier to the Viscount's desiccated Archer. Ted, the narrator tells us, 'was like a schoolboy, angry one moment, good humoured the next' (221); a coach-man remarks to Leo that 'Mr Burgess is a bit of a lad' (93). Ted, then, provides an authentic model of exuberant and unpredictable youth, continually presented outside and about his rural business, or in disarmingly intimate domestic (and deliberately feminine) scenes, making tea or tending to Leo's scrapes with 'carbolic' (81). After Ted has told him that one of his horses is pregnant because she has been 'spooning', Leo pursues the line of inquiry to the point that Ted admits that marrying someone without spooning them first 'wouldn't be natural': 'For him the word "natural" seemed to be conclusive. I had never thought of it as justifying anything' (117). Eventually betrayed by Leo and discovered 'spooning' with Marian, Ted shoots himself.

Ted's 'natural' youth, then, is destroyed by the class-ridden, death-dealing, ruling powers of England at the beginning of the twentieth century – the same powers that never allow Leo's adolescence to begin; or, perhaps, that never allow it to end. Young Leo's experiences are narrated by his older self in 1952, having returned to Brandham to find it 'had changed with all the changes of fifty years – the most changeful half century in history' (269). The past, the novel's renowned opening line has it, is 'a foreign country: they do things differently there' (7). Yet the narrative's setting is profoundly English, and its concerns recognisably contemporary to its publication. They comprise the identity of a nation caught between 'a ruined past and a menacing future' (174), riddled with uncertainties over class and gender status, and the position and potential of youth. After Ted's suicide, faced with that binary choice of mysticism or mundanity, the fantastic or the matter-of-fact, Leo Colston chose 'the life of facts' rather than 'the facts of life' (265), and as a result is rendered unable to forge an intimate adult relationship, his development arrested.

William Golding's 1954 novel *Lord of the Flies* confronts its own schoolboys with similar options, encapsulated in the podgy and bespectacled Piggy's mundane common sense, and the esoteric and nurturing Simon's rather febrile mysticism. Golding adds another alternative, however, in Jack Merridew's brutal irrationality. Leader of the choir, the red-haired Jack establishes himself at the forefront of the group of hunters, stalking the island for meat, and soon turns rogue, rejecting the authority of the mild and serious Ralph. Like Hartley with Leo, Golding positions his protagonists on the very brink of boyhood, just before 'the age of overt sex' (Golding 1996: 255). Ralph is described as 'old enough, twelve years and a few months, to have lost the prominent tummy of childhood; and not yet old enough for adolescence to have made him awkward'. Debate continues today as to the source of the evil into which the boys' behaviour descends, culminating in the deaths of Piggy and Simon. Despite a description of Ralph which notes 'a mildness about his mouth and eyes that proclaimed no devil' (15), the boys have been read as proof of the original sin of children, or of the secular and more mitigating circumstances of the atavism of human nature. Claire Rosenfield's influential Freudian analysis, for example, suggests that 'we might make the analogy to the childhood of races and compare the child to the primitive' (Rosenfield 1999: 3). Other arguments uphold the novel's suggestion that it is not primitivism but civilisation that corrupts, with the dead parachutist dropped on to the island to remind us that the boys' conflicts take place upon a larger canvas of global atomic war.

Against these understandings of *Lord of the Flies* as universal fable we can set an appreciation of the novel's social, cultural and national particularity. Ian McEwan has noted how, 'as far as I was concerned, Golding's island was a thinly disguised boarding school' (McEwan 1986: 158), and Harold Bloom claimed that 'the regression to savagery that marks *Lord of the Flies* is a peculiarly British scholastic phenomenon, and not a universal allegory of moral depravity' (Bloom 1999: 2). The island experience is not culturally neutral, but tropical with the influences of the boys' upbringings in school, at home and at play. The Lord of the Flies, Simon's hallucination prompted by a severed pig's head swarming with flies, berates him with the voice of a disapproving teacher; in 'Fable', Golding registers the irony that the novel's set-text status in schools has ensured 'that I should be treated for the rest of my days as a schoolmaster' (Golding 1996: 271). The colonial codes of decency and diplomacy of R. M. Ballantyne's classic Victorian children's novel *The Coral Island* (1857) meld with the unfettered heroic freedom of contemporary American comics:

> Jack was on his feet.
> 'We'll have rules!' he cried excitedly. 'Lots of rules! Then when anyone breaks 'em –'
> 'Whee-oh!'
> 'Wacco!'
> 'Bong!'
> 'Doink!' (44)

Unsupervised and pubescent, the central characters are prey to both their atavistic impulses and their learned cultural responses. *Lord of the Flies* can therefore convincingly be read as an account of a violent and compressed period of adolescence: the competing meanings and morals that critics have found within it as symptomatic of a presiding cultural anxiety surrounding the figure of the adolescent boy and the metaphorical work he is asked to do in the literature of the 1950s. Is he inherently evil or culturally corrupted? Is violent youth a new or ancient phenomenon? Is the teenager one of 'them' or part of 'us'?

A Revolution in Our Schools

'The most vital Report ever written on education is out today,' announced the front page of the *Daily Mirror* on Friday, 11 December 1959. 'It calls for A REVOLUTION IN OUR SCHOOLS.' Next to this headline, the symbol of an easel blackboard with '15–18' chalked upon it indicated the group of children that formed the focus of the Crowther Report. At the time this was an age-range outside compulsory schooling, but which was being increasingly emphasised as a distinct and vital period of personal and existential development. The report suggests that 'The adolescent needs help to see where he stands, but it must be given with discretion and restraint. He does not want to be "told" but he wants a guide, and a guide who will be honest in not over-stating a case' (Ministry of Education 1959: 114).

During the 1950s a number of literary works featured a protagonist directly involved in defining himself (without exception, the teacher-hero of these 1950s 'school books' is male) as a suitable guide for adolescents. In their study of the genre, Mathieson and Whiteside have distinguished between what they call 'common room novels', set in grammar schools and concerned with relationships with other members of staff rather than the blue-serged mass of pupils (W. R. Loader's 1957 *Through a Dark Wood*, for example), and representations of the Secondary Modern school (Mathieson and Whiteside 1971: 284). This latter emergent and hybrid sub-genre includes E. R. Braithwaite's *To Sir With Love* (1959), Michael Croft's *Spare the Rod* (1954) and John Townsend's *The Young Devils* (1958). Its defining features are as follows: a biographical origin that fuels some patchy polemic but is disguised with fictional names and allegorical 'slum' locations; a focus on the relationship of the protagonist with his pupils rather than with other staff; a pronounced tone of conflict; the progressive degradation of a romanticised image of young people; and a dedication to representing the deprived and debilitating nature of a working class and the increasingly commercialised environment of its children. The necessary preparation for teaching in a 'slum school' is vigorously debated. The war experience of ex-servicemen, containing as it does a mixture of both discipline and horror, is prized above new-fangled courses in Child Psychology or what the narrator of *The Young Devils* calls 'trick-cyclist stuff' from the 'Pemberton Emergency Teachers' Training College' (Townsend 1958: 32). A Damoclean cane hangs over the increasingly desperate measures of once-idealistic teachers to control their charges in these books, until the point at which, as for John Sanders in *Spare the Rod*, the personal failure signified by exercising corporal punishment 'was better than the martyrdom of patient suffering' (Croft 1954: 157). Savagery, these books set out to prove, breeds savagery, and colonial imagery is repeatedly used to signify the primitive nature of the working-class pupils' deprived existences to a middle-class readership. At Cuthbert-Hargreave Secondary Modern, across a bereft playground in the shadow of 'a large gas-holder like a squat grey buddha' (Townsend 1958: 10), 'a sound like natives chanting' (65) comes faintly to the ears of John Townsend; caught in the pupils' rush for their bus, he finds 'their shouts, cries and mob histrionics falling on my ears like the babble of tongues in a foreign market-place' (61).

Ann Jellicoe's 1958 play *The Sport of My Mad Mother* dramatises precisely this incomprehensibility and exoticism of working-class youth, its title and epigraph quotations from what she calls a 'Hindu Hymn': 'All creation is the sport of my mad mother Kali' (Jellicoe 1964: 3). In the 1964 Preface to a new version of the play, Jellicoe claimed 'it has taken me some years to understand that the play is based upon myth and uses ritual. Myth is the bodying forth in images and stories of our deepest fears and conflicts. *The Sport of My Mad Mother* is concerned with fear and rage at being rejected from the womb or tribe' (5). This brings to mind Rosenfield's influential Freudian interpretation of that other 1950s tale of youth's totems and taboos, *Lord of the Flies*, in which she suggests how:

> We might make the analogy to the childhood of races and compare the child to the primitive. Denied the sustaining and repressing authority of parents, church, and state, they form a new culture the development of which reflects that of the genuine primitive society, evolving its gods and demons (its myths), its rituals and taboos (its social norms). (Rosenfield 1999: 3)

Both Jellicoe and Rosenfield ostensibly treat young people as the 'barbarians within' society, yet as much of the dramatic experience of *The Sport of My Mad Mother* is of alienation and confusion as it is of communal identification. Its characters serve to activate in their audience the current anxieties about teenagers that inform documents as disparate as tabloid newspapers and governmental White Papers: youth violence, flick knives, consumerism, easy allegiances (in both sex and friendship), pounding 'jungle' music.

The play presents a disparate group of folk-devil delinquents whose mode of communication is frequently reduced to rhythmic patterns of syllables and weirdly repeated phrases. Fak ('about 18 years old', the cast-list gnomically informs us; Jellicoe 1964: 9) is proud of the photos of his gang in the press: 'Bottles and razors all down the Commercial road just as the flicks were coming out' (43). When he mistakenly thinks he has killed Dean, the 'young American' (9), his ecstasy is expressed in an orgy of acquisitiveness:

> Not bad. Not bad eh? . . . Killer! . . . Killer! . . . Oh! I'm gonna get a whistle sleeker than this and longer . . . new darins – narrow, narrow and dark . . . and a new shirt . . . Oh! White! With French cuffs. And a new tie – and I'll knot it broad . . . I'm gonna get a cigarette-holder, thick and stubby. Bamboo with a gold band. (28)

Patty is described as '*17 years old, a pretty little cockney girl with a lot of make-up round her eyes. She is looking at a home permanent wave outfit*' (13). Novelist and journalist Keith Waterhouse began his sensational contribution to a 1959 series entitled 'The Beanstalk Generation' in the *Daily Mirror* with a similar apprehension of perms and make-up as signifiers of how British children had changed for the worse:

PORTRAIT OF A GIRL: A natural blonde with blue eyes, a fair skin, a slim figure. She wears light powder, a pale lipstick and natural nail varnish.

There are five dresses in her wardrobe, and pin-ups of Elvis Presley on the walls of her room.

On the back of the door a hand-written notice says: 'Have you got your key? Have you got your comb? Have you got your money?' – to remind her as she goes scurrying off on her latest date. Her shoulder-length hair has a home perm.

AND SHE IS THIRTEEN YEARS OLD. (Waterhouse 1959: 12)

The play's central, yet most ambiguous character is Greta, played in the original Royal Court run early in 1958 by Wendy Craig. Jellicoe's stage directions describe Greta only as 'an Australian' (Jellicoe 1964: 9), and she remains physically and psychologically elusive up to the point at which her threat becomes overt, only appearing on stage well into the second act, mingling with the rest of the characters 'unnoticed' (51). Then suddenly, and rather like Waterhouse's horrified portrait of female youth, she is revealed in all her elaborate artifice, as she '*divests herself of part of her disguise. Her hair is long, straight and red, falling from her brow like a Japanese lion wig. Her face is very heavily made up and almost dead white*' (57). Exotic, heroic, precocious and Kali-like, she attacks the '*thin, small and tough*' nineteen-year-old Cone (13) '*in an easy, lazy, rather splendid manner*' (59).

T. R. Fyvel notes that the race riots in Nottingham and Notting Hill in the same year as Craig's performance, together with two large gang fights at London dance halls in early 1959,

> seemed to represent a definite climax in the wave of youthful violence. Well before this, however, as far as the popular Press was concerned, juvenile delinquency had for the first time in Britain become elevated to the status of a national problem. More than that, it seemed to have become curiously stylized, to have become a fashion. (Fyvel 1963: 17–18)

Fyvel uses that phrase 'curiously stylized' a number of times in relation to youth violence in his study; it is the same disquieting artifice that makes Greta's character so chilling and exotic, a quality to be inherited by Alex and his 'droogs' in Anthony Burgess's 1962 novel *A Clockwork Orange*, and controversially honoured in Stanley Kubrick's 1971 film. Her masculinity confirmed by means of the expert, 'splendid' violence she wreaks, she turns a few minutes later to reveal a pregnant belly, the father potentially any of the male characters on stage. Greta provides a fittingly ambiguous figurehead to a play about young people that is full of meaningless sounds and words, non sequiturs, enigmatic relationships and pounding drums, and as such encapsulates the confusion surrounding the motives of youth during the decade.

The play's first notices communicate this too. The year before its opening, it had won third prize (and the princely sum of £100) in the

Figure 4   The first production of Ann Jellicoe's *The Sport of My Mad Mother*, at the Royal Court Theatre, London, on 25 February 1958. All of the cast appear in this scene, with Greta, played by Wendy Craig (centre), brandishing a gun.

Observer newspaper's New Play Competition; Kenneth Tynan celebrated it as '"Godot" syncopated, a unique example of collective improvisation in the theatre' (Tynan 1957: 11). Reviewers at the play's opening, though, largely failed to relish this uniqueness. The anonymous review in *The Times* claimed that 'The author gallantly attempts to give poetic expression to the predicament of a generation ruled by fear. It is unfortunate that she appears to see life in a series of newspaper *clichés,*' while ironically going on to replicate those clichés in its reading of a 'Teddy Boy mentality' in the play's characters (Jellicoe 1958: 3). We might expect *The Guardian*, as the prize-giving *Observer*'s sister paper, to refute *The Times*'s verdict of 'a rather gritty evening of expressionism which sheds no special illumination on its theme and is not particularly entertaining', yet Philip Hope-Wallace, though praising the play's experimentalism with what he calls 'the old Expressionist manner which takes us right back to Brecht and Weil, Isherwood and Auden', shares a disappointment that the characters fail to develop. His article also replicates the reflex lapse into tabloid-speak when it comes to describing young people: 'these pubescent, delinquent wild ones speak the primal fantasies of the unaccepted. In a world of fear they play not at missiles and H-bombs but with razors, fireworks, and coshes' (Hope-Wallace 1958: 7). (One of the 'social problem' films so influential during the decade was entitled *Cosh Boy*.) In the penultimate line Dean asks, 'What's going on here?' 'Search me,' replies Steve (Jellicoe 1964: 63). The reviews, and we might assume, the play's initial audiences, echo his sentiment.

Our Children Are Changing

E. R. Braithwaite's autobiographical *To Sir With Love* (1959) documents his experience teaching at a Secondary Modern school in London's East End after his demobilisation from the Royal Air Force (RAF) in 1945. Braithwaite's class have a reputation as particularly difficult. At 15 years old they are precisely the age group that concerns the Crowther Report. Class 4B are merely sitting out the time until they reach school-leaving age. They are physically mature, variously violent and sexually provocative, and are dressed in grubby and precocious imitations of their American screen idols, a style their teacher initially condemns as 'a symbol of toughness as thin and synthetic as the cheap films from which it was copied' (Braithwaite 1992: 51). Jellicoe's Greta and her flailing, preening entourage could pass unnoticed.

Braithwaite's own experience explains the anthropological tone of his initial descriptions of these East End youths. He has come to teaching reluctantly, desperately, due to his inability to find work elsewhere. He is Caymanian, and is finding civilian life rife with a virulent racism. This experience is utterly alien to him after 'six exciting years' (37) of camaraderie and meritocracy in the RAF, and markedly different from the blatant apartheid of the United States. Braithwaite is clear that faulty education is a major contributing factor to this insidious, and particularly British, prejudice, claiming of his fellow teachers:

> It was not entirely their fault. They had been taught with the same text books that these children were using now, and had fully digested the concept that coloured people were physically, mentally, socially and culturally inferior to themselves, though it was rather ill-mannered actually to say so. (100)

This polite bigotry circumscribes Braithwaite professionally, socially and sexually – he notes wryly, that:

> It seems as though there were some unwritten law in Britain which required any healthy, able-bodied negro resident there to be either celibate by inclination, or else a master of the art of sublimation. And were he to seek solace from prostitutes or 'easy' women, he would promptly be labelled as filthy and undesirable. Utterly, inhumanly unreasonable! We were to be men, but without manhood. (96)

Yet the sexuality of the white adolescents Braithwaite teaches is similarly culturally undesirable. In 1956, *The Handbook of Health Education* was the first UK government publication in which sex education was discussed as a distinct school subject. The Birmingham Feminist History Group (BFHG) suggested that it implied that 'if you desired where you could not marry it was because you were sexually immature,' and that this 'reinforced the views that adolescent sexuality was a social problem rather than a valid expression of sexuality' (BFHG 2005: 10–11). In Braithwaite's experience, inter-racial marriage is deemed so undesirable by the British, that his sexuality as a black man becomes a 'social problem', just like that of the teenagers he teaches. This potential empathy for their experience of marginalisation is gradually introduced alongside his initial revulsion.

Braithwaite feels a betrayal by the country he was once proud to serve all the 'greater because it had been perpetrated with the greatest of charm and courtesy' (Braithwaite 1992: 42). At first this sense provokes resentment towards his deprived and disenfranchised pupils. After all, 'they were white, and as far as I was concerned, that fact alone made the only difference between the haves and the have-nots' (29). Yet over the final year of Class 4B's education he and his pupils undergo a frequently stalling, but ultimately successful, process of mutual understanding, which ends in the eponymous love. His students learn a respect for him, for learning and for themselves, and Braithwaite himself:

> was learning from them as well as teaching them. I learned to see them in relation to their surroundings, and in that way to understand them. At first I had been rather critical of their clothing, and thought their tight sweaters, narrow skirts and jeans unsuitable for school wear, but now that they were taking greater interest in personal tidiness, I could understand that such clothes merely reflected vigorous personalities in a relentless search for self-expression. (152–3)

This new appreciation of young behaviour and youth culture as a complex negotiation of emerging personal identity prompts anger at the school's treatment in a piece in the local paper that, rather than the promised engagement with the staff's progressive methods, is a piece of 'youth spectacle' (Davis 1990: 86) even more sensationalist than that of Keith Waterhouse. *To Sir With Love* provides an instructive addition to the sub-genre of 1950s fictionalised autobiography set within the school system, as its author's experience of racial injustice complicates and illuminates his relationship with his disenfranchised pupils. Braithwaite's own identity (his employment prospects, his sexual rights, his civic role) is explicitly in question – like the young people who grow to love him (and the nation in which he finds himself), he is experiencing a period of role moratorium.

The fact that 'Sir' is black in this book throws the anthropologising of young people that is a feature of 1950s social commentary into relief. The metaphorical confusion of youth as both alien to, yet indicative of, the nature of contemporary culture is rife with contradiction. We have seen how the tropical setting of *Lord of the Flies* has encouraged some critics to understand the boys' degeneracy as universally, fundamentally human. In 'Fable', Golding directly denied such a view, claiming the central horror of the novel to be not atavism, but contemporary civilisation itself:

> It is bad enough to say that so many Jews were exterminated in this way and that, so many people liquidated, but there were things done during that period from which I still have to avert my mind lest I should be physically sick. They were not done by the headhunters of New Guinea, or by some primitive tribe in the Amazon. They were done, skilfully, coldly, by educated men, doctors, lawyers, by men with a tradition of civilization behind them, to beings of their own kind. (Golding 1996: 251–2)

The creeping revelation of the reality of the death camps during the 1950s had not so much destroyed the binary opposition of civilised and savage as reversed its polarity. The image of teenager as savage, then, can be used to transmit condemnation, but we can speculate that it might also have the potential to signify hope in the shape of a new generation unsullied by the chillingly advanced technologies and failed moralities of the Second World War.

The year 1956 saw the publication of Audrey Richards's anthropological study *Chisungu: A Girl's Initiation Ceremony Among the Bemba of Zambia*. Richards's account of a 1931 fieldtrip was notable for a number of reasons. Its focus upon young women is one of them; for that reason, of course, the book was necessarily female-authored, as men were excluded from the titular ceremony. It was also one of the first works of anthropology to relate the symbolism of ritual to the structure of society and to observe the importance of symbolism in kinship roles. Chisungu, it is revealed, is not a process of intellectual education, but a ritual demanding a full emotional response: 'If the observations made here under the title of "pragmatic effects" mean anything, they point to the number and variety of emotional attitudes which can be expressed by symbolic behaviour and the multiple, and often changing, functions of such rites' (Richards 1982: 69). Though influenced by her mentor, Bronislaw Marlinowski, Richards fashions a new and self-reflexive methodological mixture of functionalist and structuralist techniques. This innovative approach lends some credence to an emerging paradigm in the literary studies of the twenty-first century: that of the 1950s as the 'start of postmodernism', the dawning of the dominance of the textually symbolic, and its resultant cultural relativity.

Richards certainly undermines the model of the objective observer so prized by more traditional social science with her disarming frankness about the perils of fieldwork – about trying to take notes and photographs at the same time, and about the exhaustion that can result in a tiny crammed hut at three in the morning, next to a huge fire, with 'the company' usually 'elated by beer': 'The observer is dead sober, nearly stifled, with eyes running from the smoke, and straining all the time to catch the words from the songs screeched around her, and to transcribe them by the firelight that penetrates occasionally through the mass of human limbs' (62). In the closing years of the decade, Colin MacInnes's journalism, like Richards's anthropological writing, was similarly engaged in emphasising the kinship significance of initiation practices – in his case, the revelation of talent of Tommy Steele, emerging English pop sensation. A 1957 article in *Encounter* describes Steele's concerts in terms strikingly similar to Richard's description of noisy, stifling nights in a Zambian hut:

> In the centre, before the mike, is a gold-haired Robin Goodfellow dressed in sky-blue jeans and a neon-hued shirting who jumps, skips, doubles up and wriggles as he sings. At certain ritual gestures – a dig with the foot, a violent mop shake of the head – the teenagers massed from stalls to gallery utter a collective shriek of ecstasy. (MacInnes 1961a: 11)

MacInnes's metaphors and similes seek to emphasise the exotic nature of modern youth whilst also contextualising it firmly within the contemporary, proudly projecting a home-grown, vibrant culture.

His work chimes with Adrian Horn's recent revisionist study, *Juke Box Britain: Americanisation and Youth Culture, 1945–60*, which confounds the perception of American influence on British teenagers of the period as anything like as profound and nationally pervasive as vociferous commentators then and since have maintained. Francis Williams's periodically hysterical 1962 text *The American Invasion*, for example, re-makes the uncontroversial statement that 'The teen-age world is pre-dominantly American. This is very natural. It is an American invention' (Williams 1962: 139). This disgust at the perceivedly imitative structure of youth culture resurfaces in Fyvel's more measured phrase 'curiously stylized' (Fyvel 1963: 18) – both critics find teenage life to be inauthentic. Yet Horn finds American cultural influences on youth style to be less influential than previously suggested, and claims that 'the influences that *were* imported had been mediated through British social, economic and cultural conditions to create style fusions that were distinctive and particular to Britain at that time' (Horn 2009: 4). In 'Pop Songs and Teenagers' (1958), MacInnes sited his cultural comparison further afield, wondering 'Could it . . . be there's something *tribal* in the teenage ideology?', as he recalls the sight of two Teds in London: 'The boys walked ahead, their expressionless faces, surmounted by Tony Curtis hair-dos, bent in exclusive masculine communion. Ten feet behind them, ignoring them completely but following on, come their twin Ted-esses. I've seen an identical sight among the Kikuyu'. (A footnote after that last sentence reads: 'To whom all apologies for this comparison'. MacInnes's joke is a strangely loaded one in the wake of Kikuyu involvement in the supremely violent Mau Mau insurrection in Kenya between 1952 and 1956.) When it came to 'the teenagers', he claimed later in the piece, 'the anthropologists have a lot of work to do (very much neglected, it seems to me)' (MacInnes 1958: 53, 55). A self-styled expert observer of teenage culture, in 1959 he was to publish a novel that set about this neglected work with extraordinary panache.

This chapter has suggested the conflicted nature of the cultural debate and literary representation of youth in Britain during the 1950s. Yet as the decade neared its end, press coverage approached consensus, and that viewpoint was profoundly pessimistic. In 1965, from a new era of optimism over the potential of young people, Peter Laurie in *The Teenage Revolution* looks back to note that:

> From 1958 on, most of the stories concern teenage sex and violence. Even with the reports and comment before one, it is difficult to recapture the aura of social catastrophe that enveloped the teenager at the end of the 'fifties. By then the teddy boys had reached and passed their peak of influence but in the public mind their image had just jelled and every reference to youth includes a side swipe at this sector. (Laurie 1965: 19)

In the 1959 novel *Absolute Beginners*, Colin MacInnes determinedly deconstructs this automatic equation of youth and negative values. The novel's unnamed narrator, himself in what he calls 'the last year of the teenage dream' (MacInnes 1984a: 12), conspicuously mocks the media sound-bites which signify youthful experience to the disapproving adult majority. His half-brother, Vernon, denied the freedom of adolescence by the war and desperate to patronise his flamboyant younger sibling, provides a mouthpiece for these dirge-like journalistic platitudes: '"It was the Attlee administrations," said my bro., in his whining, complaining, platform voice, "who emancipated the working-man, and gave the teenagers their economic privileges"' (37).

Through the narrator's picaresque pursuit of his gregarious and chaotic existence during a turbulent London summer, MacInnes contradicts these dominant discourses by mapping a more complicated social topography of urban English youth: a human geography that does not conform to traditional stratifications of class, wealth, gender and race. The clichéd catalogue of tabloid anxieties is confronted with the narrator's characteristic candour. 'SHE IS ONLY 13 BUT . . . She is wearing nylons. She has been wearing them for TWO YEARS,' spluttered Keith Waterhouse in the *Daily Mirror*, his article's illustration comprising a row of male spectators gazing and pointing at the body of the teenage girl he describes with such prurient intimacy (Waterhouse 1958: 13). Finally united with Suzette, the girl he loves, the narrator of *Absolute Beginners* discloses a teenage sexual relationship that, though outside the sanctification of wedlock, is very different from the casual promiscuity of adult fears. After rescuing her from the race riots raging in the city, he 'went and got the bowl and things, and washed her all over, and I kissed her between, and there in my place at Napoli we made it at last, but honest, you couldn't say that it was sexy – it was just love' (MacInnes 1984a: 196).

Mark Abrams's study *Teenage Consumer Spending in 1959* calculates the financial outlay of Britain's five million teenagers, after meeting State and family obligations, and contributing to their savings, to equal £830 million in 1959, or just over 5 per cent of national consumer expenditure. Abrams nominates this 'a very modest ratio for a group of people who constitute 10 per cent of the total population', yet despite this, he notes, 'the common view amongst most adults' is 'a picture of an extremely prosperous body of young people' (Abrams 1961: 4). This imbalance, his survey suggests, can be attributed to the ostentatious nature of teenage spending, with the majority of the money going on social activities and the paraphernalia surrounding them – food, drink, cigarettes, clothes and music: 'this is distinctive teenage spending for distinctive teenage ends in a distinctive teenage world' (5).

The narrator of *Absolute Beginners* does not deny the affiliation

Figure 5 'Keith Waterhouse's contribution to the 'Beanstalk Generation' series, *Daily Mirror*, 15 September 1958.

of teenagers and this specialised and hedonistic market. Rather, he celebrates it in his own flamboyant patterns of consumption:

> I had on precisely my full teenage drag that would enrage [Vernon] – the grey pointed alligator casuals, the pink neon pair of ankle crêpe nylon-stretch, my Cambridge blue glove-fit jeans, a vertical-striped happy shirt revealing my lucky neck-charm on its chain, and the Roman-cut short-arse jacket just referred to . . . not to mention my wrist identity jewel, and my Spartan warrior hair-do. (MacInnes 1984a: 32)

Vernon, like the media opinion he mouths so readily, is enraged by the perceived profligacy of this spending. Davis has noted how late twentieth-century sociological work on youth subcultures 'has argued that we should not merely view the young *en masse* as *passive* consumers but rather as at least potentially *active* in this respect, "making something out of what is made of them" through their *bricolage* of the artifacts of consumer society' (Davis 1990: 122). In *Absolute Beginners*, the narrator's consumption is characterised by a strict moral code that actively discriminates against the fetishisation of both goods themselves and the money exchanged for them. Affluence may be accelerating, but the easy equation of teenage spending and individual liberation is, in his nineteen-year-old eyes, increasingly difficult to maintain:

> This teenage ball had had a real splendour in the days when the kids discovered that, for the first time since centuries of kingdom-come, they'd money, which hitherto had always been denied to us at the best time in life to use it, namely, when you're young and strong, and also before the newspapers and telly got hold of this teenage fable and prostituted it as conscripts seem to do to everything they touch. Yes, I tell you, it had a real savage splendour in the days when we found that no one couldn't sit on our faces any more because we'd loot to spend at last, and our world was to be our world, the one we wanted and not standing on the doorstep of somebody else's waiting for honey, perhaps. (MacInnes 1984a: 12)

The narrator makes a strong distinction between his own exploitation of a booming market and the exploitation of people within a market framework. Wiz, one of his closest friends at the beginning of the novel, has a reputation as 'the number one hustler of the capital', seamlessly 'introducing A to B, or *vice versa*' (14) so that they might exchange their goods and cut him in. Later, he extends these conveyancing talents into prostitution, pimping a woman who shares his instinct for using people; she has, we are told, 'a way of *looking* at you as if you were a possibly valuable product' (137). By the time the race riots have erupted, Wiz's degeneration into the morals of a 'conscript' (one of the narrator's habitual terms of moral abuse) is confirmed by a glimpse of his sinister animation at the words of a racist, soap-box preacher: 'His wiry little body was all clenched, and something was staring through his eyes that came from God knows where, and he raised on his toes, and shot up his arms all rigid and he cried out, shrill like a final cry, "Keep England white!".' In describing the speaker as talking not to his crowd but to 'some witch-doctor he was screaming to for help and blessing' (191), the narrator turns the 'youth as primitive' symbolism on its head, wielding a racial stereotype to condemn the racism he reads as rife amongst adults.

Such an account of MacInnes's novel and its strategies to undermine predominant contemporary perceptions of teenagers risks the suggestion that it is a schematic text, sociological rather than literary in its aspirations. Yet it is in the intricacies of the novel's unusual narrative voice and structure that its most radical renegotiations of the 'metaphorical utility' of youth can be traced (Davis 1990: 86). Steven Connor has noted the way in which 'Narrative can effect an imaginative colonisation of unknown or alien spaces, allowing a fuller sense of habitation and belonging' (Connor 1996: 4). The narrative of *Absolute Beginners*, set as it is amidst the domestic race riots of a country losing its Empire, opposes 'colonisation' as too violent a process of imaginative assimilation. In *Nation and Narration*, Homi K. Bhabha and others suggested ways in which the nation, and ideas about national belonging, are predicated upon the exercise of narrative: in the establishing of origins, and the construction of a shared and sustaining story that synthesises diverse experiences. MacInnes's novel is attentive to these implications of narrative for national identity and social responsibility. So too is his narrator, who rejects a Marxist model of society precisely on the basis that it does not demand a dynamic, progressive narrative process:

> This is their thing, if I dig it correctly. You're *in* history, yes, because you're budding here and now, but you're *outside* it, also, because you're living in the Marxist future. And so, when you look around, and see a hundred horrors, and not only musical, you're not responsible for them, because you're beyond them already, in the kingdom of K. Marx. But for me, I must say, all the horrors I see around me, especially the English ones, I feel responsible for, the lot, just as much as for the few nice things I dig. (MacInnes 1984a: 127)

The title of the novel itself is a joke about the anachronistic nature of Marxist divisions of class. The narrator's attention is caught by a sign outside a dance academy:

CURRENT CLASSES
MEDALLISTS CLASS
BEGINNERS PROGRESSIVE CLASS
BEGINNERS PRACTICE
ABSOLUTE BEGINNERS

and I said out loud, 'Boy, that one's us! Although me, after my experiences, maybe I'm going to move up a category or two!' (163)

Unwilling and unable to position himself within a traditional and reified class structure, he laughingly posits a meritocracy founded on the value of varied and individual experience and the ability to reflect honestly upon that experience. This social principle is encapsulated in the novel's mode of address. Though the narrator engages his readers with a reliably charming, candid and confessional tone, emphasis is placed upon the dissonance between an assumedly adult readership and his own youthful point of view. At various points in the novel, the narrator draws direct attention to issues of narrative reliability, with interjections such as this: 'I should explain (and I hope you'll believe it, even though it's true)' (42). More frequently, the difference between his experience and that of the adult reader is emphasised precisely by the narrator's assumption of commonality. On his first trip outside London, he provides a lengthy and exuberant description of the functioning of canal locks: 'Then the lock-keeper product – with a peaked cap, and an Albert watch-chain, and rubber boots – throws some switches or other, and the water gushes in, and you'd hardly credit it, but you start going up yourself!' (151). This gambit, of course, has rich comic effect, but a serious motive too, in that it engages its reader in a repeated enactment of empathy with experiences that are, at the same time, marked as profoundly individualistic, subjective and youthful.

Connor reads this technique as 'an abandonment of the large, assimilative perspective of the nation-novel and the novel-nation in favour of the self-inventing and self-legitimating communities of style that were increasingly generated by the explosion of pop and youth culture in Britain from the 1950s on' (Connor 1996: 91). In this sense, then, *Absolute Beginners* provides a useful point of contrast to a number of the angry young male literary voices in the chapters that follow which, for all their hyped rebelliousness, rely upon narratives that demand conformity with a very particular perspective, rather than evincing and celebrating cultural and generational difference. MacInnes's novel ends, appropriately, on a note of revelry, its narrator dancing on a rain-soaked runway at Heathrow Airport, welcoming a new generation of immigrants: '"Welcome to London! Greetings from England! Meet your first teenager!"' (MacInnes 1984a: 203). Yet this is also a moment of stasis: still in the 'Absolute Beginners' class, we leave him unable to board a plane himself, and unsure as to the future of his relationship with Suzette. Just as it denies its reader an uncomplicated identification with the narrative perspective, the novel defies the *Bildungsroman* structure:

a structure which, if conformed to, imparts a universality to the youth experience. The conclusion of that definitive American adolescent text of the 1950s, *The Catcher in the Rye*, for example, suggests the beginning of a process of growing up for its protagonist Holden Caulfield:

> A lot of people, especially this one psychoanalyst guy they have here, keeps asking me if I'm going to apply myself when I go back to school next September. It's such a stupid question, in my opinion. I mean how do you know what you're going to do till you *do* it? The answer is, you don't. I *think* I am, but how do I know? (Salinger 1979: 220)

With this hint of a new start of conformity, Holden's often-savage critique of adult society is circumscribed as 'just a phase'. *Absolute Beginners* offers no such sense of impending closure. In the open-endedness and dissonance of its narrative it both enacts and critiques the cultural anxieties surrounding young people in Britain during the decade. Simultaneously the 'litmus paper' indicative of a fast-changing society, and alien and incomprehensible to that society, a beacon of hope for postwar humanity and its potential nemesis: youth is made to bear a metaphorical burden so heavy and contradictory that it animates and aggravates 1950s writing across all literary genres.

Chapter Three

First Writing: 1950s Fiction

'Ask the young: they know everything': this Spanish proverb begins a 1952 article assessing new novelists, 'Uncommitted Talents', in the *Times Literary Supplement*. Julian Gustave Symons continues: 'No words could be more exactly belied by the British literary scene at present as far as its youthful practitioners are concerned. For it is the admission, or almost, quite frankly, the boast, of our young novelists that they know precisely nothing.' Of all the writers currently on what he calls 'the bright side of forty', Symons summons a modicum of enthusiasm for Angus Wilson, who that year had published his first novel *Hemlock and After* following two short story collections, claiming, 'There is no doubt at all about Mr. Wilson's fine talent, only about its possible limitations of theme and application' (Symons 1952: 572). Writing two years later in the *Listener*, the talented Mr Wilson noted that:

> It has for some time now been customary to use the title 'The Future of the English Novel' as the conventional introduction to the announcement of its death. To a considerable section of the population the news of the imminent death of any form of art is always pleasing. (Wilson 1954: 746)

Yet running counter to these intimations of the morbidity of fiction during the decade in Britain was another narrative, driven from the middle of the decade by the trumpeted emergence of an allegedly new breed of (anti-)hero: the Angry Young Man. Harry Ritchie traces the catchphrase from its inception in 1956 in the Press Office of the Royal Court Theatre to promote John Osborne's first play, *Look Back in Anger*. Ritchie documents its frenzied application to a thoroughly disparate grouping of writers and their characters, crossing and re-crossing another journalistic invention for the literary scene – the Movement (considered in Chapter 6), and onwards to its own demise, exhausted through overuse: a then-unprecedented exercise in literary publicity.

The 'Angry Young Man' label was applied to writers by the media with little respect for semantics. From an original triumvirate of John Osborne, Colin Wilson (whose philosophical tract *The Outsider* was published in 1956) and Kingsley Amis, it was extended to include, amongst others, Richard Hoggart, Nigel Dennis (Osborne protested he was 'the most charming, kindest and mildest of men, who is over forty and the father of teenage children'; Osborne 1957a: 4), John Wain and Doris Lessing (the latter's essay was included in the 1957 collection *Declaration*, the 'ill-fated climax' to the hype; Ritchie 1988: 42). All this sensation about a fictional 'Angry' movement, together with its now-required refutation, has tended to obscure a particularly striking facet of 1950s British fiction: the extraordinary number of first novels published by authors whose careers would endure well beyond the decade – Kingsley Amis, John Braine, William Golding, Doris Lessing, Iris Murdoch, V. S. Naipaul, Alan Sillitoe, Muriel Spark and Angus Wilson. As Stuart Laing has suggested, this renaissance within fiction of the 1950s lies at the heart both of the Angry Young Man phenomenon and its conceptual failure:

> This new wave of writers . . . stimulated the quest for a unilinear account of "the novel". In fact, if there is a common feature here, it is an uncertainty about the role and voice of the novelist and a tendency to incorporate such issues into novels. But they are unevenly perceived and diversely expressed. (Laing 1983a: 241)

This chapter takes (with a little licence) a selection of first novels published between 1950 and 1960 as a means of exploring the uncertainty identified by Laing, that of the role of fiction within society, together with fundamental issues of its narrative voice, style, structure and content. Critical, rather than journalistic, accounts of the decade's fiction assuage the sense of anger with one of quietism, both stylistic and political, finding in the 1950s a postwar reaction against experiment in the novel, and a taking of refuge in realism. Bernard Bergonzi's influential *The Situation of the Novel* emphasised the technical superiority and aesthetic self-awareness of American novelists at the expense of British writers, calling the literature of the 1950s and 1960s 'backward- and inward-looking' (Bergonzi 1971: 56). Looking back on the fiction of the 1940s, of course, was a peculiarly disjointed experience, but one novel in particular was apparent as a significant precedent for new novelists. The influence of the parable in George Orwell's *Nineteen Eighty-Four* (1949) of a political future in which language is drained of all humane experience, together with the deliberately plain style of Orwell's wider writings, can be detected in the narrative voice and content of a novel hailed by many of the alleged Angries: William Cooper's 1950 *Scenes From Provincial Life*.

To call this a first novel is somewhat disingenuous: it was the first published under the pseudonym William Cooper, but the fifth by author H. S. Hoff. John Braine, author of *Room at the Top*, one of the decade's most hyped debuts (considered in Chapter 10), was to call *Scenes from Provincial Life*

> the novel in its empirical form. It could and did stand for an important swing away from the stylistic backlog of modernism, or what William Cooper calls the 'Art Novel': a swing towards an art of reason, an art of lived-out and recognisable values and predicaments. (quoted Bradbury 1969: iii)

'Seminal is not a word I am fond of,' he claimed; 'nevertheless I am forced to use it. This book was for me – and I suspect many others – a seminal influence' (i). For those under the influence, the perceived empiricism of Cooper's novel – or the emphasis it placed upon the primacy of verifiable experience in human thought – was especially influential. So too was the reluctance it showed overtly to engage in politics, a decision heightened by Cooper's choice to set his novel just as the Second World War breaks out: 'I am writing a novel about events in the year 1939, and the political state of the world cannot very well be left out. The only thing I can think of is to put it in now and get it over' (Cooper 1969: 18).

Having done so, the novel goes on as a *Bildungsroman*, tracing the tumultuous relationship between its hero Joe Lunn, a reluctant schoolmaster, and his girlfriend Myrtle, his search for his vocation, and a depiction of a fraught homosexual love affair between two of his friends. Joe's first-person, self-conscious narration foregrounds the tightness of its focus amidst the horror of world events:

> In spite of what the headlines told me every morning, in spite of what I reasoned must happen in the world, I was really preoccupied most deeply with what was going on between me and Myrtle and between Tom and Steve. People can concentrate on their private lives, I thought, in the middle of anything. (172)

In his review of the immediate postwar period, Anthony Hartley noted how the making of 'this sort of mythical virtue out of necessity' can, for a novelist, 'take the form of a praiseworthy preoccupation with the material around him, but the attitude in itself becomes narrow and banal after a while' (Hartley 1963: 48). Joe's narration jests provocatively with such accusations; he claims at one point to feel 'I was being hunted by Hitler and Myrtle in conjunction' (Cooper 1969: 238).

The narration may admit world politics only at a tangent, but this is not to say that the novel is unpolitical. Laing claims that 'its pre-war setting and tremendous smugness deprive it of the critical edge of John Wain's *Hurry on Down* and Kingsley Amis's *Lucky Jim*' (Laing 1983a: 243). However, *Scenes from Provincial Life* is a key document for a number of the decade's male-authored first novels in its support for the personal as important and singularly worthy of fictional treatment, and its recognition that, for much of the time, life is lived at the level of individual reality, and not the abstract and removed. Yet beneath the tone of comic realism that Joe Lunn adopts is a complex process of self-justification. The irony and humour he exercises upon his younger life are carefully underpinned by the authority of the retrospective narrative, and its empirical 'proof' in the novel we are reading; it ends with the Orwellian touch of Joe reaching for a notebook and picking up a pen, his true vocation – that of writer – now apparent. Appeals to shared, 'reasonable' codes of value are frequent throughout the text, and though they purport to universality, they are actually precariously particular, depending upon the reader's assent to a range of assumed masculine and heterosexual judgements, as here: 'I was faced with an inescapable truth: you cannot have a mistress and read' (Cooper 1969: 40, and see Ferrebe 2005). The narrative tone is akin to that of the mass art that so worries Richard Hoggart in *The Uses of Literacy*, for its ability to dupe working-class people into compliance, 'because they have been approached in a personal, friendly and homely manner' (Hoggart 1958: 83).

For all its reasonable and realistic register, and professed surety of the reader's verification of the experience it depicts, the narrative voice that Cooper produces is an anxious one. The sense of dissembling forms an important theme within the novel, as Joe seeks a profession and a way of being that mirrors his authentic feelings. In receipt of a letter from the headmaster asking him to reconsider his profession, he realises that

> It might well be that a schoolmaster really ought to behave like a schoolmaster. If I could not behave like a schoolmaster, perhaps I ought not to be one. This left me faced with the most alarming question of all. 'What *can* I behave like?' (Cooper 1969: 137)

This feeling of social life demanding the acting of a part (usually for which one is woefully miscast) is increasingly important within the sensibility of the 1950s. It is no accident that, in John Braine's *Room at the Top*, Joe Lampton's hobby in his aspirational new life in Warley is amateur dramatics. American sociologist Erving Goffman's pioneering *The Presentation of the Self in Everyday Life* (1959), based upon a field trip to the Shetland island of Unst, was a precursor to the theories of performativity so dominant today: 'The perspective employed in this report', he began, 'is that of the theatrical performance; the principles derived are dramaturgical ones' (Goffman 1990: 9). In Britain, Stephen Potter's spoof self-help books on how to act yourself to success, including *One-Upmanship* (1952), were comic interpretations of the same theory.

So too was John Wain's first novel, *Hurry on Down* (1953), the story of another educated young man trying to find his place, which rejects first-person narration for the omniscient narrative of conventional realism. Randomly choosing Stotwell after graduation as a suitable 'everyplace', Charles Lumley tries out in a diverse number of roles – as window-cleaner (the result, apparently, of the same aspiration to proletarianism as Jimmy Porter's to his sweet stall in *Look Back in Anger*), drug runner, bouncer and hospital orderly. On a personal level, he is competing for Veronica with Bernard Roderick, a rival he recognises as 'smoothness itself. He was giving a first-rate performance in the role of himself being smooth' (Wain 1970: 150). The often-anguished comedy of the novel ends in a distinctly dark resolution. Lumley is offered a sizeable salary as a joke-writer for a radio show, a professional means of exploiting the disjunction between reality and a pretence of happiness. When Veronica chooses him, and expresses her regret at the time she spent with Roderick, Charles welcomes her in a new spirit of cynicism: 'mentally he translated this into: *You're rich now, you're doing as well as Roderick. And you're fifteen years younger*' (251). *Hurry on Down* features one of Charles's university peers, Edwin Froulish, a self-styled genius who is writing a novel, the style of which festers somewhere between a pastiche of the work of James Joyce and that of Dylan Thomas. Like Charles, Froulish ends with a job as joke-writer (though on considerably reduced terms to Charles's); Wain's own cynicism as to the role of the 'experimental' writer in contemporary culture is clearly legible.

Kingsley Amis's *Lucky Jim*, published a year later in 1954, exercises similar contempt for the pretensions of a perceivedly outdated High Culture through its treatment of the clash of Jim Dixon, probationary lecturer in History at a provincial red-brick university, and the donnish Welch family, whose patriarch professor is Jim's boss. In interview with an American academic in 1958, Amis claimed that if Jim Dixon:

> were closely questioned about this, he would probably admit in the end that culture is real and important and ought not to be made the property of a sort of exclusive club which you can only enter if you come from the right school – culture ought to be available to everyone who can use it; but such an avowal would be very untypical of him and you would probably have to get him very drunk first. (quoted Kynaston 2009: 360)

The novel shows a similar awareness to Wain's of the need for pretence if a reasonable young man is to survive the society in which he finds himself. The reviewer for the *Times Literary Supplement* recognised him as 'the anti-, or rather, sub-hero who is beginning to figure increasingly as the protagonist of the most promising novels written by young men since the war', 'an intelligent provincial who, after getting a scholarship and an Oxford or Cambridge degree, finds his social position both precarious and at odds with his training' (Ross 1954: 101). Jim is always acting a part, suppressing what he wants to say in favour of what he thinks he should, and often avoiding saying anything at all: 'he began eating the largest surviving gherkin and thought how lucky he was that so much of the emotional business of the evening had been transacted without involving him directly' (Amis 1976: 21). Like William Fisher in Keith Waterhouse's later novel *Billy Liar* (1959), Jim works off his frustration in elaborate bouts of fantasised triumphs. His other emotional outlet, a barrage of pulled faces (including his 'Edith Sitwell face'; 102), is uniquely his.

For Jim, this sham-selfhood is a necessary survival strategy for a world, social and professional, to which he does not belong. For those around him, he judges it a despicable pretence. He is miserably romantically involved with Margaret Peel, a fellow lecturer, and constantly deplores the histrionics she affects in an attempt to make theirs a 'real' love affair: 'Don't be fantastic, Margaret. Come off the stage for a moment, do' (159). The peak – or trough – of inauthenticity in the novel (and its comic climax too) comes with the one instance in which we are shown Jim (mal)functioning in his professional capacity. Forced into it by Welch, he gives a public lecture on 'Merrie England', rehashing some spurious and superseded ideas that were never his in the first place. He is drunk, and unknowingly produces a series of mocking imitations of the speech patterns of his institutional superiors before passing out. Yet the professional apocalypse of this ventriloquist act is rendered harmless by an epiphanic incident occurring immediately before it. Jim has fallen in love with Christine Callaghan, girlfriend of Bertrand Welch, one of the Professor's pretentious sons. Finally enraged to the point of physical action, Jim knocks the baying Bertrand down with a punch, then proceeds to top his triumph by giving voice to his exact (if characteristically whimsical) thoughts:

> It was clear that Dixon had won this round, and, it then seemed, the whole Bertrand match. He put his glasses on again, feeling good; Bertrand caught his eye with a look of embarrassed recognition. The bloody old towser-faced boot-faced totem-pole on a crap reservation, Dixon thought. 'You bloody old towser-faced boot-faced totem-pole on a crap reservation,' he said. (209)

As the novel ends, Jim gets the girl, and gets a job. Christine is certainly at least a social class above Jim, but she is an aspirational figure because she is naturally beautiful in a way that the desiccated, fussy Margaret is not. The true hypergamous relationship at the heart of the comedy's ending is that between Jim and Julius Gore-Urquhart, a mysterious character who offers Jim an undefined position that will allow him to cultivate his sham-self for substantial financial gain. Joe Lampton in *Room at the Top* lurks as a possible prototype for what Jim could become.

In order ostensibly to remove him from the class hierarchy Jim refutes, Gore-Urquhart is Scottish, yet he is still unmistakably posh, and distinctly manipulative: 'I want to influence people so they'll do what I think it's important they should do. I can't get 'em to do that unless I let 'em bore me first, you understand' (215). Altogether sunnier in aspect than *Hurry on Down*, *Lucky Jim* none the less ends on a note of anxiety as to the prospects of its young protagonist. Its narrative, however, is constructed in such a way as to banish uncertainty over the validity of his point of view. Richard Bradford suggests:

> It is as though there are two Jims: one inside the narrative, struggling with his own impatience, frustration and feelings of contempt; the other controlling and orchestrating the narrative, ensuring that the reader will share his perspective – on the idiocies of the Welches and the pretensions of Bertrand and Margaret. (Bradford 1998: 12)

Amis's use of a free indirect discourse, which voices the third-person narrator in the hero's own idiom, coaxes a close identification with that narrative voice at the same time as its more traditional omniscience lends an authority to Jim's judgements on all those around him. It is this technique that lies at the centre of an enduring tendency to associate author with hero in Amis's texts. 'In many of his narratives,' claims Robert Bell, 'Amis seems massively ubiquitous, his characters articulating the author's likes and dislikes' (Bell 1998: 2). As a result, a reference to, for example, 'some skein of untiring facetiousness by filthy Mozart' (Amis 1976: 63) is read not as a hung-over Jim's bad-tempered response to the whistling of his despised and pretentious boss who is hogging a bathroom he desperately needs to access, but as Amis's philistine rejection of cultural excellence itself.

The 'Angry' novels of the 1950s have been routinely accused for their quietism with regard to the public politics of their contemporary scene. Such an accusation is undoubtedly just, yet this brief survey has shown their intense engagement with other political issues – those entwined in personal relationships and in narrative authority – that are to reach ideological prominence in the noisier public debates of the following decade. The power at stake in a novel's narrative voice may perhaps be dismissed as negligible in fictions featuring (failed) English schoolteachers and lecturers, but another highly comic first novel with another failed teacher as its hero makes its political machinations much plainer – in fact, they lie at the heart of its (tragi-)comedy. V. S. Naipaul arrived at Oxford University from his native Trinidad in 1950, and graduated with a degree in English Literature. He went on to a spell as an editor for the influential literary BBC radio programme 'Caribbean Voices', which was broadcast from London back to the Caribbean, and played an important role in defining the new literary grouping of emigrant / immigrant writers examined in Chapter 8. His novel *The Mystic Masseur*, published in 1957, is a parody *Bildungsroman* and mock biography of Ganesh Ramsumair, Trinidadian Hindu, who moves through the roles of masseur, healer and national politician to that of statesman G. Ramsay Muir, Esq., MBE, visiting Britain in 1954 (Naipaul 2001: 208).

Ganesh himself is well aware of the symbolic power of books, building his reputation in the backwater of Fuente Grove by deliveries that include 300 volumes of the Everyman Library (his wife's tears at the expense of the full set of 930 curtail his ambition for 'seventy-seven feet' of shelved books; 68). The novel's narrative voice, that of a fellow Trinidadian who is taken to Ganesh as a child for (quack) healing, exposes the textual power dynamics by making overt the influence of free indirect discourse in a third-person voice that foregrounds a fawning partiality towards the eponymous anti-hero. His narration parodies omniscience in pseudo-prophetic glimpses of the future that themselves parody Ganesh's own fallacious autobiographical technique. '"I suppose," Ganesh wrote in *The Years of Guilt*, "I had always, from the first day I stepped into Shri Ramlogan's shop, considered it as settled that I was going to marry his daughter. I never questioned it. It all seemed preordained"': yet we already know that Ganesh only decides to marry Leela after her father has enumerated all the wealth and possessions she will inherit (35). Such instances emphasise the narrator's blinkered refusal of the benefits of hindsight to judge Ganesh for what he is – a deceiver of the vulnerable within his community, an exploiter of his own religious heritage, and ultimately a betrayer of his nation who prefers the pomp bestowed by the coloniser to the political graft of Trinidad's gathering independence.

Just as the narrative mocks the elaborate deceptions of Ganesh's various careers, so too does it draw attention to the untruth inherent in the traditional realist structure, with the tyrannous authority of a third-person narrative voice, and the unavailable, unexamined sources of its omniscient information. Naipaul's novel evidences an awareness of the fundamental instability of narrative, however realist, and an intense resultant ambiguity surrounding the act of writing and works of fiction. The tension in the early part of the novel is Ganesh's failure to write and publish. When he becomes a politician, however, he destroys all his former publications, fearing they will discredit the persona he has now adopted. This suspicion of both writer and narrative as inherently corrupt, however comically communicated, is predicated upon the experience of colonisation, in which the coloniser's control of the printed word – and thus of the 'truth' about 'reality' – is paramount. Lalla notes how the novel's unresolved ending perpetuates 'the vacuum constructed by colonialism' (Lalla 2007: n.p.); King suggests that, within this vacuum, 'The materials for personal and national advancement are not available' (King 2003: 35). Both critics, together with Homi Bhabha, find in Naipaul's work an intriguing and productive ambiguity in response to the colonial experience (see Bhabha 2005), while Edward Said is numbered among a postcolonial critical majority which casts Naipaul as a writer 'who has allowed himself quite consciously to be turned into a witness for the Western prosecution', as desperate for the coloniser's approval as Ganesh (Said 1986: 53). Such a complex debate lies outside the scope of this study, but placing *The Mystic Masseur* alongside texts in the established 1950s canon helps to illuminate their own, less explicit, political engagements.

Novelists as Metaphysicians

Alan Sillitoe's short story, 'The Loneliness of the Long Distance Runner', and the collection to which it gives the title (1959), are similarly engaged in experimenting with the authenticity of traditional literary voices. Rather than the politics of colonialism, it is those of class that Sillitoe seeks to deconstruct. Placing Smith, his Borstal inmate hero, in the position of narrative authority is in itself a transgressive act, and Sillitoe continually undermines literary conventions throughout the story. Smith authors a complex and exclusively first-person narrative that self-certifies its own philosophical sophistication with reference to the activity that forms its focus and informs its flow – running, or rather the freedom of thought that running inspires in him. Like Naipaul, he parodies omniscience, this time with the strange observation on an early morning run that there is 'not a sound except the neighing of a piebald foal in a cottage stable that I can't see' (Sillitoe 1985: 19). The story's ending overturns all his claims of a new and hard-won wisdom with the revelation that we can only be reading the story because Smith has been imprisoned once again: 'I'm going to give this story to a pal of mine and tell him that if I do get captured again by the coppers he can try and get it put into a book or something' (54). Yet it is perhaps the unfamiliarity of Smith's act of heroism within traditional literary conventions that forms Sillitoe's more daring rebellion: he chooses to lose the story's climactic race for the Borstal Blue Ribbon Prize Cup for Long Distance Cross Country Running (All England) (39), emphasising his decision by slowing to a halt before the uncomprehending crowd so as to exhort the maximum humiliation of his Governor.

Smith's act is conspicuously existential in its intent to wrest an independent identity from free choice. In *Existentialism*, John MacQuarrie understands the philosophy to be antithetical to British (or at least, English) experience:

> existentialism has flourished in those lands where the social structures have been turned upside down and all the values transvalued, whereas relatively stable countries (including the Anglo-Saxon lands) have not experienced this poignancy and so have not developed the philosophizing that flows from it. (MacQuarrie 1982: 60)

Alan Sinfield has noted 'a conservative interpretation of existential freedom' repeated in many works of the 1950s, and although throwing a race in a children's home may not equate to the shooting of a randomly selected man on a beach (as does Meursault, the hero of Albert Camus's 1942 *The Outsider* [*L'Étranger*]), Sillitoe's story provides one of the more committed existential acts in British literature of the decade (Sinfield 1989: 92). Colin Wilson's non-fictional tract, *The Outsider*, an exposition of what he called his own 'religious existentialism', will be examined in Chapter 12. His close friend Bill Hopkins's 1957 novel, *The Divine and the Decay*, features Peter Plowart, a hero whose sense of his own genius exceeds that of Colin Wilson: 'I'm the greatest man of our time,' he announces. 'That's the cause of the trouble' (Hopkins 1957: 76). For commentator Kenneth Allsop, the trouble was rather the uneasy combination of existentialism and Fascism in the pair's writing, which he read as 'propagating their Religious Existentialism which they say requires a higher type of man, a superman, to thrust humanity through to safety out of civilization's big crash. It is probably unnecessary to add that they see themselves as the super-men' (Allsop 1958: 22).

Iris Murdoch had contributed a number of radio programmes on the French philosophy to the BBC Third Programme in 1950. In one, she suggested that its most prominent exponent, Jean-Paul Sartre, would never reconcile existentialism with his Marxist beliefs, even in fiction. In 'The

Novelist as Metaphysician' she pointed out that Marxism claims to know the world, while existentialism is concerned with the 'point at which our beliefs, our world pictures, our politics, religions, loves and hates are seen to be discontinuous with the selves that may or may not go on affirming them' (Murdoch 1950). Her first novel, *Under the Net* (1954), demonstrates this disjuncture in its hero Jake Donaghue, a composite of an existentialist hero and a concerned citizen of the Welfare State. His narration contains characteristics of both these personas, as here, when he assesses his relationship with girlfriend Madge: 'I tried in an instant to grasp the whole essence of my need of her. I took a deep breath, however, and followed my rule of never speaking frankly to women in moments of emotion' (Murdoch 1963: 12). (Murdoch's first novel replicates the Angry Young Man blueprint in one respect – its female characters remain peripheral throughout.) Like Jimmy Porter and Charles Lumley, Jake makes deliberately counter-cultural decisions in an attempt to cast off his formal (scholarship) education and demonstrate his own freedom, and chooses to work as a manual orderly in a hospital. His work of adolescent philosophy, *The Silencer*, undermines Wilson's *The Outsider* two years before it appears, and, Murdoch suggests, it also constitutes the betrayal of Jake's friend Hugo. Hugo's philosophical explorations are less compromised than Jake's fashionable dabblings, and culminate in an extreme scepticism over language as an authentic tool for conveying experience – Jake's book is a pretentious dialogue between Tamarus and Annandine, stand-ins for himself and Hugo respectively. Tamarus's argument that literature must treat language more practically contravenes his friend's uncompromising conclusion that 'It is in silence that the human spirit touches the divine' (81). Jake loses Hugo to the most extreme demonstration of contingent job-seeking in the novels of the decade – he randomly decides to go and be a watchmaker in Nottingham. The novel's existence suggests, however, that he wins the argument, albeit partially, and its resolution occurs within a broadly humanist framework and a commitment to writing as a meaningful act.

Nigel Dennis's novel, *Cards of Identity* (1955), sets out to discredit Sartrean theories of the self as it does all contemporary theories of identity. These include traditional identifications with nation, class or gender, and also with what he called 'our modern Identity clubs' like 'the Marx club' (Dennis 1958: 31). By comically debating them within the plot device of a conference of the pseudo-scientific Identity Club, in a crumbling country pile reminiscent of a dilapidated Brideshead, he deftly manages a *reductio ad absurdum* which exposes the weaknesses of all. One character, Vinson, suggests current thinking, and his own, to be dominated by an existentialist (de)construction of self:

> The nearest I can get to defining the new identity is to say that the one I lacked previously is now lacking on a much higher level. It's as if with a single leap I had mounted a full flight closer to the Realization of Nothingness. (137)

Yet existentialism undergoes a still more intrinsic critique than Dennis's satire in the work of another new author of the decade. William Golding's first novel, *Lord of the Flies*, was considered in Chapter 2; his second, *The Inheritors* (1955), was an imaginative reconstruction of a primal human society yet to develop language. His third, *Pincher Martin* (1956), functioned to destroy the possibility of coherent selfhood at the same time as it undermines narrative's ability to communicate it. Golding's work, of the 1950s and well beyond, is particularly difficult to categorise, inviting yet resisting as it does both the realist label and the experimental one.

A first reading of the narrative as (fairly) conventionally realistic is overruled by a need revealed by what disapproving critics have called its '"gimmick" ending' to reinterpret all the supposedly empirical evidence we as readers have received. As Arnold Johnston puts it, the novel's conclusion 'points up the danger of a single, solipsistic viewpoint of which the limitations are unacknowledged' (Johnston 1978: 103). An existential interpretation might suggest that Christopher Martin's thoughts, speech and actions, which constitute a vast proportion of the narrative, do constitute 'existence' outside conventional understandings of the term, but there is no suggestion that such an interpretation should receive validation. As Laing has noted, Golding's novels of the 1950s all combine a secure narrative position with a radical shift of perspective at the end – to that of the naval officer in *Lord of the Flies*, for example – and the first three wreak respective violence upon what he calls 'texts of high-bourgeois optimism' (Laing 1983a: 242): Ballantyne's *The Coral Island* (1857), H. G. Wells's *Outline of History* (1919) and Defoe's *Robinson Crusoe* (1719).

The Appalling Strangeness of the Mercy of God

Pincher Martin is littered with relics of a Christian symbolism – the fortunate fall of Christopher (Christ-bearer) is a kind of salt-water baptism, and his naming of himself, the rock and its scattered landmarks an echo of Genesis – but like the narrative construction itself, they offer little hope of reliability. Other novels of the decade which deal specifically with religious issues are similarly bleak. Brian Moore's *The Lonely Passion of Miss Judith Hearne* (1955), a coruscating account of an alcoholic Catholic spinster in a Belfast she feels to be oppressively Protestant, finally provides no confirmation as to whether Miss Hearne is wrestling with a crisis of faith or one of mental illness. Graham Greene is routinely judged as what Mark Bosco has called 'the gold standard of ... the "Catholic Novel" in English literature' (Bosco 2005: 3). *The End of the Affair* (1951) offers no explicit Catholic consciousness, and is predominantly narrated by Maurice Bendrix, abandoned and harshly resentful lover. The woman he loves, Sarah Miles, makes a pact with God after an air-raid that she will end their passionate and (for her) adulterous relationship if Bendrix's life has been spared. The novel features a late shift in perspective that is more muted but no less radical than Golding's in *Pincher Martin*, providing access to Sarah's diaries after her death to both Bendrix and the reader. They detail her struggle to accept her vow to sacrifice her love for Bendrix, and end by addressing God as a spiritual lover. As Bosco puts it, 'The reader, like Bendrix, finally succumbs to the aura around Sarah's diary' (60). A series of instances of healing that seem to imply Sarah's posthumous involvement, and her mother's late revelation that Sarah had been secretly baptised a Catholic at the age of two, offer up a reading of Sarah as saint. Yet the dominance of Bendrix's harsh but romanticised rationalism through the greater part of the novel, and the hatred and jealousy that he transfers from Sarah to God after reading her diaries, do not allow an unwavering faith in that conclusion. *The End of the Affair* is arguably the last in a cycle of 'Catholic Novels' that began with *Brighton Rock* in 1938 (although after *The Quiet American* (1955) took the ethics of American involvement in Vietnam as a prescient focus, Greene returned to a Catholic *milieu* in the despairing *A Burnt-Out Case*, 1960). The final novel's ultimate ambiguity upholds nothing more certain than what a priest in the first calls the 'appalling ... strangeness of the mercy of God' (Greene 1971: 246).

Muriel Spark's *The Comforters* was published in 1957, three years after her religious conversion. She cast this decision in notably prosaic terms as merely the confirmation of an existing psychology: 'The Catholic Church for me is just a formal declaration of what I believe in any case. It's something to measure from' (Spark 1961: 60). Her first novel was, by her retrospective account, a reluctant enterprise:

> I was asked to write a novel, and I didn't think much of novels – I thought it was an inferior way of writing. So I wrote a novel to work out the technique first, to sort of make it all right with myself to write a novel at all – a novel about writing a novel, about writing a novel sort of thing, you see. (Kermode 1977: 132)

At the centre of *The Comforters* is Caroline Rose. She has lived with her lover, Laurence Mander, for six years, but her recent conversion to

Catholicism has induced her to set up home separately. Laurence's own Catholicism, though lapsed, coupled with his love for her, is sufficient for him to bear with this new celibate arrangement. Spark's title points tangentially to the Book of Job, in which Job receives the attentions of an array of complacent, solipsistic souls offering comfort inapplicable to the torment with which God is testing him. Caroline's own suffering, though less pronounced, is complex; she begins to hear concerted voices and the insistent sound of typing. At times they reference her past, at times predict her future, and sometimes state information concerning the characters around her that is predicated upon the omniscience of the third-person narrator of conventional realism. Caroline's heightened conjunction of religious and metafictional awareness provides a model for Spark's approach to the influence of her faith upon her writing that endures throughout her long career. Religion is a way of confronting reality rather than retreating from it. As Joseph Hynes perceptively suggests, this constitutes a reversal of the

> usual rendering of 'Catholic' and 'catholic'. That is, where speakers are customarily quick to say 'with a small *c*, of course,' and thereby to insist that they mean bigness rather than smallness, Spark's books implicitly and regularly suggest the reverse idea of smallness and bigness, of container and contained. (Hynes 1988: 36–7)

The substance of the plot of *The Comforters* is the Ealing-esque 'case' of Louisa Jepp, Laurence's seventy-eight-year-old grandmother, and her suspected jewel-smuggling ring, a tale so hokey as to parody the straightforward pleasures of the detective story in which investigation leads to the uncovering of a hidden empirical order. Its inevitability brings to mind Bendrix's bitter conclusion at the conclusion of *The End of the Affair* that 'We are inextricably bound to the plot, and wearily God forces us, here and there, according to his intention, characters without poetry, without free will' (Greene 1970: 182), and it gradually ceases to be the plot, becoming an intrusion into Caroline's wider investigations into 'the boundlessly real' (Hynes 1988: 137). Caroline is herself a novelist, currently engaged on a study called *Form in the Modern Novel*. She is 'having difficulty with the chapter on realism' (Spark 1987: 57), yet her trouble pales in comparison to that which 1970s critics, in the first bout of sustained attention to Spark's work, find with the disruption to orthodox realism. 'It leaves the reader puzzled and baulked of his normal reaction to a story,' tutted Patricia Stubbs in a British Council pamphlet (Stubbs 1973: 6), and the otherwise relentlessly approving Peter Kemp called the novel's metafictional aspects 'an attention-catching gimmick but not functional at all: and, as one of those things nourishing the fallacy that Mrs Spark is basically no more than a roguish purveyor of teasing trivialities, it is especially to be regretted' (Kemp 1974: 29). Yet Spark's positioning of her narrative somewhere between the need to present a contingent reality and the infinite freedom of the novelist is indicative of an awareness shared by so many of the new novelists of the 1950s: that of a lack of faith in conventional fictional realism, with its inured assumptions of authority, to convey the truth of their contemporary social experience. For Naipaul, Golding and Spark, in particular, but also for Amis, Sillitoe and Murdoch in their tinkerings with narrative voice, realism becomes an experiment in itself.

Chapter Four

Angering Aunt Edna: 1950s Theatre

In 1955 John Wain, novelist, poet, academic and journalist claimed that:

> What is successful on the stage is a very direct index of the taste and preoccupations of an epoch; a great novel or poem can lie dormant, having its major success a generation or more later, but a dramatist, to stay in business, has to hit the target with every shot. (Wain 1955a: 339)

Certainly, of all literary genres, it is drama that has most noticeably assumed, or been assigned, a representative status for the cultural life of the 1950s in Britain. And of all the cultural activities of the decade, it is theatre that demonstrates the most insistent (and perhaps the most consistent) invocation of a generation gap between the values of old and young, or the old and the new. It is also in critical accounts of the decade's drama, at least since the publication of John Russell Taylor's book *Anger and After* in 1962, that the 1950s has been shaped into a narrative of artistic revolution, with its crisis in 1956, at the first performance of John Osborne's play *Look Back in Anger* at the Royal Court Theatre in London. This dynamic tale contrasts sharply with the sense of stasis that pervades established understandings of the decade's other genres.

At the beginning of the 1950s, Ivor Brown was claiming mildly in the *Observer* that 'It is vaguely felt that we need a new style: T. S. Eliot and Christopher Fry have gone off into poetry, which is one way out: the radicals are rightly groping for some way to freshen the sociological play' (Brown 1950: 6). By the middle years of the decade, journalistic criticism had reached an urgent state of anxiety over the cultural value and legacy of contemporary theatre. Brown's successor, Kenneth Peacock Tynan, whose national reviewing career began in 1954 when he was 27, summoned anger at what he called 'the peculiar nullity of our drama's prevalent genre, the Loamshire play. Its setting is a country house in what used to be called Loamshire but is now, as a heroic tribute to realism, sometimes called Berkshire.' Tynan begged, 'We need plays about cabmen and demi-gods, plays about warriors, politicians and grocers – I care not, so Loamshire be invaded and subdued. I counsel aggression because, as a critic, I had rather be a war correspondent than a necrologist' (Tynan 1954a: 6).

A particular object of Tynan's freelance disgust was an ageing figure ensconced in the theatre seats of London's West End: Aunt Edna. Playwright Terence Rattigan, whose plays had enjoyed enormous commercial success since the end of the war, had spawned Edna's comely person in the preface he wrote for the second volume of his collected plays, published in 1953:

> Let us invent a character, a nice, respectable, middle-class, middle-aged maiden lady, with time on her hands and the money to help her pass it. She enjoys pictures, books, music and the theatre, and though to none of these arts . . . does she bring much knowledge or discernment, at least, as she is apt to tell her cronies, she 'does know what she likes'. Let us call her Aunt Edna. (Rattigan 1953: xii)

She was, he suggested, a type prevalent enough in London audiences to oblige playwrights to cater to her preferences in order to survive commercially. Sure enough, the playbill for the West End in 1955 provided by Taylor in *Anger and After* had plenty to lure Edna and her middle-aged kin. It features some formulaic 'American fare', a few rather creaking British revivals, and 'an unusual number of artless musicals' (Taylor 1968: 17), together with a raft of 'makeshift comedies, turgid melodramas and endless whodunits' (Marowitz et al. 1981: 39). Agatha Christie's *The Mousetrap* had opened in London on 25 November 1952, and is yet to close at the time of writing. Two months before the opening of *Look Back in Anger*, Rayner Heppenstall struck a note of desperation in the *New Statesman* as the decade's years ticked by: 'More than half of the Fifties is now behind us. We ought be able to guess at the myth they will leave': 'a butlers' and antique-dealer's cult of gracious living' (Heppenstall 1956: 377). As Brown had noted, verse drama was continuing its revival from the immediate postwar years, with the reappearance of T. S. Eliot (*The Cocktail Party* in 1949 and *The Confidential Clerk* in 1953), and the continuing success of Christopher Fry (*Venus Observed* in 1950 and *The Dark is Light Enough* in 1954), albeit partly attributable to the participation of acting luminaries such as John Gielgud and Laurence Olivier. We might also note an unusually heavy emphasis on Shakespearean drama during the decade (and on the casting of Gielgud and Olivier within it); Dominic Shellard remarks wryly that 'there now seemed to be no male Shakespearean role that Gielgud could not rescue from critical or academic indifference.' At the *Sunday Times* in 1953,

Harold Hobson alone reviewed twenty-four different productions of Shakespeare plays (Shellard 2000: 37).

Yet, rather than this bardic impasse, it was the decade's array of 'new' British drama which so piqued Tynan's sense of a culture that could look only backwards. The arrival of Arthur Miller's *Death of a Salesman* in London in 1950 had prompted a sense that it was only American playwrights who could unflinchingly scrutinise contemporary society. Five years on, this seemed to be confirmed by a West End dominated by established writers working in their trademarked, and distinctly genteel *milieus*; Rattigan's *Separate Tables* was continuing its run from the previous year, and Noël Coward's *South Sea Bubble* and J. B. Priestley's *The Scandalous Affair of Mr Kettle and Mrs Moon* opened. This prominence of older writers during the first half of the decade has been routinely attributed to the malign influence of H. M. Tennent Ltd, the production company then controlling much of the commerce of the West End, and its managing director, Hugh 'Binkie' Beaumont. The accusations directed at 'the Group', as the corporation became rather sinisterly known, have been amassed with often dubious accuracy to bolster the sense of a 1956 theatrical insurrection. The Group refused to allow contemporary political concerns to sully its sparkling and financially successful stages, and it restricted the lower classes to the cheap seats, barring their appearances in the writers' credits and leading roles. As Dan Rebellato points out, 'This is history as fairy-tale; the smooth villainy of "Binkie" Beaumont, the self-evident wickedness of the West End, and the Court's fresh-faced triumph against all the odds are there in every history' (Rebellato 1999: 38).

Yet pantomime villainy aside, the financial structure of 1950s theatre did have considerable impact upon artistic endeavour. Most theatre managements, in and outside of the Group and of London, had long realised that maximum profits came from long runs of proven plays in their own theatres, rather than risking the production of untested work or the vicissitudes of touring. Arts Council policy during the decade had completely abandoned the 'Art for the People' ethos of its first incarnation, the Council for the Encouragement of Music and Art, founded in 1939. CEMA had placed emphasis on touring areas not served by theatres, galleries and concert halls, and on support for amateur work. Instead, the Arts Council aim of maintaining cultural standards for the nation during the decade translated into the majority of its modest funding (its entire government grant for 1955 to 1956, for example, was £820,000, but £9,300,000 for 1964 to 1965) going to national, professional (and almost exclusively metropolitan) companies (Laing 1983b: 138). A chirpy Q and A in a 1950 Arts Council leaflet encapsulates this ideological shift in relation to theatre: '"Are Drama Societies associated with the Council?" "No. These are almost invariably amateur societies; and the Council, being unable to cover all the ground, has adopted a deliberate policy of directing its financial help towards the professional aspect of the arts"' (quoted Rebellato 1999: 43).

Two new companies entered London's theatrical scene during the 1950s – Theatre Workshop and the English Stage Company – and although debate still rages as to the relative weight of their contributions, their work inarguably both produced and evidenced a shift in metropolitan culture. The founding of each was a direct response to a prevailing economic climate in which bricks and mortar (a theatre of one's own) trumped touring every time. Theatre Workshop had been established as a touring ensemble in 1945 in Kendal, Cumbria, by Joan Littlewood amongst others, but the group settled permanently in London in 1953. They opened with a production of *Twelfth Night* at the Theatre Royal, Stratford East, a moribund building that was painted by the group between performances (they frequently slept there, too, to conserve money). Their innovative approach came to prominence, rather ironically, after touring the Jacobean classic *Volpone* to great acclaim in Paris in 1955. On 24 May 1956, 16 days after the opening elsewhere of *Look Back in Anger*, Brendan Behan's *The Quare Fellow* brought them more acclaim and higher public visibility. 'Miss Littlewood's company have performed a better play than I wrote,' claimed a gracious Behan at the curtain call (Behan 1956: 3).

His comment was validation for the ensemble's distinctive practice, with its emphasis on improvisation and the reworking of texts during rehearsal. Tom Milne claimed that: 'Joan Littlewood's rehearsal method . . . is invaluable. In her rehearsals for *Macbeth*, for example, the actors began by playing at cowboys and Indians, moving gradually to an improvised battle, and finally to the opening scene of the play' (Milne 1981: 82). Similarly childlike qualities had been celebrated in George Devine's review of *The Caucasian Chalk Circle*, one of three productions brought to London by Bertolt Brecht and the Berliner Ensemble in August 1956, the month of Brecht's death; Devine suggested that 'the actors seemed to be like children playing' (Devine 1981: 15). This youthful freedom contrasted sharply with established British acting styles, which Charles Marowitz found to be reduced to 'a mechanical process of Buzz and Flash. Buzz: the cliché-symbol is transmitted; Flash: the cliché-symbol is received' (Marowitz et al. 1981: 20). The old star system was being challenged both by a new, Brechtian disapproval of performances that ostentatiously spotlighted actorly versatility, and by the influence of a fresh transatlantic realism. This latter was inspired by the theories developed by Stanislavsky and the 'Method' technique derived from them by Lee Strasberg, which demanded that actors drew upon their own memories and emotional experiences to give psychological realism to the characters they portrayed. This new brand of stage work aspired to a newly understood authenticity of performance recently appearing on cinema screens, in particular in the directorial work of Elia Kazan and the acting styles of American actors such as Marlon Brando and James Dean.

All the critical quotations in the above paragraph are taken from one publication: *Encore*, which quickly became the house journal for the change of direction in British theatre. Its ideology tended towards the kind of dynamic but vague vocabulary of 'life' and 'feeling' we will go on to find in the rhetoric of the New Left. The magazine's subtitle was 'The Voice of Vital Theatre', and, as Lacey puts it, that concept of the 'vital'

> had a set of immediate and colloquial connotations – of youth and energy, as well as of being necessary and urgent – that place it on a landscape of fifties iconography. It also alluded to a possible social role for theatre, but one which was hard to define in the available languages. (Lacey 1995: 38)

As per the new acting style, this 'social role' depended upon a move beyond a perceivedly outdated naturalism to an updated realism. John Arden's introduction to *Serjeant Musgrave's Dance*, which opened at the Royal Court in 1958, announces it as 'a realistic, but not a naturalistic, play' (Arden 1987: 11), and the play, which confronts its audience with the cruelty of Britain's imperialist warfare, demands a Brechtian style of performance, withholding any focus upon individual motivations in order to present a wider truth.

The English Stage Company (ESC), which took over the Royal Court Theatre in April 1956, was the other important London theatre company founded during the decade. Like Theatre Workshop, they were notably attentive to Brecht; six months after the opening of *Look Back in Anger*, John Osborne was acting as a member of the 'stoic peasantry' in the ESC production of *The Good Woman of Setzuan* (Osborne 1991: 28). Yet whereas Theatre Workshop was an acting / directing / producing ensemble with a commitment to popular forms and a (loosely) shared political outlook, the ESC was a writer's theatre; as artistic director Devine put it, it represented an 'attempt to provide a theatre and conditions where the contemporary dramatist could express himself without having to submit to the increasing hazards of the commercial theatre'. The company aimed to encourage new British writing that was, Devine confidently claimed, 'in touch with contemporary attitudes, with the contemporary searching for new values' (Devine 1957: 152). They commissioned novelists to write plays (Angus Wilson's *The*

Mulberry Bush was the company's first production), as well as advertising for new works, and collaborating with the *Observer* newspaper in a playwriting competition. They ran Sunday night 'Productions without Décor' of plays considered too risky for full staging, presenting them rehearsed and directed, but without costumes or sets. Yet, as for Theatre Workshop, artistic innovation was funded by more traditional endeavours. As Devine confessed in his review of the company's first year:

> We lost a considerable amount of money in our first nine months, and if we consider it ironical that the fortunes of The English Stage Company were, in fact, turned by the presentation of a classical comedy, Wycherley's *The Country Wife* for Christmas, we can only be thankful that, in the theatre, such ironies do exist. (155)

Foreign influence on the British stage during the 1950s was not restricted to that from Germany and the US. Work by both Eugène Ionesco and Samuel Beckett featured prominently in the early years at the Royal Court in particular, yet the work of both these playwrights had already been trialled by director Peter Hall in 1955. *The Lesson*, Ionesco's 1951 play about the illogical murder of a student by her professor, was produced at the Arts Theatre Club in London in March 1955, the private nature of the venue ensuring freedom from censorship of the play's sexually charged material by the Lord Chamberlain's Office. (This official surveillance was to continue, albeit with increasing liberalism, until 1968.) Five months later, Hall's production of Beckett's *Waiting for Godot* opened to an audience of barely 300. Like *The Lesson*, *Godot* played upon the fundamental impossibility of human communication, with its tramp-like characters conversing in an empty, repetitive banter. Almost endlessly elusive, its Absurdism directly contradicted the impulse towards explicit engagement with contemporary society that Tynan, for one, envisaged as a means of revitalising 1950s British theatre. A printed spat with Ionesco on the civic responsibilities of theatre was to follow in 1958 (see Ionesco: 1958b). None the less, the critic immediately recognised the play's dramatic implications: '"Waiting for Godot" frankly jettisons everything by which we recognise theatre . . . It forced me to re-examine the rules which have hitherto governed the drama, and, having done so, to pronounce them not elastic enough. It is validly new' (Tynan 1955b: 11).

An Audience of 6,733,000

Despite its performance in a private club, the Lord Chamberlain still sent one of his censors to watch *Godot*, after receiving a complaint about its obscenity. C. D. Heriot wrote on 30 November: 'The general feeling seemed, like mine, to be one of acute boredom – except for a sprinkling of young persons in slacks and Marlon Brando pullovers with (according to sex) horsetails or fringes, who applauded pointedly' (quoted Shellard et al. 2004: 150–1). This identification of youth (albeit a heavily clichéd vision of it) with the culturally unfamiliar was not restricted to the old guard, but celebrated by the new theatre companies and the publications that celebrated them. Devine identified as 'products of the new Education Act' a group of young people who 'came stream-ing into the tired metropolis, they woke up everything they touched . . . For all these, the Royal Court became a symbol, even if they did not bother to patronise its plays' (Devine 1962: 12). Lacey notes how 'In retrospect, this image of a theatre inhabited by a young public does cor-respond to real changes in audience composition, changes which were to become more apparent in the sixties and seventies' (Lacey 1995: 55–6). During the 1950s, however, these new playgoers remained as idealised (and as fictionalised) as Aunt Edna herself. In one of his final pieces of the decade, 'Summing-Up: 1959', Tynan wrote of a performance of Arnold Wesker's *Roots* that:

> The theatre, I noticed, was full of young men and women who had been dis-tracted from the movies, from television, and even from love-making by the powerful lure of a show that concerned them and that could help as well as amuse. (Tynan 1964: 87)

Yet it is, of course, another play, and another Tynan review, that loom over any account of 1950s drama: John Osborne's *Look Back in Anger*, submitted to Devine at the Royal Court in response to an advertisement in *The Stage*.

The performance on Tuesday, 8 May 1956, along with Osborne's play as a wider phenomenon with all its paraphernalia of criticism, counter-criticism, adaptation and publicity, is an indisputably mythic cultural event – *the* presiding cultural event of the British 1950s. As such, the play has been the subject of some intense recent critical revi-sionism (see, for example, Rebellato 1999; Shellard 2000). What it indu-bitably was *not* was an iconoclastic creative event, at least at the level of theatrical form. The sense of the 1950s as a genuinely transitional period between the conservative and the radical has been borne out by the financial sustenance of its two most innovative theatre companies by Jacobean and Restoration comedy, and it is underlined again by the formal traditionalism of its supposedly most dissident play. In this way, at least, *Look Back in Anger* maintains a claim to represent the zeitgeist. We might also note how the conventional status of the play's form – its well-madeness and legible naturalism – allowed it to be taken up so instantly and vehemently by critics as an articulation of contemporary cultural anxieties, in a way that the allusive *Godot*, for instance, was not. Yet the focus of claims for the play's representative status, both then and now, was on the decade's most freighted symbol: youth. John Barber, reviewing the play in the *Daily Express*, concluded: 'It is intense, angry, feverish, undisciplined. It is even crazy. But it is young, young, young' (Taylor 1983: 46).

Another of the myths surrounding *Look Back in Anger*, now largely scotched, is that it was Tynan's review that rescued the play from universal condemnation. In fact, most critical responses, like Barber's, followed an attention to the play's flaws in construction and characterisation with a final and resounding approbation of its energy, language, youth, modernity and promise. Only the *Evening News* ('putrid bosh') and the *Birmingham Post* ('an extension of some feebly rancid short story in a highly contemporary idiom') were unreservedly negative, and that latter condemnation at least acknowledges that the play's language sounds up-to-date (Taylor 1983: 43, 45). Tynan's article, 'The Voice of the Young', published on the Sunday five days after opening night, was later denigrated by Osborne as 'the most hedging rave ever written' (quoted Kathleen Tynan 1988: 125). It is certainly noticeably lacking in the fearless polemic and insouciant style of Tynan's responses to innumerable other plays. To his review of Rattigan's *Separate Tables* in 1954, he gave the form of a spoof dialogue between 'A Young Perfectionist' and the 'universal and immortal' Aunt Edna herself. The youth grants that 'the play is as good a handling of sexual abnormality as English playgoers will tolerate.' 'For my part,' Edna responds, 'I am glad it is no better.' 'I guessed you would be,' says the Y. P., 'and so did Mr Rattigan' (Tynan 1954b: 11). Tynan's deftly satirical touch contrasts sharply with Rattigan's misjudgement in creating Aunt Edna. This has to do with context; the preface to a *Collected Plays* is, of course, an entirely different textual environment to that of the *Observer* arts page. It is also, perhaps, a question of professionalism. Young wrote of Rattigan's 'light-hearted' prefaces that 'They almost give the feeling, in spite of the importance he attaches to technique, that he thought of himself as an amateur' (Young 1986: 123). For all his light-hearted mode of expression, Tynan, a successful dandy at Oxford but a failed actor and director after it, was deadly serious about his reviewing career, and as we shall see in Chapter 12, professionalism was a crucial standard for young critics of the 1950s.

Until the final paragraph of 'The Voice of the Young', however, Tynan's tone is troubled. He seems to feel obliged to respond to the negative points in reviews by the daily papers, fending off accusations that the marriage of Jimmy Porter and the upper-class Alison is unrealistic, that Osborne is insufficiently critical of Jimmy, that the play has no action, and only budging to allow that the final scene is one of 'painful whimsy'. The real nature of Tynan's burden is the difficulty of manipulating contradictory contemporary discourses surrounding youth to Osborne's unfettered advantage. He even begins the piece by defending *Lucky Jim* against Somerset Maugham's verdict that the new breed of State-aided university students are 'scum', pronouncing *Look Back in Anger* to be 'all scum and a mile wide' (Tynan 1956: 11). Such a clunky Americanism only proves Maugham's point about cultural denigration to a reader predisposed to agree with him.

Tynan's review is fraught with contradiction. He tries to mobilise Jimmy both as a figure representative of youthful disregard for class through his 'realistically' hypergamous marriage, and as a member of a very precisely located, young, 'non-U intelligentsia' that has been damaged by the social necessity of leaving its origins behind. He cites Jimmy's 'evident and blazing vitality' (*Encore* magazine's most cherished quality) to refute accusations of a lack of action in the play, but without evidencing it, then follows it with a rueful confession that Osborne 'certainly goes off the deep end'. And he aligns Jimmy with a swathe of topical concerns that the media have hyped as characteristic of youth – 'leftishness', jazz, corporal punishment, sexual promiscuity – while trying to enshrine him as an unmediated voice of the young. Tellingly, many of the contradictions in his piece – an overwrought 'realistic' idiom, the clash between Jimmy's classlessness and class obsession, the affectless effect of his constant ranting and the shifting terms of his social critique – reproduce those of Osborne's play itself. As we have seen, they are also characteristic of the metaphorical burden placed upon youth more generally.

In his final paragraph, Tynan finally casts his defensive stance with a flourish. 'I agree that *Look Back in Anger* is likely to remain a minority taste,' he writes, seeming still to hedge, then: 'What matters, however, is the size of the minority. I estimate it at roughly 6,733,000, which is the number of people in this country between the ages of twenty and thirty.' It is no matter that the vast majority of these young people live outside London, and no matter that most of them will never set foot in a theatre, drawn instead to the flickering screens of cinema and, increasingly, television.[1] And it is no matter that the Royal Court could accommodate only 480 of their youthful bottoms on its tatty, limited seating. Tynan had invoked the new audience of the 1950s – the young – who did not need to show up at the theatre in order to have their presence felt in its auditorium. He finishes with a return to his characteristically hyperbolic tone, sealing a relationship between Osborne's play and the spirit of the 1950s which endures today: 'I doubt if I could love anyone who did not wish to see *Look Back in Anger*. It is the best young play of its decade.' *The* play of the British 1950s has now been comprehensively worked over by those determined to debunk its revolutionary status. It is a testament to the enduring power of Tynan's writing, at least, that those closing sentences of his review can still inspire a sense of the powerful pleasure of myth-making.

Domestics' Space

The curtains open on 'a fairly large attic room, at the top of a large Victorian house'; in the house's heyday, this would have been the servants' quarters. The stage is littered with furniture for storing clothes, books and food, and for sitting, dining and sleeping, most of it 'simple, and rather old'. Two men are slumped in armchairs. Tatty domestic appliances are also in evidence – a gas stove, a storage tank, and an ironing board placed before the only woman on the stage (Osborne 1989: 9–10). Though such a scene was not necessarily new (Priestley's *The Scandalous Affair of Mr Kettle and Mrs Moon*, playing London in 1955, was set in the living room of a flat in Brickmill, North Midlands, for instance), it was certainly intended, as Lacey puts it, as 'an act of semiotic vandalism, challenging almost point by point the iconography of the bourgeois living-room and the country-house drawing room' of the Loamshire play (Lacey 1995: 29). Its off-stage equivalent was certainly very familiar to many of that audience of 6,733,000. George Scott's autobiography, *Time and Place*, documents how the 'anxieties of finding a place to live and bring up our families in post-war Britain have been chronic' amongst those in their twenties during the 1950s; rather than renting houses, 'It was furnished rooms and furnished flats only – and almost always there should have been inverted commas around the furnished' (Scott 1956: 175, 171). The Porters' one-room flat provides both a material realism and an emotional potential. In *Look Back in Gender*, Micheline Wandor notes how 'the cluster of kitchen, eating, entertaining and sleeping areas suggests a hothouse of interpersonal relations' (Wandor 1987: 8).

As this study will go on to attest, both 'home' and 'the family' were intensely politicised concepts during the 1950s, polemically charged as they were with the task of postwar reconstruction. Onstage, Arnold Wesker's trilogy, incorporating *Chicken Soup with Barley* (1958), *Roots* (1959) and *I'm Talking about Jerusalem* (1960), provided the most explicit examination of the relationship between family and political activism, in an epic dramatisation of the negotiation of the changing terms of Socialism by three generations of the Kahn family. (*Roots* is examined in greater detail in Chapter 10.) Rather than this overt treatment, the plays examined in this chapter share the tendency to transpose collectivist political issues on to personal experiences of generational and gender conflict. As such, the family forms their epicentre, together with 'something of an index of the way in which personal and political interact – or do not' (Wandor 1987: 36).

As Wandor's study persuasively examines, *Look Back in Anger* presents us with numerous familial configurations and kinships, the first being that 'facsimile of the family' with Jimmy and Alison Porter and their surrogate 'child', Cliff (47). The play performs a series of substitutions. Alison's mother, snobbish and domineering, is a dominant presence despite the fact she never appears, and Jimmy nicknames the centre-stage storage tank after her (Osborne 1989: 85). By contrast, his own mother is a central absence, invoked only so that her selfish disapproval can further sour his father's death on his return from the Spanish Civil War (57), and replaced by surrogate Mrs Tanner, who sets him up with the inexplicable sweet stall business. Jimmy pays lip service to despising Alison's father, Colonel Redfern, but this is softened by his rueful envy of the Edwardian certainties of the older man's past, to the extent that the two mirror each other in their rejection of the present. Helena replaces Alison in Jimmy's bed, and at the play's conclusion when Alison loses their baby, Jimmy is able to subsume his status as her husband in the childish Bears and Squirrels game.

In *The Uses of Literacy*, Richard Hoggart claims of the figure of the 'scholarship boy', educated, like Jimmy, beyond the presiding mean of his class, that 'he now tends to be closer to the women of the house than to the men' (Hoggart 1958: 295). The feminisation of young men is a spectre that haunts Jimmy Porter (and the literature of the decade more widely; see Ferrebe 2005), and one that finds voice in the vehement misogyny of his tirades against his wife. Coaching Emma Thompson to play Alison in Judi Dench's 1989 revival of the play, Osborne is still desperate to maintain the urgency of this threat:

> I tried to explain that it was she, not her husband, who was the most deadly bully . . . The ironing board was not the plaything of her submission, but the bludgeon and shield which were impenetrable to all Jimmy's appeals to desperate oratory. (Osborne 1996: xii)

The home as battleground, with women as the foe; in Errol John's *Moon on a Rainbow Shawl* (1958) this is also the case, although rather than a

Victorian house, the embattled domestic scene is a Trinidadian yard (its space similarly divided between its residents).

John's play was composed in London in 1955 (Westall 2005: n.p., par 3) but came to prominence, and production, when it won the 1957 *Observer* / Royal Court play competition. The young man Ephraim is struggling to free himself from the yard, and a life, that seem dominated by women. There is the bossy matriarch, Sophia Adams, her preternaturally intelligent twelve-year-old daughter, Esther, promiscuous Mavis, and Eph's girlfriend, Rosa, who has just discovered that she is pregnant ('TRAP!' Eph screams wildly when she tells him; John 1985: 53). Sophia's husband, Charlie, first appears drunk from a party for returning troops, '*carrying a glass half full with Coca-Cola*', with a small Union Jack hanging from his jacket pocket and a Royal Air Force officer's cap askew on his head. Charlie, once a fast bowler of international promise, is now a tottering, '*big, bloated, brown-skinned man*' (39), his size and softness reminiscent of his wife's plumpness, decked out in the symbols, corporate and military, of the occupying powers. Richard Burton has emphasised a structuring dialectic at work within the Caribbean traditions of both cricket and calypso, which places the feminine domesticity of the yard against the masculinity of proving oneself in the public space of the street (and the pitch) (Burton 1997). To Eph, Charlie functions as a vision of his own feminised and colonised future if he does not leave the island. As he leaves a desperate Rosa for passage on a tanker at the end of the play, the only hope left in Trinidad is tentative, partial, female and that of a still younger generation: Esther calls 'Ma-ah!' in a voice that '*has warmth – a certain intimacy – strength. It should give the impression that the future could still be hers*' (85). That the tanker is bound for Liverpool, one of the key ports of the slave trade, suggests Eph's future freedom is far from assured.

Doris Lessing's *Each His Own Wilderness* was first produced as a Sunday night performance without décor at the Royal Court in 1958, and in it Ephraim's vision of a feminised generation of young men has come to pass in the character of twenty-two-year-old Tony Bolton, who has just returned home from National Service. The play is predicated upon a generational divide over which causes are good, brave and worthy. For Tony's mother, Myra, and her friend, Milly Boles, everything is worth fighting for, as it is the fight that counts; as Tony puts it, 'Milly will help Mother to battle with the Bomb when she's not attending to racial prejudice and the Chinese peasantry . . . I simply cannot endure them. It's their utterly appalling vitality' (Lessing 1968: 107). Like Jimmy Porter, he wants to opt out of the 'respectable' employment available to a man of his education in favour of a gesture of self-sacrifice;

like Jimmy's, Tony's cynicism sounds more like a plaintive hysteria. As with Jimmy, we are offered the unjust death of his father (killed in a bombing raid) as partial justification for his habitual anguish. Each young man, we are told, was 'born out of his time' (129; Osborne 1989: 90).

Lessing's play affords considerably more insight into her female characters than is bestowed upon Alison, and they are allowed to prick Tony's misogyny with an irony that Osborne cannot allow. Having slept with Milly, Tony swerves from posturing aggression to craven submission in an instant:

> TONY [*guilty*]: Of course women are so much better than men.
> MILLY [*grimly*]: Is that so?
> TONY [*sentimental and shrill*]: You're so much stronger.
> MILLY: That's very nice for you, isn't it? (Lessing 1962: 149–50)

However, there are moments of the play in which Tony is allowed a genuine critique of his mother's generation, suggesting their frenetic empathy and the loudness of their political causes to be no more than empty gestures in the wake of disillusionment with Socialism. This is an apathy just as noisy and exhausting as Jimmy's has proved to some of his audience and commentators. 'I've spent a good part of what are known as my formative years listening to the conversation of the mature,' Tony tells his mother. 'You're sloppy and corrupt. I'm waiting for that moment when you put your foot down about something and say you've had enough. But you never do. All you do is watch things – with interest' (114). After the death of the husband she adored (the Bomb has distinctly personal ramifications for Myra), she has steadfastly refused to compromise her feelings in a long-term relationship of lesser love. Though the play suggests a certain heroism in this, it also upholds the failed family as the source of Tony's hysteria and his fetishisation of his mother's house. The only 'cause' that Tony is able wholeheartedly to place himself behind is that of giving their home a new lick of paint (160). His need for security is the direct result of his mother's strident insistence upon his freedom, but he also reads his limited horizons as the product of the older generation's compromised and pusillanimous socialist vision:

> Do you know what it is you've created, you and your lot? What a vision it is! A house for every family. Just imagine – two hundred million families – or is it four hundred million families? To every family a front door. Behind every front door, a family. A house full of clean, well-fed people, and not one of them ever understands one word anyone else says. Everybody a kind of wilderness surrounded by barbed wire shouting across the defences into the

other wildernesses and never getting an answer back. That's socialism . . . To
each man his own front door – to each man his own – refrigerator! (123–5)

This speech, tracing the divide between grandiose political aspirations
and their narrow realisations, can itself serve as metaphor for the dramatic technique of the most representative plays of the 1950s. They
deal with the wider ideological issues in the narrow confines of crowded
domestic spaces, rooms that in their tatty décor and degraded appliances
are a direct confrontation, not only of the Loamshire drawing room, but
also of the shiny efficiency of the advertisement kitchens, the efficient
heart of a happy home.

Lessing's play does not provide anything like a corrective answer to
the skewed gender politics of Osborne's. Rather, it reproduces much
of the emotional confusion of *Look Back in Anger*, as well as reinforc-
ing Jimmy's perception of a lack of good, brave causes that speak to
the young. It ends with a young couple, Tony and Rosemary, in the
same kind of fey stasis as Jimmy and Alison in their game of Bears and
Squirrels. Tony suggests, 'Supposing we all said to the politicians – we
refuse to be heroic. We refuse to be brave. We are bored with all the
noble gestures,' and Rosemary concurs: 'Yes. Ordinary and safe.' Tony
ends the play by continuing their cocooning fantasy: 'Leave us alone,
we'll say. Leave us alone to live. Just leave us alone. . .' (167).

Osborne's subsequent and infinitely subtler play, *The Entertainer*
(1957), centres upon yet another failing family, the Rices, with each
member held helplessly in emotional stasis. Not one of these plays is
able to offer even a partial solution to the generational conflict upon
which their drama is predicated. In this way they voice the genuine
sense of uncertainty about issues surrounding youth that we traced in
Chapter 2. In 1958 Alan Brien wrote disparagingly of another *Observer*
competition winner, *A Taste of Honey*, that:

> Twenty, ten, or even five years ago, before a senile society began to fawn
> upon the youth which is about to devour it, such a play would have remained
> written in green longhand in a school exercise book on the top of the
> bedroom wardrobe. (Brien 1958: 729)

The ill-tempered tone of his piece might conceivably be attributed less
to the play itself, which is both well made and innovative, than to the
furore of publicity that hyped author Sheila Delaney's own youth,
gender and (working) class as debilitations miraculously overcome.

Once again, Delaney's play is set within a shabby domestic interior,
and once again it presents a challenge to expectations of appropriate
behaviour, both within that space and under the slightly more roomy

auspices of 'the family'. Very little conventional domestic activity takes place within the stage space, and when it does, it is never performed by its traditional practitioners. The play elicits sympathy for a number of characters already burdened with contemporary cultural and social pressures: the teenager Jo who gets pregnant, the black boy with whom she is in love, 'semi-whore' Helen, her (now-)single mother, and Jo's friend Geof, who is homosexual (Delaney 1982: 7). Unruly sexuality is a key concern for everyone in the play, even Helen, whose apparently careless promiscuity overlays a desperate need to regain some measure of respectability in an enduring relationship with Peter (an alliance which fails in the course of the play). Ultimately, though, it is the (socially validated) mother / daughter relationship which endures, and the uncomfortable intimacy initially forced upon Jo and Helen in the sharing of the stage's double bed deepens into authentic kinship. Indeed, as Shellard has shown through his work on theatre censorship, the character of Geof was the first practical consequence of a secret memorandum of 31 October 1956 from the Lord Chamberlain that lifted the ban on the representation of homosexuality on the stage, largely because, in the assessor's view, Geof satisfactorily 'explains that he is really quite a normal young man, only not very strongly sexed, and with a very real desire to marry and settle down and have a family' (Shellard et al. 2004: 159).

A Taste of Honey breaks another theatrical taboo. As Wandor states, 'here is a play, in a domestic setting, which follows the fortunes of the women at its centre' (Wandor 2001: 61). Women also lie at the emotional centre of George Munro's *Gay Landscape*. The play's three acts are set in 1908, 1914 and the 'Present Day' respectively, and they span three generations of a family as they come and go from John and Magdalene Gascoyne's home in Glasgow's shipbuilding district, Govan.[2] It was first performed in 1958 at Glasgow's Citizens' Theatre, an organisation that gives the lie to the idea of Theatre Workshop's collaborative ethos and dedication to working-class art forms as unique in Britain in the 1950s. So too does the city's Unity Theatre, which produced Robert McLeish's *The Gorbals Story*, filmed in 1950. In fact, as Randall Stevenson has noted, Joan Littlewood's group might well have settled in Glasgow after successive successful visits to the city during the Forties (Stevenson 1987: 349). *Gay Landscape* itself was to transfer to the Royal Court in London.

Munro's play charts a number of extraordinarily intense and malevolent family feuds. The Reverend Ian Alastair Forbes, married to Anne Gascoyne, and the only empathetic and compassionate male in Munro's piece, asks despairingly at one point: 'Is every family gathering to take on the air of clan clash?' (Munro, Act II: 26). This malevolence is driven by a wide range of bitterly contentious contemporary issues – sexuality, education, socialism, religion – which, as in *A Taste of Honey*, are mapped on to generational conflicts by means of the representation of the domestic space and the role of women within it, specifically regarding their reproductive capacities. The setting of Magdalene's tenement kitchen in the inaptly named 'Harmony Row' inexorably deteriorates from the 'antiseptic cleanliness' and glossy grate of 1908 (Act I: 1) to the squalor of the present day, with a scuffed grate, table littered with empty beer bottles and fish and chip papers, and granddaughter Liz sprawled in slatternly fashion in the hole-in-the-wa' bed (Act III: 1). To a Scottish audience, rather than a London one, of course, one-room living, with alcove beds and a shared, not just exterior, toilet, had been a reality in an urban setting since the Industrial Revolution.

The play also traces the progressive denigration of the Gascoynes' approach to and behaviour at the religious ceremonies that mark the changes in family life. They proclaim themselves 'a strong Presbyterian family always' (Act II: 8), and Munro, himself brought up in the Brethren, notes dryly in his fulsome opening directions that 'a Catholic might sooner forfeit a right to Extreme Unction than a Gascoyne his or her right to attend a family christening, marriage, funeral or feud' (2). In Act I, they observe a fairly traditional public ritual at their father's death. Act II centres upon the christening of Martha's illegitimate daughter, fathered, is revealed to the audience, by her brother-in-law, Josef; it is a rushed, private affair, performed out of a mixture of compassion and shame by Ian. Act III, on the day of Magdalene's funeral, contains a still less salubrious 'christening' of sorts, in which the father of Martha's daughter is revealed to the family at large, just after she has spent the night in the tenement flat with Joseph Savage, now revealed as her half-brother. (It is fairly swiftly confirmed that incest, the ultimate family taboo, did not take place; asked, 'There was no haymaking here last night?', Liz replies, 'savagely', 'Only a hieland christening,' Act III: 34).

Wandor has noted of the Wesker trilogy that it features

> a fascinating contradiction: on the one hand the women are given a powerful political and cultural voice which in most other plays is the prerogative of men. On the other hand, the conventional gender roles within the family are seen to be under strain. (Wandor 1987: 25)

As we have seen, this inability to validate a revisioning of the family is the case in *Each His Own Wilderness* and *A Taste of Honey*. Munro is more radical. Despite the mouthy and aggressive allegiances sworn by her various aunts towards family and decency, it is Liz who visited and cared for her grandmother in 'Merryflats Asylum' where her daughters put her 'among the demented and the derelict' (Act III: 20), and Liz who held her as she died. At the end of the play Liz rounds on her family with the final judgement of her taciturn grandmother:

> D'you want to know what she said to me at this hearth, the last time I combed her hair? I'll tell you. 'Elizabeth Margaret', she said, 'from my womb there never came woman good enough to wipe the stour from your shoes. For I know that you never brought your grandmother a girning look or a crookit bawbee.' Away with you. All of you. You're naebodies! (28)

Magdelene's only support and real kinship at the end of her life has come from a disowned granddaughter, 'a wean' born 'out of wedlock' (Act II: 2) but bound by strong ties of love. The play ends by confirming the tyranny of the existing family structure, as well as the pathos of Liz's loss; alone and drinking again, she tries out her newly revealed name, 'A name to nod me into mourning everlasting', then gives a 'Throbbing, heartrending wail' for her granny (Act III: 35).

Stevenson notes the 'strangely rhythmic, alliterative language' of *Gay Landscape* that moves it 'beyond the naturalism of his other work' (Stevenson 1987: 350). The various idiolects of Munro's characters are sites of inscription for the same social and cultural conflicts that incorporate the play's plot. Eldest brother Archibald is a riveter in the shipyard, and we are told that his 'muscular look advertises his trade ... He is big, black and ruddy. Only his voice bewilders. It is reedy' (Act I: 8). At home, he is frequently made inarticulate and impotent by the anger aroused in him by his confident and garrulous sisters. The way all the Gascoynes speak is testament to their clan history, their loss, and the pretensions that blight their morality; an Author's Note reads, 'Although living in tenement setting, the Gascoynes cling to inherited highland speech: their talk may borrow from tenement vocabulary but not their accents. Thus their speech is "English as read", made attractive by a slight Invernessian accent' (Cast List: 1). These linguistic politics ensure a place can be made for *Gay Landscape* within an alternative history of British drama to the one focused upon in *Look Back in Anger*: one which traces the development of a (postmodern) theatre that explores language itself as the site of meaning (or its absence), and performance as the moment of production of that meaning (or its lack). Cultural movements rarely have clearly defined beginnings, and postmodernism's origins have a claim to being some of the most indeterminate of all (see, for example, Eagleton 1996). This study, by its nature as a contextually situated survey of the decade's literature, reads its selected plays as both reflecting and defining their social and cultural background, while recognising that such a reading, like that of the 1950s as representing in some way the 'beginning of postmodernism', is always a partial one.

The plays that Harold Pinter produced during the 1950s can be situated at precisely the point at which these two differently inflected readings meet. In *Anger and After* Taylor gives Pinter a chapter all to himself; Lacey suggests that this indicates 'that even at this early stage his work was considered important, and also difficult to insert into the main modes of contemporary theatre' (Lacey 1995: 140). Pinter's work can be placed in an Absurdist tradition alongside that of Beckett and Ionesco, with a common refusal of any knowable representational function. Debate continues as to whether Pinter's stylistic innovation was domestic or imported. *The Times* review of *The Birthday Party* (1958) called the play an 'essay in surrealistic drama ... [that] gives the impression of deriving from an Ionesco play which M. Ionesco has not yet written' (Pinter 1958: 3): Pinter himself denied this aping of the continental avant-garde.

If Pinter's plays defy easy categorisation it is because they provide the appearance of social realism, with none of its explanations. Yet Alan Sinfield certainly has no problem in situating Pinter's plays within a legible realist context: 'His sense of idiosyncratic detail in the speech of different classes and of the dynamics of psychological tension suggest naturalistic rather than absurdist drama' (Sinfield 1983a: 183). *The Birthday Party* and *The Room* (1960) explore the gendered dynamics of power at work in a boarding house and a rented room respectively. The pitch of unease and virulent helplessness of their older female characters, Meg and Rose, both make a mockery of psychoanalyst D. W. Winnicott's breezy contemporaneous claim that

> Talk about women not wanting to be housewives seems to me to be just nonsense, because nowhere else but in her own home is woman in such command. Only in her own home is she free, if she has the courage, to spread herself, to find her whole self. (Winnicott 1957: 88)

Both plays rehearse, in their disjointed and frequently non-comprehending conversational exchanges, the role of the scholarship boy (for the superior speakers in both are always men), elevated in education and eloquence. In these plays, words are not absurdly empty of meaning, but chillingly effective as social weapons.

In its melding of a bleak social critique with a wider, unnerving, existential malaise, Pinter's work unsettles any simple dichotomy between realism and Absurdism in 1950s British theatre. Periods of transition disrupt staunch binary oppositions in this way. We might even return to the maligned Terence Rattigan's plays to suggest that they similarly defy clear-cut categorisation, notably within the terms of the decade's most trammelled symbolic opposition: that of old and young. By the time of Rattigan's preface to the 1964 third volume of his collected plays, Aunt Edna, motivated perhaps by desperation, has undergone 'a rejuvenation operation in 1955', and now attends and enjoys the challenge of plays by John Osborne, Harold Pinter and Arnold Wesker (quoted Young 1986: 125). Yet there is certainly no debate that Rattigan's work provided a sense of counterpoint for a number of emerging playwrights during the 1950s; Innes claims that it was 'outraged disgust at seeing Margaret Leighton wasting her talents in Rattigan's *Variation on a Theme* [1958] that moved Shelagh Delaney (still a schoolgirl in 1958) to write her first play, *A Taste of Honey*' (Innes 2000: 54), and Wansell reports Rattigan remarking at the premiere of *Look Back in Anger* that the play could have been entitled 'Look, Ma, I'm not Terence Rattigan' (Wansell 1995: 270). It becomes harder, too, to chalk Edna up to a misjudgement of the readership's mood when we consider her against a series of controversial public statements by Rattigan. In 'Concerning the Play of Ideas', published in *New Statesman and Nation* in 1950, for example, his explicitly anti-political championing of character and narrative above 'Ideas' had triggered an outcry and prompted responses by playwrights including George Bernard Shaw, Christopher Fry and Sean O'Casey. Of Rattigan's two major plays of the 1950s, *The Deep Blue Sea* (1952) most obviously upholds a privileging of character above all else, narrative included, in its study of Hester Collyer. As Gross points out, 'contemporary social realities are used as secondary elements that underscore primary, psychological processes' (Gross 1990: 398), like the finely pathetic irony that Hester's suicide attempt fails because she did not have enough coins to put in the gas meter.

Separate Tables (1955) however, explores contemporary social realities more explicitly in its presentation of the Beauregard Private Hotel, near Bournemouth, and the focus shifts from an individual to a society in transition. The hotel's postwar residents range across ages and classes, all of them homeless, or rather forced to make the various public rooms in which we view them function like a private home. Like all of the self-consciously realist plays examined in this chapter, issues of environmental and economic determinism are, as Lacey puts it, 'made concrete in the stage space itself, which ceased to be simply a location for the action, and became a tangible representation of the oppressive force of a constraining social and natural order, limiting the possibilities for change and growth' (Lacey 1995: 69). Once again, the dissonance between the

'ideal home' (and family) of the decade's postwar propaganda and commercial iconography and the characters' situation is obvious. Yet unlike
most of the plays produced by younger writers, an alternative to the traditional familial configuration is offered by the conclusion of *Separate
Tables*. Its nominal climax is the defiance of Age (and class hierarchies)
by youth, as Sybil refuses her mother's order that she snub 'Major'
Pollock. A more subtle and communal triumph is reached, however, by
the guests at large, as, old or younger, Tory or Socialist, they adjust their
reflex moral absolutes to produce a more tolerant environment. This tol-
erance may provide only a thin veneer over a mass of social conflicts (the
generational divide being the most turbulent), but its formation denies
the idea of Rattigan as simplistically bourgeois, ignoring unsavoury
swathes of the contemporary world.

Recent re-evaluations of Rattigan's work in the centenary year of his
birth, 2011, drew heavily on the motif of generational divide, and a sense
of Rattigan's unfair treatment at the hands of insensitive youth – Simon
Heffer in the *Daily Telegraph* suggested that 'Brutal realism, shouting,
emotional incontinence, confrontation and other forms of psychological
savagery seemed suddenly to revolutionise the English drama. The herd
went along with Osborne; Rattigan's reputation seemed to evaporate
overnight' (Heffer 2011). This is, of course, a recognisable journalistic
tactic – any story of the revival of an artist's work requires a back story
of that work's unfair repression – but playwright David Hare suspects
a more sinister motive. He reads Rattigan's most recent redemption as
part of a current flourishing of Right-wing art in what he calls, writing
in *The Guardian*, a contemporary 'national festival of reaction', and
attempts to counter it by denying once again the narrative of a 1956
theatrical insurrection:

> To this day our dramatic ecology is much as it has always been: apolitical
> formalist experiment and classical revival jostling in pleasant diversity along-
> side vehicles for jetted-in Hollywood stars and evenings of musical uplift. The
> glories of the British theatre remain the brilliance of its actors and the vibran-
> cies of its small spaces. At no point have revolutionaries from Sloane Square
> looked like taking over the show. (Hare 2011: 28)

Tynan, despite being one of the loudest voices crying for change
in 1950s drama, provides us with a more measured approach to
Rattigan's role in the disputed revolution: 'Mr Rattigan', he wrote in
1955, 'is the Formosa of the contemporary theatre, occupied by the old
guard, but geographically inclined towards the progressives' (Tynan
1964: 32–3).

Notes

1. For the role played by television in the success of *Look Back in Anger*, see Chapter 12.
2. To date, *Gay Landscape* remains inexplicably unpublished. All references are to the undated manuscript copy in Glasgow's Mitchell Library, with the pagination of that manuscript's various divisions.

II.

The Less Deceived

Chapter Five

Women, Children and Home

On 24 July 1959, US Vice President Richard Nixon and Soviet Premier Nikita Khrushchev had a televised discussion at the opening of the American National Exhibition in Moscow. The Cold War was escalating, and this was the first high-level meeting between the two superpowers since the Geneva summit of 1955. Their rumbustious conversation began outside the television studio, in the kitchen of the cross-section of a $14,000 house the exhibitors claimed that, in the new affluent America, every citizen could afford. Nixon's pitch for the superiority of the capitalist system puts much emphasis on the 'new inventions and new techniques' apparent in the room. On the gleaming Formica work surface sits a box emblazoned 'SOS' (full of 'interwoven soap pads') but neither man, each belligerent but good-humoured, gives signals of distress. 'In America', Nixon claims before Khrushchev interrupts him once again, we like to make life easier for women . . .' (Nixon 1959: n.p.).

The location for these ideological wranglings – a set dressed as a capitalist kitchen – seems irresistibly appropriate for a decade for which, in Britain as well as in the US, the real influence of so much of global, national and personal politics was felt within confined domestic spaces. As we have seen in Chapter 4, the dramatic stage with its kitchen sink is an obvious symbol of this influence, but perhaps the readiest of the emblems of the British 1950s to spring to mind is that of the housewife courtesy of 'Admass', redolent of baking and fulfilment, beaming ecstatically at the bounty of a groaning refrigerator, a fragrant washing machine or a laden tray hot from the oven. For all their relentless joy, the visuals of these advertising campaigns carry a touch of residual heroism from the determined housewives of war propaganda, making them still more unnerving to the jaded twenty-first-century eye. In reality, it was women who were much more intensively exposed to both the privileges and pressures of increasing affluence throughout the 1950s, though

Figure 6   US Vice President Richard Nixon and Soviet Premier Nikita Khrushchev argue in a mock-up kitchen at the American National Exhibition in Moscow, 1959.

as Wendy Webster makes clear, this viewpoint, and the chapter that follows here, are selective, as 'A focus on black women produces a very different story – of poorly paid, low-status, full-time employment, separation from family through the process of migration, a search for accommodation in which the sign "no coloureds" was repeatedly encountered' (Webster 1998: x). As Nixon's assertions echoing across the Pond attest, it was (white, middle-class) women who came to bear a kind of psychological burden of capitalist affluence. Domestic electrical apparatus had taken on a powerful symbolic significance, both of national regeneration and gender equality. This metonymy, the faintly hysterical smiles of the advertising models hint, is suspect even if your home is crammed with appliances; and the majority of British homes were not. The commentary for Richard Hamilton's exhibition, *This Is Tomorrow*, at the Whitechapel Art Gallery in 1956 is prescient in its expression of this dominant new relationship between woman and domestic things:

> The worst thing that can happen to a girl, according to the ads, is that she should fail to be exquisitely at ease in her appliance setting – the setting that now does much to establish our attitude to woman in the way that her clothes alone used to . . . This relationship of woman and appliance is a fundamental theme of our culture. (Russell and Gablik 1969: 73)

Figure 7   The 1950s housewife of the advertisers' dreams.

In their important sociological study, *Women's Two Roles: Home and Work* (1956), Alva Myrdal and Viola Klein noted the way in which 'Memories of a long obsolete social pattern linger on and as well as colouring our dreams they distort our attempts at rational thinking' (Myrdal 1962: 4). The coloured dreams of the newly ebullient advertising industry have played an important part in the idea that, during the 1950s in Britain, feminism was dead.

Elizabeth Wilson's 1980 book, *Only Halfway to Paradise: Women in Postwar Britain: 1945–1968*, remains the key analysis of the position and perception of women during the period, and sets out precisely to reject popular perceptions of an era of uncomplicated domestic bliss. Though Wilson is at pains to refute the idea of feminism as moribund during the 1950s, her conclusions suggest it is, at best, in a comatose state: 'Feminism led an underground or Sleeping Beauty existence in a society which claimed to have wiped out that oppression' (Wilson 1980: 187). Vera Brittain, one of the most prominent of British feminists in the wake of the First Wave, upheld the idea that the Welfare State embodied the goals of female liberation. In *Lady into Woman*, she named it 'both the cause and consequence of the second great change by which women have moved within 30 years from rivalry with men to a new recognition of their unique value as women' (Brittain 1953: 224). In its exposition of a system of Social Security, the 1942 Beveridge Report, founding document of the Welfare State, had explicitly recognised the role of the housewife in the success of the economy, furnishing a sense of her as, if not straightforwardly equal with the male breadwinners, at least equal but different, demanding the 'Recognition of housewives as a distinct insurance class of occupied persons with benefits adjusted to their special needs' (Beveridge 1997: Section 30, paragraphs 107–17, n.p.). Striving for the good, brave causes of women as a distinct group seemed to some too sectarian, or simply churlish after the brutal separations and sacrifices of war-time.

It is the kind of ideological and rhetorical manœuvre performed by William Beveridge in relation to the figure of the housewife that Wilson reads as indicative of the decade as a whole: 'In the fifties Britain was a conservative society described in the rhetoric of a radical ideology. This held out in one hand the image of social revolution achieved, a political achievement, while with the other it demolished politics as a valid activity' (Wilson 1980: 6). Nowhere is this more explicit than in the plethora of magazines aimed at women published during the era. Five out of every six women read at least one each week, and many saw several (White 1977: 9). Editorials, features and advertising couched a newly aggressive materialism as cosy and traditionalist, and the debates we can recognise as being most traditionally, explicitly feminist were subsumed in a Conservative rhetoric of purportedly 'natural' gender behaviours. Monica Dickens asked of the working woman in *Woman's Own*:

> Will her children love her more if she is an efficient career woman who pops in and out of the house at intervals, knows a lot of stimulating people, and

can talk about everything, except pleasant, trivial, day-to-day matters that are the breath of family life? . . . She is not cheating her children by staying at home. She is giving them the supreme gift – herself. Long after they have left home, they will be grateful to her. (Dickens 1956: 28)

To a society emerging from World War II, 'normality', defined in a very traditional way, seemed to many of its citizens to be a radically unfamiliar experience.

Children First

The literature surrounding the raising of children, including the highly influential 1953 text, *Child Care and the Growth of Love*, which emphasised the significance of parental care in a child's early years for future mental health, was similarly welcomed as radical. John Bowlby's was a study of institutionalised children, but in a society so ideologically invested in the psychological and political importance of family for postwar reconstruction, it was read as a general report on the effects of maternal deprivation. His report's reactionary elements are very plain: Myrdal and Klein note that '"Children First" is the motto writ large over all discussions of the merits and demerits of married women's employment,' adding with characteristic but meaningful mildness that 'it is rather unfortunate that the rights of children should ever have been put in opposition to the "Rights of Women"' (Myrdal and Klein 1962: 116). It is, however, possible to appreciate how the approach of Bowlby and his followers, which enshrined child care as a site in which femininity carries special types of skill and knowledge, had its appeal for some contemporary women.

The emphasis upon caring femininity extended into a new phenomenon in British publishing during the decade – children's literature as a specialist genre. As Kimberley Reynolds notes, 'During the 1950s British publishers began consciously to establish children's lists and to appoint staff with responsibility for working only in this area' (Reynolds 1998: 23). As was the case with 'feminine middlebrow' literature (the term is Nicola Humble's, 2001), staff and books within the genre were still marginalised within the industry, and as a result children's publishing offered unprecedented opportunities for women. Valerie Krips has suggested how, 'Among marginalized formations, children's fiction can claim a kind of precedence since it is, after all, a production of two formidable branches of what Louis Althusser would call the "ideological state apparatuses": education and publishing' (Krips 2000: 23). In response partly to the rise of television, and partly to the exaggerated concerns surrounding youth more generally, State and professional concern with children's reading was greatly heightened. 'The Ministry of Education had issued a directive to schools to improve their libraries, and the "teacher-librarian" [a female figure] appeared for the first time as an important factor in the economics of book-production' (Crouch 1962: 111) Marcus Crouch's study *Treasure Seekers and Borrowers: Children's Books in Britain 1900–1960*, written at the decade's turn, provides a useful document of the period's approach to children's literature, and it is a divided one. Crouch bemoans the fact that 'The earnestness, the purposeful professionalism of the 'fifties produced books for which teachers and librarians ask; it was less likely to produce the book of individual genius' (111). (When two of these did arrive, they came in translation, and from Scandinavia, in the unruly shapes of Tove Jansson's *Finn Family Moomintroll* (1950) and Astrid Lindgren's *Pippi Longstocking* (1954), the latter the most transgressive and atavistic heroine since Alice.) Crouch, then, might be expected to celebrate the elaborate fantasy of the seven-book series that began in 1950 with *The Lion, the Witch and the Wardrobe*. (Fellow Inkling J. R. R. Tolkien's fantasy series for adults, *The Lord of the Rings*, began four years later.) Yet Crouch says of C. S. Lewis's *Chronicles of Narnia* that they

> were great in conception, rather less than great in execution. The grandeur of the central theme was marred by occasional trivialities of expression and by a fundamental improbability; it was always difficult to accept the translation of the schoolboy Peter into the High King Peter of Narnia. (115)

His point of comparison is immediately revealed to be Mary Norton's *The Borrowers* (1952), in which the reader 'makes one concession to probability, in accepting the existence of such tiny creatures; after this everything is worked out in strictly naturalistic terms' (116). As for adult literature in the 1950s, it would seem, realism is the order of the day.

Within this order, one children's author in particular was famously found wanting during the decade: Enid Blyton. In the early 1950s she was beginning to top children's lists of favourite authors and publishing in huge volumes – averaging over fifty titles a year (Ray 1982: 38). With this popularity and profligacy came a critical backlash. In 'Dear Little Noddy: A Parent's Lament' in *Encounter* in 1958, Colin Welch berated Noddy (whose series of books began in 1949 with *Noddy Goes to Toyland*) as an 'unnaturally priggish . . . sanctimonious . . . witless, spiritless, snivelling, sneaking doll' who appeared within an 'unintentional yet not wholly inaccurate satire on – or parody of – the welfare state and its attendant attitudes of mind' (Welch 1958: 22, 21). For the gatekeepers of children's reading, the teachers and librarians, however, Blyton's work was derided as escapist – too far removed from the contemporary experience – and as too simplistic, using a vocabulary 'drained of all difficulty until it achieves a kind of aesthetic anaemia' (Stoney 1974: 164). The racism inherent in the golliwog characters in the Noddy books in particular continues to be debated.

David Rudd attempts to counter some of this critique by aligning Blyton's writing with standards of oral, rather than literary, fiction. He also provides a semi-serious, but none the less convincing, reading of the influence of contemporary context upon the Noddy books – their nascent consumerism, for example, and the legal wranglings over Noddy's status when he arrives in Toyland: 'There are certainly echoes of the plight of refugees and immigrants here. There is a general sense of people finding where they belong' (Rudd 2000: 71–2). There is, of course, an extent to which such a theme – finding a place in an unfamiliar world – is the underpinning grand narrative of all writing for younger people, yet one children's character debuting during the decade seems to provide the most explicit allegory for issues of immigration and the colonial past. In *Colour in Britain* (1958), James Wickenden notes of the epicentre of the capital's race riots that 'To the east of Notting Hill lies Paddington, a centre for coloured immigrants where most of the available accommodation had been filled before the peak influx of 1955–6' (Wickenden 1958: 36). Arriving in 1958, the eponymous hero of Michael Bond's *A Bear Called Paddington* is renamed after the station in which he is first glimpsed by the eminently upper middle-class and liberal Mr and Mrs Brown, in preference to his original name, 'a Peruvian one which no one can understand' (12). Paddington, of course, functions on important levels of identification other than that of immigrant – as adopted (or evacuated) child, for example, as well as teddy bear. And although the bear's origin is carefully selected to be outside the British Empire, Mrs Bird, the Brown's redoubtable housekeeper, hints at her knowledge of an economic colonialism, that makes foreigners fluent in British brands and products:

> 'Where was it you said you'd come from? Peru?'
> 'That's right,' said Paddington. 'Darkest Peru.'
> 'Humph!' Mrs. Bird looked thoughtful for a moment. 'Then I expect you like marmalade. I'd better get some more from the grocer.' (Bond 1958: 24)

Yet it is Philippa Pearce's *Tom's Midnight Garden* (1958) that best fulfils the decade's preference that children's fiction should debate the issues of the day whilst challenging its readers' imaginations and vocabularies. Tom Long is sent to stay with his uncle and aunt for the summer to avoid his brother's dose of measles. They live in East Anglia in an environment fraught with contemporary symbolism: 'a big house now converted into flats. The house was crowded round with newer, smaller houses that beat up to its very confines in a broken sea of bay-windows and gable-ends and pinnacles. It was the only big house among them' (Pearce 2008: 4). In the shared hallway there is a grandfather clock that belongs to the elderly Mrs Bartholomew in one of the upper flats, and which has a pendulum engraved with the pronouncement of an angel in the Book of Revelation. When it strikes thirteen one night, Tom makes the first of his journeys into the past, and the garden of the big house in 1895, now home to an aristocratic family. Hatty, the youngest child of the family and their only daughter, seems to be the only one who can see Tom, and they forge a sporadic friendship until Hatty, who is older each time they meet, falls in love with a boy her own age. She, and the garden, seem lost to Tom, until he realises that Mrs Bartholomew is Hatty, and that their friendship endures, just as her childhood does in her dreams: 'Tom said: "We're both real; Then and Now. It's as the angel said: Time No Longer"' (224). Krips has noted how:

> The situation of a children's book is ... peculiar in its temporal reference, which is both to the present and past, to memory and the promise of a memory. This strange placement ensures that children's fiction has the potential to be profoundly enlightening about the understanding of place and memory at the period of the book's individual creation and production. (Krips 2000: 25)

Tom's Midnight Garden refuses the stasis of *The Go-Between* to offer a dynamic relationship between past and present, childhood and adulthood, and individual and collective memory, as well as forging a sense of continuity between contemporary children's literature and that of the Golden Age; the novel is, on some level, a rewriting of Frances Hodgson Burnett's *The Secret Garden* (1911). In its central bond between an elderly woman and a pre-adolescent boy, it also offers a negotiation of the competing demands of gender conformity and self-individuation rarely glimpsed elsewhere in the decade's literary representations of gender.

The Feminine Point of View

In its pioneering attempt to reinterpret feminism during the decade, the Birmingham Feminist History Group concluded in a 1979 paper that 'feminism in the fifties was constructed through dominant notions of femininity. Feminists in the period could not escape from the social democratic stress on the "equality" already achieved and the rights won – "mopping up" was all that was required' (BFHG 2005: 21). Their hypothesis, though inarguably true, fails fully to convey the resultant rhetorical strain placed on the definition of women's roles, particularly as these roles were defined by women themselves. Olwen W. Campbell's draft of *The Report of a Conference on the Feminine Point of View* (1952) makes this stress very evident. A summation of the discussions of a group of professional women (including teachers, academics, a journalist, a union officer and the founder of the Married Women's Association), this text is dense with the explicitly feminist issues that will later drive the Women's Liberation Movement. The conference vows early and rather elegantly to avoid debating whether the 'feminine point of view' derives from nature or culture, so as to concentrate on the effects of gender difference rather than its causation. The women claim their work to be a response to a history of violent reigns and usurpations of Western civilisations, which have made it seem 'imperative both for feminist and humanist reasons to examine the question whether women have any special approach to human problems. Men seem to think that they have,' they add ruefully, 'for better or for worse' (Campbell 1952: 13).

Their survey includes a consideration of the whole cultural apparatus of gender: of the representation of women in media, films and literature, their sexuality, their positioning in the economy, the workplace and the home, and the question of women's complicity in these inferior positions. Some defiant calls are made to disrupt the patriarchal family – for example, with recourse to *'a greater variety of marriage patterns'* which include periods of house-husbandry that allow wives lengthy trips away from the home to pursue professional projects. 'Marriage', they assert, 'should not have to appear as a cage to men and women of talent and spirit' (57). Yet ultimately these discussions terminate in a single strategy:

> The wrong attitude of mind has mostly to be changed by the individual wife and mother within her own home. The woman who spends most of her life in a small group of family and friends has a big part to play. We believe that the world desperately needs her point of view. (60)

We might tinker with Elizabeth Wilson's formulation to suggest that this document ends by describing feminist social reform in the rhetoric of a conservative ideology. Or perhaps, more accurately, an individualistic one: one of the few confident claims the conference participants make for female difference is that 'the deeply-rooted individualism of women makes them less likely to think in terms of masses at the cost of cruelty and cynical indifference towards the claims of the individual' (21). The 'feminine point of view' (its wording making it a more dynamic concept than the immanence of 'femininity') is most clearly defined in its individualised opposition to mass movements and their resultant mass destruction. I want to suggest, then, another way of thinking about female identity during the 1950s – as a foment of competing ideologies in which a model of feminism predicated upon shared priorities and a mass politics is confronting and negotiating a model of individual liberation. It is this latter understanding of political purpose, of course, that is to define the culture of the West during the 1960s, and beyond.

As a genre dedicated to the expression of the interior life of individuals, we might look to female-authored novels to engage with the kind of gendered debate that informs *The Feminine Point of View*. Wilson is condemnatory of the 'women's novels' of the 1950s. Damning *The Echoing Grove*, Rosamund Lehmann's 1953 novel, with faint praise, she judges it 'successful in connecting the general atmosphere of retreat to a special sense of women's peculiar situation' (Wilson 1980: 149). Its representation of women, in other words, is of interest only for the particularity of the experience it describes, rather than as an insight into more revealing social truths. Myrdal and Klein are struck by:

> An astonishing fact, in itself worth speculating upon, that in this era of social investigations so little systematic research has been done on the vital problems concerning women in contemporary society. Tremendous changes in their way of life, and in their position in family and society, have taken place during the life-time of the present generation.
> We are, in fact, the unobservant participants of a social revolution. (Myrdal and Klein 1962: 183)

Discussing what they consider to be 'the characteristic feminine dilemma of to-day', between career and family, the authors note how, in the absence of external obstacles, 'the conflict has become "internalized" and continues as a psychological problem which may assume many different variations and shades' (137). This chapter will consider a range of 1950s women's novels as the work of highly observant participants of social change, which trace those variations and shades of conflict to produce insights relevant to the experience of both women and men during the decade.

The motif that begins Elizabeth Taylor's novel, *A Game of Hide and Seek*, published in 1951, is a smudged photograph that horrifies the central character, Harriet Claridge. It is of her mother Lilian when she was young, with her best friend Caroline, taken whilst the two women were being dragged up some steps by policemen:

In the background, shop-windows showed great holes like black stars. Harriet, not able to bear this picture nor to ignore it, heedless of former sacrifice, as history makes all of us, saw only that her mother had exposed herself to mockery and ridicule, that she looked ugly, wild, a little mad, her mouth darkly open, her hat sideways. (Taylor 1986: 3)

The novel opens in 1925 (we are told that *Mrs Dalloway* is Virginia Woolf's 'latest'; 14), at a time in which it seems to Lilian and Caroline that feminism has become 'a weird abnormality; laughter was easily evoked at the strange figures of suffragettes with their umbrellas raised, their faces contorted and, one supposed, their voices made shrill with fury and frustration' (3). 'One supposed': the narrator is mocking the perception of First Wave feminism as necessarily a screeching, ugly business, the very antithesis of femininity. Yet though empathy for the women's long-standing friendship is strong in the novel, Lilian and Caroline, now with children of their own, do not escape a similarly gentle mocking; they disapprove of a change in the style of evening frocks, we are told, as 'long skirts, they feared, would threaten the status of women' (82). *A Game of Hide and Seek* conducts a fascinating survey of a range of female lives at a range of stages and ages, the novel's scope spanning a period from just after the First World War to a few years after the Second, when things are beginning to come back into the London shops (220). For both Harriet and the narrator, a suspicion of feminism stems from the fact that the *modus operandi* of suffragism stands in antithesis to a fundamental creed of individualism, vital to both Harriet's education and the novel's mode of expression. On a train, Harriet is bemused by a fellow passenger beginning his small talk with 'I'm a fairly ordinary chap, but it strikes me . . .'. By contrast, she believes, 'I represent no one. I am typical of no one. No one else thinks my thoughts or understands my hopes or shares my guilt. I am both better and worse than I would admit to other people' (193). Much to the disappointment of her mother, Harriet forges a life of controlled and comfortable convention, choosing to marry the dependable, affluent Charles Jephcott rather than subject herself to the vicissitudes of the mutual passion of her relationship with her cousin Vesey.

Harriet and Charles have a daughter, with whom 'the real *trouble*', the narrator informs us, 'was that nothing was explicable, even to herself. When she wept, it was from confusion. Her ravelled emotions fatigued her. She was overwrought from uncertainty, more than from any specific cause' (228). Betsy's febrile nature functions as a portrait both of the violent hopelessness of female adolescence, and of a femininity in which feeling is always indulged over thought. Her emotions unravelling in front of her Classics teacher, Betsy, 'with one of her grandmother's

gestures, which, if Miss Bell could have recognised it, would have cancelled out all that had been said, put her wrist against her throbbing
brow' (232). Readers can recognise how the gesture affiliates Betty with
Julia, her paternal grandmother, a vain and theatrical woman to whom
sisterhood is no more than a coy platitude: '"Silly Charles! Women
understand one another." Her smile warmed as it included Lilian, suggested complicity. Lilian's answering smile was the faintest tremor' (53).
Miss Bell, Betsy's teacher, is a Girton graduate, yet has a narrow life,
able to inspire ardour only in a semi-hysterical teenage girl. 'She was no
feminist,' we are told, 'but did not like to waste her capabilities, which
she had not so far found less than any man's' (129). By the end of the
novel, however, she has found her capabilities lacking in one respect,
and is punished for her failings. An ardent student but a poor teacher,
she is 'let go' from Betsy's school, condemned to London to teach, not
passionate Greek, but functional Latin. We leave her as she stares 'ahead
of her at the long, deserted street which appeared as dull as her own
future' (242). *A Game of Hide and Seek* is a woman's novel that tanta-
lises with a proffered female community and feminist continuity which
is never satisfactorily forged. Sitting at her desk, Harriet catches sight of
her face reflected in the glass of a photograph of Betsy: 'In some respects
the two faces were the same; Betsy's eyes – large, candid – matched her
own; the blonde hair hung pale against the darker; but timidity was
absent from the girl's expression' (131). Her sense of herself, it seems,
matches neither the photograph of her mother, flailing in the arms of a
policeman, nor that of her daughter, on the brink of growing up.

Angelica Deverell, protagonist of Taylor's later novel, *Angel* (1957),
is a prodigal publishing sensation in Victorian England. Aged just fifteen
and feigning illness, she produces the lavish romance *The Lady Irania* in
her bedroom above her mother's grocery shop. Angel's writing methods
confirm the most derogatory critical assumptions about the romance
genre:

> The words flowed without effort all the evening and she seemed to be in a
> trance . . . By bedtime, she was both excited and exhausted. Her right arm
> and shoulder were aching and her fingers were cramped. She had scarcely
> paused, either to consider what she should write or judge what she had
> written. Day-dreaming had paved the way. (Taylor 2001: 29)

One of her publishers firmly aligns these writing practices with equally
feminine reading practices – aping Angel's style, he tells how his wife
'devoured and gobbled every iridescent word' of the novel. 'So will other
women,' predicts his colleague, and he is proven right as sales boom
(51). Taylor portrays Angel as a woman who both writes and reads the

world entirely wrongly, yet she is able to generate not only a sense of preposterousness (this is lavish and joyful throughout the novel), but also one of pathos in relation to her heroine. Elizabeth Bowen's 1955 novel, *A World of Love*, conducts a more ambiguous critique of the romance genre. Set in a contemporaneous Ireland, the novel's world is none the less under the influence of the First World War as much as the Second. Fred and Lilia work the land for Antonia, who inherited it from her cousin Guy. Killed in the Great War and dying intestate, he was engaged to Lilia. A bundle of his love letters is discovered by her daughter, Jane, who breaks the band holding them together: 'gathering them up, she endeavoured to put them into their former order – for that there had *been* an order, and that it was significant, she did not question – but found that it could not be done' (Bowen 1955: 47). Jane's conviction that there must be an ordering narrative to the letters suggests the potentially delusional influence of romance reading. Jane's younger sister, Maud, has an imaginary friend, 'the non-dimensional Gay David' (213), a comedic double of Jane's fantasy of the long-dead Guy. The intense attraction Jane develops towards her mother's lost lover can be read as symbolic of the pernicious influence of a masculine dissembler, but at the same time demonstrates the emotional potential of human desire. The letters do not bear Lilia's name, and suspicions of Guy's infidelity to his fiancée are rife. Yet, as the narrator asks, 'Who desires to know what they need not? So why continue to wonder, so why suffer? Yes, but if not the Beloved, what was Lilia? Nothing. Nothing was left to be' (143).

Lilia's identity is invested in that romantic (and Romantic) feminine archetype – the 'Beloved'. Yet her allegedly prepossessed and inert beauty is revealed to be not without its efforts and occasional collapse, as here, in the high heat of summer: 'Sweat broke out on her forehead and upper lip: it was afternoon, most brutal phase of the day, which had leapt upon and was demolishing the poor snow-woman' (60). Supplied with *Woman* magazine in the hairdresser's, Lilia 'did nothing more than contemplate, with her head aslant, prototype Woman on the cover' (134). In contrast to this modern prototype, Lilia's neighbour, Lady Latterly, with her symbolic name, emphasises the kind of femininity the elderly woman dons like an outdated costume. Lady Latterly prepares herself in a bedroom Jane supposes to be 'a replica, priceless these days, of a Mayfair *décor* back in the 1930s' (81), then glides down to her guests: 'her face by being worn tilted back brought the more into notice a flawless jawline, which her eyes, turning down under varnished lids, would have contemplated were it but in their view' (84). Femininity in the novel, then, is presented as an artificial construction of various degrees of precariousness. At twenty, Jane's identity is similarly uncertain. The novel ends with a meeting arranged for her by Lady Latterly – hardly an auspicious start – but when Richard Priam's eyes meet Jane's, 'they no sooner looked but they loved' (224). Jane's youth gives her the potential for change; this is undoubtedly the beginning of a romance, but its ability to exceed Lilia's doomed model of the love relationship is left uncalibrated.

Rejecting Romance

The 1950s fiction of authors such as Bowen, Lehmann and Taylor, together with that of decade debutants Elizabeth Jane Howard and Penelope Mortimer, would seem to confirm that:

> Feminism of the fifties seemed to be more concerned with the integration and foregrounding of femininity in a masculine world. Those aims demanded certain modifications of femininity, to be implemented, but not a thorough appraisal. Feminism was, therefore, bound by femininity in such a manner that we as feminists today do not easily recognize its activities as *feminist*. (BFHG 1979: 6)

Ideas surrounding female identity, and the narratives in which they are presented, are under scrutiny in these novels, but it is certainly the case that an explicitly political discourse is avoided in favour of scrupulous examinations of interior life. In a self-fulfilling process, as middle- and upper-class women are traditionally considered better able to be feminine than those from the working class, the fiction that takes femininity as its focus is dominantly from and about the upper / middle classes, and these upper- / middle-class novels come to serve as definitive of femininity. Both Doris Lessing's origins and her writing serve to disrupt this easy equation, just as her life experience runs counter to the traditional feminine trajectories of marriage, home and family. Born in Iran and brought up in Rhodesia, she arrived in London with her son from her failed second marriage and a manuscript – *The Grass is Singing* – which was published in 1950. The novel begins with the death of Mary Turner, in her youth an independent white Rhodesian urbanite, who was frightened by gossip about her spinsterhood and gauche sexuality into marriage with an incompetent farmer, Dick. A complex relationship between Mary and a servant, Moses, concludes in her murder.

Mary Turner's domestic life is extremely hard – isolated and poor, with a husband she is unable to respect and servants who do not respect her. The deprivations of her life are more emphatic in their contrast to her earlier and prolonged single life, when 'she was a most rare phenomenon: a woman of thirty without love troubles, headaches, backaches, sleeplessness or neurosis' (Lessing 1972: 45). Married life is utterly alien, making her feel 'as if she had been lifted from the part fitted to her, in a play she understood, and made suddenly to act one unfamiliar to her. It was a feeling of being out of character that chilled her' (119). Worse, the particular situation of the Turners' settler life in Southern Africa warps Western domesticity in a profoundly *unheimlich* way. Alison Ravetz has argued 1950 to be a watershed in British women's history in relation to domesticity due to the fact that, 'By then, two things of profound significance for women had occurred: the middle-class wife had finally and irrevocably lost her servants and the working-class wife had gained, or was in the process of gaining, a whole house to look after' (Ravetz 1989: 189). Mary's house is dirt poor, yet relies upon servants still lower in the economic hierarchy than the mistress herself. The houseboy system completely disrupts any definition of the role of the housewife, making her more stage manager than actress in the scene of her home. In fact, Mary proves to be utterly unable to maintain any 'proper' hierarchical relationships on the property, as class and race boundaries dissolve in her intense involvement with her servant Moses, which is certainly sexually charged, even if the extent of its consummation is unclear.

Communism played an important role in Lessing's life and education before she arrived in London. In postwar Britain, Communist rhetoric and party practice were emphasising the role of wife and mother for women. Jackie Kay, whose father worked full-time for the British Communist Party during the 1950s, remembers that 'the party for my dad did come before his wife, his family, and everything really. He spent much more time with the party doing party things than he spent with his wife or family' (Kay 1997: 35). Contrary to Khrushchev's belligerent optimism in that mock-up kitchen, the 'woman problem', and women's problems, were ascribed by Communist thinkers to the problems of the capitalist system, rather than any gendered experience of oppression. Mary's initial urban inexperience leads her into similar confusion: '"Class" is not a South African word; and its equivalent, "race", meant to her the office boy in the firm where she worked, other women's servants, and the amorphous mass of natives in the streets, whom she hardly noticed' (Lessing 1972: 42). Mary 'had inherited from her mother an arid feminism, which had no meaning in her own life at all, for she was leading the comfortable carefree existence of a single woman in South Africa, and she did not know how fortunate she was'. As in other moments of political and personal crisis in the novel, the narrator addresses her readers directly: 'How could she know?' (41)

It is the failure of this desiccated, inappropriate feminism to provide Mary with a way of analysing and justifying her happy, independent life, that leads to her marriage, and a death that begins as metaphorical and ends as literal. As a collective term, 'women' has pejorative implications in the novel, linked as it is to constrictive stereotypes of female existence. Mary's instinctive rejection of a life dominated by motherhood is distorted into a revulsion towards the native women gathered around the 'kaffir store': 'there was something in their calm, satisfied maternity that made her blood boil' (116). Not long before she dies, Mary briefly views her desperate self objectively, but her potential epiphany ends in alienation and incomprehension:

> while she saw Mary Turner rocking in the corner of the sofa, moaning, her fists in her eyes, she saw, too, Mary Turner as she had been, that foolish girl travelling unknowingly to this end. I don't understand, she said again. I understand nothing. The evil is there, but of what it consists, I do not know. Even the words were not her own. (241)

Mary herself has neither the articulacy nor the authority to express or defend her own individual experience, and the collective vocabulary available to her is useless and debilitating. Her mother's feminism is no more than misandric resentment, her husband's Marxism inapplicable to their situation in Rhodesia and disfigured by racism. On some level, Mary's predicament might be seen as a grotesquely phantasmagoric version of that experienced by women in Britain during the 1950s, caught as they were between a First Wave feminism intent upon overt legal reform, and a Second Wave that transfers its critique to the cultural systems of representation themselves. Simone de Beauvoir's 1949 work, *Le Deuxième Sexe*, can be justifiably marked as the beginning of this latter movement – the book was first published in Britain in 1953. Lessing's 1962 novel, *The Golden Notebook*, can equally surely be upheld as the most important British fictional engagement with the relationship between gender and literary expression in the immediate postwar period. This engagement is, however, already apparent in *The Grass is Singing*, where it is suggested at one point that Mary's powerlessness is attributable to her reading history, its flawed development entirely halted by her move to the farm:

> Five years earlier she would have drugged herself by the reading of romantic novels. In towns women like her live vicariously in the lives of the film stars. Or they take up religion, preferably one of the more sensuous Eastern religions. Better educated, living in the town with access to books, she would have found Tagore, perhaps, and gone into a sweet dream of words. (163)

Lessing's language in describing the African landscape can be as lushly exotic as that of Bengali poet Tagore. However, Mary's story and its irresolutions reject the conventions of the romance genre with its traditionally writerly nature, characteristically cosseting the reader with all the direction and information she could desire. The narrative of *The Grass is Singing* is one of roving free indirect discourse, but the emotions that colour its account are exclusively white – those experienced by Mary, Dick, Tony, Charlie Slatter and his wife, and the chattering middle classes of the town. The novel ultimately denies any possibility of valid collective expression or understanding. In the next chapter we will turn to a masculine genre – the poetry of that much-debated group, 'the Movement' – that similarly rejects romance at the same time that it vehemently appeals to precisely the kind of communal experience that the women's novels in this chapter are left unable to access.

Chapter Six

The Sensation of Movement: Poetry in the 1950s

The title of Philip Larkin's collection of poetry, *The Less Deceived* (1955), was taken from his poem 'Deceptions', dated 1950 (Larkin 1990: 32). The poem's epigraph is attributed to Henry Mayhew's mid-Victorian documentary survey, *London Labour and the London Poor* (though a recent article corrects this attribution to author Bracebridge Hemyng; Robinson 2009). It consists of the words of a young woman who has been raped: 'Of course I was drugged, and so heavily I did not regain my consciousness till the next morning. I was horrified to discover that I had been ruined, and for some days I was inconsolable' (Larkin 1990: 32). The pathos of her ruin is intensified by the weird existential non-equivalence of a final desperate plea either to be 'killed or sent back to my aunt'. The speaker of Larkin's poem is not immune either to pity or to the harrowing gravity of her situation ('I can taste the grief,' 'I would not dare / Console you if I could'). However, that emotional distance between speaker and subject is then vertiginously widened, as the poem's voice goes on to use the incident as an exercise in reasoning:

> What can be said,
> Except that suffering is exact, but where
> Desire takes charge, readings will grow erratic?

The speaker conducts a calibration of the rational value of experience of both victim and rapist, finally acknowledging to the former that 'you would hardly care / That you were less deceived, out on that bed, / Than he was.' In its process, if not its subject-matter, the poem is indicative of a definitive feature of Larkin's poetry: the arousal of an unfamiliar emotion which is then figured out into some kind of everyday truth – in this case, that male sexual desire (for this is assumed to be the rapist's motivation) is an irrational, ungovernable force. Its direct address to a long-dead female 'you' is certainly unusual in Larkin's work, but it is complicated by a more familiar appeal to a contemporary reader to agree that 'what can be said' *has* been said. Four years later, in 'Success Story', Larkin is to root the idea of failure etymologically in deception. The poem claims of the verb '*to fail*': 'They trace it from the Latin *to deceive*' (Larkin 1990: 88). In the earlier poem, the ideal reader and I-speaker, unlike the desperate woman, can appreciate the modest but important victory of being 'less deceived'.

These different roles (speaker / reader) are very deliberately gendered. The speaker and his reader, by virtue of their gentle exercise of reason, maintain a masculine viewpoint on the encounter that is unavailable to the woman in her piteous emotional intensity. The poem has under- standably prompted numerous troubled critical responses to its gender politics, particularly for the apparent suggestion that the rapist is as much a victim as his victim (see Booth 1992: 111; Holderness 1989: 122–9; Rossen 1989: 70). One of the poem's most sinister aspects is a pattern of domestic imagery that runs from a 'bridal London' that averts its gaze from the rape, to the woman's damaged mind as 'a drawer of knives', then culminates in the rapist 'stumbling up the breathless stair / To burst into fulfilment's desolate attic'. Cumulatively these domes- tic images suggest that we witness only an aberration of heterosexual relationships, an uncanny imbalance of the correct matrimonial model. Mary Macaulay's handbook, *The Art of Marriage* (1957), would seem to corroborate such a sense: 'It is a shocking thing to hear a woman say that ... she will not be raped even by her husband. Such an attitude would be impossible in any woman to whom loving and giving were synonymous' (quoted Wilson 1980: 93). This sense of a kind of skewed normalcy is upheld by the speaker's matter-of-fact tone and the routine rhythm of the predominant iambic metre. Though the poem can, and has, been read as an apology for rape, it lacks such animated motivation. Still more disturbing, perhaps, is its calmly calculating use of a violent, far-off incident to make out a method for writing. Emotional control is here confirmed as a crucial part of literature and of literacy; the raw experiences of the 'desiring' rapist and his drugged, terrified victim are rendered illiterate by the speaker's rational standards. Such a gambit demonstrates how much there might be at stake for Larkin in his need to demonstrate a measured 'common sense'.

In 1953, John Wain was chosen to edit and present the poetry pro- gramme, *First Reading*, on BBC Radio's Third Programme. His selec- tion of poets such as Larkin, Kingsley Amis, Elizabeth Jennings and Thom Gunn, later to be identified as part of 'the Movement', did much to promote them *as* a poetic movement, with shared techniques and a definitive ideology (see Morrison 1986: 42–5). This ideology was influenced by the thinking of F. R. Leavis and William Empson (this philosophical relationship will be examined more closely in Chapter 11). During the 1950s, a number of British writers took up the concerns of Logical Positivism, a school of thought combining empiricism with a version of rationalism, and applied its debates about the limits of scientific and philosophical assertions to literature. At the centre of this idea is the conception of the processes of reading and writing as being essentially empirical, or rooted in proof in the 'real world'. Alfred Jules Ayer had claimed in *Language, Truth and Logic* (1936), one of the school's founding texts, that:

> It will be shown that all propositions which have factual content are empirical hypotheses; and that the function of an empirical hypothesis is to provide a rule for the anticipation of experience. And this means that every empirical hypothesis must be relevant to some actual, or possible, experience, so that a statement which is not relevant to any experience is not an empirical hypothesis, and accordingly has no factual content. (Ayer 1967: 41)

From this position, authoritative knowledge, or what we might (more poetically) call 'truth', is apprehended through experience, yet can also be rationally hypothesised and stated in advance, providing 'a rule for the anticipation of experience'. The experiencing self, therefore, is simultaneously the objective assessor of its own experience, keeping any emotions in check. Chapter 3 traced the implications of this belief for fictional form.

Robert Conquest's edited collection, *New Lines*, published in 1956, was the first Movement anthology widely available in Britain. (D. J. Enright's earlier *Poets of the 1950s: An Anthology of New English Verse*, containing most of the same poets, was published in Japan and difficult to come by elsewhere.) Those poems in *New Lines* we might call 'philosophical' are concerned with the relationship between language and experience that animates the debates of Logical Positivism (see, for example, Conquest's 'Epistemology of Poetry' and Wain's 'Who Speaks My Language?'; Conquest 1956: 73–4, 85–8 respectively). Yet the kind of wholesome objectivity espoused by Ayer is less in evidence than the volume's editor, confident of 'a new and healthy general standpoint' (xiv), supposes. In the second edition of *First Reading* (broadcast 24 May 1953), Al Alvarez suggested the need for 'a revival in poetry of what Donne called "masculine persuasive force" and intellectual objectivity' (quoted Morrison 1986: 45). Placed alongside Larkin's 'Deceptions', this makes for an uneasy juxtaposition. Despite the reasonable tone cultivated by these poets, the advocation of 'masculine' force and objectivity as a priority in literature is a profoundly exclusionary tactic. It is a tactic that draws again to our attention the fact that the gendered assumptions which suffuse the dominant literary modes of this allegedly apathetic decade have complex political implications. The trauma undergone by the woman in the epigraph of Larkin's poem is indisputable and outside the literary discussion here. Yet the poet's calculated use of her situation should serve as a disturbing reminder that the way in which particular modes of thought are gendered has much larger cultural and personal consequences than the particular poetics of a literary movement.

On 1 October 1954, an anonymous leader in the *Spectator* entitled 'In the Movement' (later revealed to be written by the magazine's editor, J. D. Scott) identified a 'new movement' in British poetry. Its participants had much in common – all had been born between 1917 and 1929, with three (Kingsley Amis, Donald Davie and Philip Larkin) in 1922. During the decade, all the Movement poets were working in the recently expanded university environment, most as lecturers – a fact that aided them to create and espouse a more general taste for their own particular vision of poetry. As Blake Morrison puts it, 'Perhaps the most interesting indication of the Movement writers' sense of belonging to a small academic audience is the recurrence of the pronoun "we" in their poetry: nearly half of the poems in *New Lines* use this form of address' (Morrison 1986: 120). It is this collection that best serves to encapsulate any shared poetics, and Conquest's introduction defines the group with direct reference to the empiricism of the poetry: 'It is free from both mystical and logical compulsions and – like modern philosophy – is empirical in its attitude to all that comes' (Conquest 1956: xiv–xv). 'Mystical and logical compulsions' seem at first a peculiar pairing, but as logic may be defined as a well-tested pattern of reasoning applied without reference to context, what Conquest is claiming is his poets' rejection of explanations exterior to lived experience itself. Their literary technique is one of a simultaneous process of description and rationalisation that defies both supernatural references and scientific inferences.

Of the latter, it is perhaps Freud's psychoanalytic logic that forms the most obvious target. 'Was Freud entirely right?' asks D. J. Enright at the beginning of 'Baie des Anges, Nice' (54), the faux mildness of the question signalling, in mannered Movement discourse, the necessary resounding and negative response. Conquest's introduction notes that 'In the 1940s the mistake was made of giving the Id, a sound player on the percussion side under a strict conductor, too much of a say in the doings of the orchestra as a whole' (xi). Despicably 'mystical compulsions' are read by these writers in other, older, literary movements considerably more cohesive and coherent than their own. Kingsley Amis's poem, 'Against Romanticism', assembles Romantic tendencies alongside

Modernist intellectualism and Freudian sensationalism in order to pit his homespun rhetoric against them all:

> To please an ingrown taste for anarchy
>   Torrid images circle in the wood,
> And sweat for recognition up the road,
>   Cramming close the air with their bookish cries. (45)

As his published correspondence attests, Amis's ire was repeatedly aroused during the 1950s by his encounters with the flamboyant stylistics of Dylan Thomas, both in print and in the flesh. He was to parody the poet in novels as far apart as *That Uncertain Feeling* (1955) and *The Old Devils* (1986). Thomas's *Collected Poems* was published in 1952, and the poet's verse prologue for the collection is, in parts, not easy to distinguish from Amis's later caricatures:

> Seaward the salmon sucked sun slips,
> And the dumb swan's drub blue
> My dabbed bay's dusk, as I hack
> This rumpus of shapes
> For you to know. (Thomas 1952a: viii)

In contrast to that of his closest friend, Philip Larkin's reaction to the most influential British writer of the Forties was one of qualified admiration. Responding to Amis's ringing judgement of 'GONORRHEIC RUBBISH' in a 1947 letter (Leader 2000: 109), Larkin's own mild beef, he wrote back to Amis, was the Welsh poet's tendency towards linguistic obfuscation: 'Dylan Thos. just makes you wonder what he means, *very hard*' (Thwaite 1993: 133). Trying to calm his own reaction to the public mourning of Thomas's sensational, drunken death in 1953, Amis produced the relatively measured assertion that Thomas had been 'A Bloomsburyite to his *dirty* fingernails, that was him, and only sentimentalising, ignorant horsepiss about his Welchness can conceal the fact' (Leader 2000: 345) (Playing directly into Amis's hands, the review of Thomas's *Collected Poems* in the *Times Literary Supplement* opined sentimentally, 'It is said that he does not speak Welsh: it is certain that he thinks Welsh'; Thomas 1952b: 776.) Like the Welch family in *Lucky Jim*, Thomas functioned for Amis as a compact source of outrage at literary and intellectual pretension, both Romantic and Modernist, and the media spectacle of Thomas's untimely death in 1953 on the fourth of his notoriously riotous lecture tours to the United States ensured, for Amis, his continued cultural irritancy throughout the 1950s.

So the Movement poets wrote, they would have us believe, in opposition to a broad and disreputable church, one which incorporated all literary tendencies towards the mystical, Romantic, Modernist and symbolist, and easily classed as feminine in relation to a masculine, rationalised empiricism. As a devout Roman Catholic, Elizabeth Jennings (b. 1926) therefore seems a surprising choice to open *New Lines*. As religious faith is defined by its dedicated reliance upon a cause outside human understanding, it might be expected to disrupt the empiricism upheld to be characteristic of Movement writing. However, her poem, 'Not in the Guide Books', could serve as a poetic rewrite of Conquest's introductory manifesto in the measured, plain diction it upholds. It describes a place without an elaborate 'ruin or statue to sustain / Some great emotion in their stone', where a weary but discerning visitor can find restoration:

> Yet good, a place like this,
> For one grown tired of histories
> To shape a human myth,
> A story but for his
> Delight, where he might make the place
> His own success
> Building what no one else had bothered with –
> A simple life or death. (Conquest 1956: 6)

The visitor is notably male, and emphatically *not*, in Larkin's memorable phrase, a 'ruin-bibber, randy for antique' (Larkin 1990: 98) who will conjure a landscape into a frenzy of subjective and spiritual response. The metaphor is suitably muted; life (like the poem) is styled as a modest construction achieved by a sensible, essential self. Yet from the disruptive gender of its very first poet, *New Lines* swiftly seems less than uniform in its artistic priorities and practices. Another of Jennings's poems, 'Identity', retains a motif of construction, but begins from an entirely contrasting model of selfhood:

> When I decide I shall assemble you
> Or, more precisely, when I decide which thoughts
> Of mine about you fit most easily together,
> Then I can learn what I have loved. (Conquest 1956: 2)

An intellectual love poem, it explores a sense of the beloved as consisting of a collection of images assembled by the lover, and the idea of love as a dynamic process of the mutual exercise of will and imagination. Such a concept is obviously influenced by existentialism, which rejects the rational observation inherent in an empirical viewpoint for a selfhood that is incessantly and precariously evolving. Other, radically different philosophies are already creeping in, and Jennings's poem can again be upheld to make an argument that is becoming familiar in the course of this study – that British literature of the 1950s was as often postmodern in its project as it was parochial, deconstructing traditional concepts of fixed human identities.

Jennings was not alone in the collection in her attraction to existentialist sensibilities. Of the eight poems by Thom Gunn that Conquest chose for *New Lines*, seven came from *The Sense of Movement* (1957). The collection's title might have seemed a kind of serendipitous guarantee of Gunn's belonging to the Movement, yet of all the various *New Lines* contributors his poetic allegiances seem the most conflicted, as his reader moves from the mystic drama of 'Merlin in the Cave: He Speculates Without a Book' (34–7) to the determined anti-whimsy of 'Puss in Boots to the Giant' (39–40). Born in 1929, and much the youngest poet in the grouping, Gunn had moved to California in 1954, the year of publication of his first collection, *Fighting Terms*. That leader in the *Spectator*, also in 1954, that attempted to define the 'new movement' in British poetry, saw it as 'part of the tide which is pulling us through the Fifties towards the Sixties' (Scott 1954: 1); this is certainly, if not exclusively, applicable to Gunn's work. His particular poetic voice during the 1950s sounds somewhere between neo-Augustan discursiveness and Romantic intensity, and between English tradition and US innovation. And there is Continental influence too: Gunn was to say of *A Sense of Movement* that it contained 'a great deal of raw Sartre' (Gunn 1982: 177) (the 'movement' of its title is that of existential dynamism), and *New Lines* includes some uncooked Sartrean philosophy in the poem 'Human Condition', with its claim 'I am condemned to be /An individual' (Conquest 1956: 33). Gunn's poetic interpretation provides another interesting example of the British reworking of existentialism's original tenets.

In *Existentialism from Within*, E. L. Allen attempts to 'hazard a definition of existentialism in a sentence', and comes up with the following: '*Existentialism is an attempt at philosophizing from the standpoint of the actor instead of, as has been customary, from that of the spectator*' (Allen 1953: 3). The implications of this shift for empirical thinking and, by implication, the objective tone of Movement poetry, are immediately apparent. Gunn's poem, 'Carnal Knowledge', from *Fighting Terms*, is a coruscating exposure of Sartrean bad faith and sexual inauthenticity:

> Even in bed I pose: desire may grow
> More circumstantial and less circumspect
> Each night, but an acute girl would suspect
> My thoughts might not be, like my body, bare. (Gunn 1962: 20)

Gunn's poem is prescient of a marked shift in understandings of sexuality between the 1950s and that cultural construct, the Sixties; it anticipates a critique of sexual liberation before that liberation has really begun. Gunn was later to say that at Cambridge he developed 'a rather crude theory of what I called "pose", based partly on the dramatics of John Donne, somewhat perhaps on W. B. Yeats's theory of masks, and most strongly on the behaviour of Stendhal's heroes' (Hayman 1977: 140). This existential tenet of 'pose', we can interpret, then, allowed him to combine a hybrid literary tradition with an excitingly new philosophical template, and (irresistible with the hindsight of Gunn's homosexuality) a nascent understanding of sexual identity as performance rather than essence.

'Carnal Knowledge' dramatises a number of crises: sexual, existential, phenomenological (in its mistrust of the body's responses), but also empirical. The poem 'Helen's Rape', also in *Fighting Terms*, might serve as a companion piece to Larkin's 'Deceptions' in the surety it places upon violent violation as a catalyst for self-knowledge: 'Hers was the last authentic rape / From forced content of common breeder / Bringing the violent dreamed escape' (Gunn 1962: 17). For the sexual partners of 'Carnal Knowledge', there is a painful dissidence between language and experience, the dissembling male speaker abandoning his taut metrics and precise diction at the end of the first stanza for the mumbled suspicion that 'You know I know you know I know you know.' There is a strong sense in the poem that the inauthenticity of their experiences together is in part attributable to the fact that they are conducted with mutual consent, or rather that the 'girl' is rapacious in her desire, albeit her desire to be passive: 'Lie back. Within a minute I will stow / Your greedy mouth.' The doubt of the opening stanza as to whether the girl is 'acute' enough to realise the falseness of their encounter is soon dissipated with that verse's final line: he knows she knows. That word 'acute' generates numerous associations: sickness, similarly, can be acute, and 'cute', the Americanised approbation that echoes here, has its etymological roots in a darker sense – of cunning, or deception. But who is the less deceived? She is the one accused of attempting a useless rationality – 'Your intellectual protests are a bore' – and the poem ends with his deciding their mutual culpability in pretence: 'And even now I pose, so now go, for / I know you know.' With its truncated, tolling rhythm, this is a conclusion rather of clunking and despairing instinct than rational finesse. Empiricism, like their relationship, is proven wanting.

Time to Change

Unsurprisingly, perhaps, for a group of academics, the prospect of being marked a failure haunts the work of the Movement. *New Lines* includes the poem 'Rejoinder to a Critic', Donald Davie's reply to Martin Seymour-Smith, who had criticised Davie in the journal *Departure* for 'constantly seeking a critico-academic excuse for postponing an attempt to write poetry of a wider range' (Seymour-Smith 1955: 16). Davie does not deny his failure to confront a wider world, but rather justifies the limits of his poetic stance as the only decent response to a still-recent war: '"Alas, alas, who's injured by my love?" / And recent history answers: Half Japan!' When recent passions have run so high and cruel, Davie concludes, 'How dare we now be anything but numb?' (Conquest 1956: 67). The speaker of Nissim Ezekiel's poem, 'In Emptiness', from his first collection *A Time to Change* (1952), is similarly afflicted with numbness: 'Waiting now in emptiness, / Annulled, cancelled, made a blank', yet 'Resolved to find another way' (Ezekiel 1989: 11). As this resolve gathers momentum in the poem, the speaker becomes convinced of the need to draw upon both reason and emotion for a full and moral way of life, ending with a secular prayer to:

> let me always feel
> The presence of the golden mean
> Between the élan of desire
> And the rational faculties,
> Brooding on design and colour
> Even in this emptiness. (12)

Bruce King has described Ezekiel's work as 'rather a poetry of mind thinking about feelings than the expression of emotion' (King 1987: 94) – as good a summary of the ethos of Movement poetry as there is. The above stanza practises precisely the poetic technique espoused by *New Lines*, with the poet's intellectual control of the anxieties he confronts maintained in an exact diction and a calm conversational tone.

In 1992 the publication of Larkin's letters uncovered what Northern Irish poet, playwright and critic Tom Paulin called 'a sewer under the national monument' (Paulin 1992: 15). Larkin's private self was revealed to be 'a casual, habitual racist and an easy misogynist', and Lisa Jardine suggested that the voice of Larkin's poems had duped its readers: 'the very familiarity of the poetic tone, its easy reference to what we know and love', she claimed, 'masks its implications for those who "don't belong"' (Jardine 1992: A4). Nissim Ezekiel's sense of belonging was intricate and unusual; born into Bombay's Jewish community in 1924 and raised a secular rationalist by his father, a scientist, he was always outside Hindu–Muslim culture, and spent two-and-a-half years in England (from 1948 to 1952), in the thick of the vertiginous end of Empire. Historical accounts of modern Indian poetry in English tend to begin with *A Time to Change* as the volume that cast off any Romantic tendencies in favour of a more rational poetic (see, for example, King 2004: 62). The eponymous poem begins 'We who leave the house in April, Lord, / How shall we return?' (Ezekiel 1989: 3), and Ezekiel's response to London is steeped in the symbolism of T. S. Eliot. The Modernist aim of finding objective, poetic correlatives for both subjective experience and abstract ideas clearly informs 'In Emptiness', and the volume as a whole. Yet Ezekiel's striving for self-definition soon rejects that Modernist model of a lost unitary self (so vital an absent presence in the poetry of Eliot), and the collection he publishes at the end of the decade bears an existential philosophical stamp and title: *The Unfinished Man* (1960).

A Time to Change and its affinities with Movement mores emphasise the way in which a particular assertion of selfhood and national identity can be concealed within a modest poetic tone. Rather than a muted response to history, the rational, reasonable register of Ezekiel's poetic voice is actually an amplified political and personal statement in response to a dominant Indian poetic that was, according to King, 'obsessed with mythology, peasants and nationalist slogans' (King 1987: 92). An Indian writing in English at this point in history signified a stance of modernisation, urbanisation and Westernised education. By not 'sounding Indian', Ezekiel is asserting his own particular Indian identity; in his first volume of poetry, Movement poetics become metonymic of the new, secular nation of India to which he returns in 1952. Reading Ezekiel as a Movement poet reminds us how the 'easy tone' of so much of this poetry is a political device. Movement writing has habitually been upheld as characteristic of 1950s British literature, but assuming the Movement voice to be typical is an act of exclusion, and itself typifies the reflex imposition of a particular English, male experience as a shared, nationwide one. Yet despite an identity so diasporic we might assume his sensibility to be inclusive, Ezekiel too is not without misogyny; in her preface to Ezekiel's *Collected Poems*, Leela Gandhi writes of 'the bitter masculine self-regard to which he is prone especially when writing of women and desire' (Gandhi 1989: xvi). A misogynistic bent, it would seem, is often characteristic of those who consider themselves 'less deceived'.

More recent literary historiography marks Movement poetry as provincial in its scope, but is usually charitably understanding of its deliberately unambitious response to the emotional barrage of war and its overweening rhetoric. Charles Tomlinson's fizzing contemporaneous review of *New Lines*, 'The Middlebrow Muse', is piqued not by the Movement's apathy but by its sensationalism. Tomlinson takes impassioned exception to 'the ingratiating image of the average man' produced by the poems and the laddish publicity surrounding them: 'the beer-mug (we learn from the *Educational Supplement*) "is never far from Mr. Wain's hand"' (Tomlinson 1957: 208). Tomlinson's own first volume, *The Necklace*, was published in 1955, beginning a long and critically neglected career in a presciently ecological poetry that defies an anthropological view of the universe for its arrogance and destructive tendencies. He loathes what he sees as the cynicism of the Movement's poetic exercise in 'militant middle-cum-lowbrowism', reading *New Lines* as we might a copy of a late twentieth-century 'lad-mag' like *loaded*, as a publication in which 'the errors of the tribe and the errors of the market ally themselves in impregnable confidence' (209). The superficial, 'second-hand responses' (215) of this blokeish pose, he contends, is interrupted only once in this anthology of 'O.K. names' (213), with the inclusion of 'Miss Jennings', 'so *determined* to be feminine and nice' (212). The opposition of the *New Lines* poets to other literary agendas, according to Tomlinson, is similarly stagy and false. The poets' professed anti-modernism is no more than a chummy philistinism, an attempt to 'make friends with the reader by assuring him how decent you and he are and how these chaps like Eliot lay it on a bit thick' (212), their anti-romanticism mocked by the fact that 'there is at work an unconscionable amount of self-regard, of acting up to one's mirror image of one's self' (213). Unable even to dignify it with a capital letter, Tomlinson concludes: 'The "movement" was in the first place a journalist's convenient generalisation. It is only our total relativity of standards, our want of high and objective criteria that can cause us to mistake it for a significant literary fact' (216).

Philip Larkin, for one, did not disagree with the accusation of 'the Movement' as a product of the press. In a 1956 letter to Robert Conquest, he spoofs a revised introduction to *New Lines*: 'Now we have had time to take a second and closer look at the poetry of this self-styled and already disintegrated "movement" . . . ' (Thwaite 1993: 260). To Tomlinson's review and its more vicious criticisms his response was couched in just that tone of studied blokeishness that fuelled the critique: 'Oh dear,' he wrote, again to Conquest, 'what a gunning from Chas Tomlinson!' (274). Dated 1958, 'The Whitsun Weddings' (published in the eponymous collection in 1964) is a far more complex hybrid of influence than any of Larkin's work in *New Lines*. The poem's Movement characteristics are plain – it is, in fact, a key text in establishing that received identikit of the 1950s British poet: a mildly disapproving middle-class male observer, travelling by train (or sometimes bike, courtesy of 'Church Going'). S. H. Clark calls this figure 'the characteristic persona of his poetry: the excluded onlooker slightly wistful, yet nonetheless resolute in his self-conserving attachment' (220), going on to call *The Whitsun Weddings* as a whole 'a vivid and somehow appalling evocation of socially constructed and responsible masculinity' (226), with a special horror reserved in this respect for 'Self's the Man' (Larkin 1990: 117–18).

In their study of twentieth-century British women's poetry, Jane Dowson and Alice Entwhistle suggest a 'postwar neo-Romantic return to a fixed lyric personality, albeit unheroic' (Dowson and Entwhistle 2005: 110). The Romantic roots of this construction of personality in Larkin's poetry can be set against the profoundly anti-Romantic landscape of 'The Whitsun Weddings', with its countryside crossed by 'Canals with floatings of industrial froth' (Larkin 1990: 114) and piles of scrapped cars at the edge of towns. This contradiction, together with the poem's symbolist conclusion of 'A sense of falling, like an arrow-shower / Sent out of sight, somewhere becoming rain' (116), hints at the folly of confining Larkin's poetry to any particular literary agenda. And for all his personifications of 'responsible masculinity', the writer's *œuvre* as a whole suggests that it is young women (whom he would call 'girls') who 'get to' Larkin most profoundly. It is they whom he uses most readily to communicate a sense of vulnerability: witness his novels *Jill* (1946) and *A Girl In Winter* (1947), the ephemeral school stories collected in *Trouble at Willow Gables* (2002), and poems such as 'Lines on a Young Lady's Photograph Album' and 'Maiden Name' (Larkin 1990: 71–2; 101). Certainly it is this gambit that lies at the centre of the emotional success of 'The Whitsun Weddings', in which it is 'the girls', 'Marked off . . . unreally from the rest' in their synthetic fabrics, who bear the brunt of contemporary society, with its modern stresses of consumption and its ancient gendered rituals, with marriage as 'religious wounding' (115). Despite the mordant pun on 'dying' in its Jacobean inherent in that phrase, Larkin's poems seem ultimately to advocate the (albeit chequered) celibacy that recent publication of his correspondence with Monica Jones suggests was his own frustrated experience of life (Larkin 2010).

Blake Morrison's 1980 study *The Movement* professes its

> main purpose is to show that, for a time at least, there was considerable agreement and interaction, and that out of these was established a Movement consensus. The view that the Movement was a journalistic invention or agreed fiction can no longer be allowed to stand. (Morrison 1980: 6)

Still the presiding definitive critical work on this group of writers, Morrison's text achieved success in this aim. Since its publication, if anything, the Movement has come to dominate perceptions of 1950s British literature as a verifiable literary event, rather than the shaky consensus it always was. Classing Movement poetry as representative of the decade does an injustice, both to the urgent engagement with issues of aesthetics and economics of critics like Tomlinson, and to the poetry itself, which, as this chapter has begun to show, is more emotionally complex and ideologically conflicted than this metonymy allows. It does injustice too to the much wider scope of writing during the 1950s, if the regional identity of the English provinces is allowed to stand for the British nation. As we saw with the poem 'Deceptions', the mores enshrined in Movement writing have cultural consequences well beyond aesthetics.

Anything but Numb

The outstanding British poetic debutant of the decade had a very different experience of life and of poetry from that of Larkin. As we have seen, Charles Tomlinson's assessment of the shortcomings of the *New Lines* poets was unstinting.

> They show [he claimed] a singular want of vital awareness of the continuum outside themselves, of the mystery bodied over against them in the created universe, which they fail to experience with any degree of sharpness or to embody with any instress or sensuous depth. (Tomlinson 1957: 215)

The dearth he identifies was redressed in the work of a poet whose first volume, *The Hawk in the Rain*, was published that same year. Tomlinson's term 'instress' comes from the journals of Gerard Manley Hopkins, where it is used to indicate the force that maintains and communicates another neologism, 'inscape' – the unity of characteristics that make each thing or experience unique. The eponymous poem which begins Ted Hughes's first collection immediately evokes Hopkins through its avian subject – a hawk, rather than the falcon of Hopkins's 'The Windhover' (1877) – and through the drubbing of its alliteration: 'I drown in the drumming ploughland, I drag up / Heel after heel from the swallowing of the earth's mouth.' It is already apparent how far we stand from the rhythmic restraint of Movement poetry. The powers of observation in this poem do not belong to its speaker, mired in mud, and bludgeoned by wind:

> the hawk
>
> Effortlessly at height hangs his still eye.
> His wings hold all creation in a weightless quiet,
> Steady as a hallucination in the streaming air. (Hughes 1968: 11)

Yet even amidst the sudden calm of these short vowels and neat frica-tives, the bird's omniscience is thrown into question by that phrase 'steady as a hallucination'; its hovering form takes on an unearthly, unstable quality over the visceral reality of the 'I' on the ground. This is not so simple a metaphor, however, as a mind / body, hawk / human split. Rather, the poem forms a complex image that mocks the maintenance of such a binary when so many different experiences are in play.

The earth has a 'mouth' and the wind 'thumbs my eyes': it is not the creature but the environment itself that is anthropomorphised. This unusual tactic, and the pronounced aural changes, the first at the enjambment of the first stanza, present us not with the description of an empirical experience, but with a world created in language, rather than reported and rationalised by it. Hughes's linguistic universe is a daunting, shifting terrain, but the final victory belongs not to the brutal elements, nor to the still and hanging bird, but to the embattled, mud-spattered speaker. The hawk is described as 'The diamond point of will that polestars / The sea drowner's endurance', yet the poem ends with its star falling:

> the ponderous shires crash on him,
> The horizon traps him; the round angelic eye
> Smashed, mix his heart's blood with the mire of the land.

In a final, wilful act of the imagination, the speaker poet proves the fragility of his central image, the hawk, by dashing it to the ground, or rather by crushing it within the landscape, in a literary equivalent to the crumpling and balling of a vigorous painting. The Romantic impulse of transformation is fused with a Modernist awareness of the provi-sionality of human perception to announce the complexity of Hughes's agenda; both stand in obvious opposition to the conversational poetry of rationalised experience.

Hughes's positioning of his work in relation to that of the Movement treated the group rather more mildly than had Tomlinson. In a 1971 interview in the *London Magazine* he remarked that:

> One of the things those poets had in common I think was the post-war mood of having had enough ... enough rhetoric, enough overweening push of any kind, enough of the dark gods, enough of the id, enough of the Angelic powers and the heroic efforts to make new worlds. They'd seen it all turn into death-camps and atomic bombs. All they wanted was to get back in civvies and get home to the wife and kids for the rest of their lives ... Now I came a bit later. I hadn't had enough. I was all for opening negotiations with whatever happened to be out there. (Hughes 1971: 10–11)

His poetry shuns the numbness Donald Davie deemed necessary, 'opening negotiations' between the present and pasts both recent and primal. Another hawk poem from Hughes's next volume, *Lupercal* (1960), embodies the scope of this time-scheme. As in 'The Hawk in the Rain', the anthropomorphic project of 'Hawk Roosting' is once again skewed from the expected gambit of likening creature to human:

> I sit in the top of the wood, my eyes closed.
> Inaction, no falsifying dream
> Between my hooked head and hooked feet. (Hughes 1989: 43)

As the bird speaks from its pinnacle of superiority over trees and universe ('It took the whole of Creation / To produce my foot, my each feather'), the delusions of its grandeur reveal human fascism as bestial, rather than animal impulse as human. In counteraction to the dynamic of the end of 'The Hawk in the Rain', here it is the hawk who owns and orders the world: 'Now I hold Creation in my foot / Or fly up, and revolve it all slowly.' He shuns 'sophistry' and 'arguments', and the poem concludes with his ultimate error – he imagines himself omnipotent, and his viewpoint dominant and eternal: 'My eye has permitted no change. / I am going to keep things like this.' The hawk's voice is used to explore precisely the mode of rhetoric and the 'overweening push' Hughes understood the preceding poetic generation to be shy of, harnessing the power of its certainty at the same time as it exposes its deluded instability.

Seamus Heaney was to contrast the work of Hughes and Larkin as stemming from utterly different understandings of indigenous English identities. Hughes he claimed as pagan, Anglo-Saxon and bardic, while for Larkin, the 'proper hinterland is the English language Frenchified and turned humanist by the Norman conquest and the Renaissance, made nimble, melodious and plangent by Chaucer and Spenser, and bosomed clean of its inkhornisms and its irrational magics by the eighteenth century' (Heaney 1983: 15). Entwined with these conceptions are differing models of masculinity, and initial responses to Hughes's work celebrated its perceived revival of a primitive virility so different from the cerebral rationalism of the Movement's main men (Gunn's macho 'pose', with its strong American flavour, being an exception).

Stevie Smith, in her 1957 collection *Not Waving But Drowning*, gave her own diagnosis that 'Many of the English';

> The intelligent English,
> Of the Arts, the Professions and the Upper Middle Classes,
> Are under-cover men,

But what is under the cover
(That was original)
Died; now they are corpse-carriers.
It is not noticeable, but be careful,
They are infective. (Smith 1988: 84)

The poem's judgement is uncharacteristically unequivocal for Smith's work, which tends to defy the quick condemnation of the characters it includes, revelling in their mixed motives and moral ambiguities. Here, however, the Establishment (as the matrix of official as well as social power was commonly known) is uncompromisingly sinister, male, moribund and best avoided, as 'They are infective.' Smith's work has traditionally been read as mindful of this poem's warning, quarantining itself from its immediate cultural context. In a 1979 article 'Why Stevie Smith Matters' (its title indicating the prevailing critical assumption that she didn't, very much), Mark Storey noted approvingly that the writer 'stands outside any tradition of the day, and in so doing, acts as a comment on what is happening elsewhere; she becomes a touchstone' (Storey 1979: 42). The anonymous reviewer of *Not Waving But Drowning* in the *Times Literary Supplement* was quick to justify Smith's cultural marginalisation with reference to gendered failings: 'Largely depending for its effects upon mood and flavour, her verse offers somewhat informal commemorations of markedly feminine yieldings to impulse or capricious fancy' (Smith 1957: 588). Sylvia Plath, who married Ted Hughes in 1956 and published her first volume, *The Colossus*, in 1960, was never accused of femininity, despite the determinedly confessional voice of her poetry. This is perhaps because her work, like that of her husband, interrogates the power of masculine rhetoric at the same time as it exults in reproducing it – the poem 'Daddy' (Plath 1985: 60–2) providing a case in point.

More recently, Smith has been more confidently championed as a prescient post-structuralist; Romana Huk claims her poems and novels 'were, quite early on in the century, taking part in what literary studies considers a postmodern project: deconstructing the traditional concept of a "closed, fixed, rational and volitional self"' (Huk 2005: 4). It is now critically orthodox, yet still undeniably productive, to read Smith's strikingly multivocal, multivalent writing in the light of Bakhtin's theories on textual politics. Debates around her political motives for this poetic, be they postmodern feminist or retaliatory romantic, take far more space than is available here. Smith's elaborately cultivated public persona may have contained elements of that isolated madwoman in the attic figure, but to read her poetry only as outside its historical context seems a dubious tactic, not least because many of her poems engage so directly with the Movement and other masculine poetic mores examined in this chapter.

'Magna est Veritas', also included in *Not Waving But Drowning*, begins by aping that 'statement of self-evident truth' stylistic recognisable from the poems of Amis, Davie, Larkin, Wain et al.: 'With my looks I am bound to look simple or fast I would rather look simple' (Smith 1985: 148). Andrew Crozier nominates the defining characteristic of Movement poetry to be the 'guiding and controlling presence of a speaking subject constructing the poem's framework of interpretation around its personal authority' (Crozier 1983: 228). In Smith's poem, the nature of such personal authority is immediately at odds with the archetypal speaking subject familiar from, for example, Larkin's poetry. The binary opposition 'simple or fast', presented as commonsensical, is false, and the fact that both terms suggest numerous possible interpretations destabilises its referential qualities still further. Furthermore, that 'fast' – its colloquial sense defined by the *Oxford English Dictionary* as 'Often applied to women in milder sense: Studiedly unrefined in habits and manners, disregardful of propriety or decorum' – establishes a female speaker, and one of a particular eccentric bent. She walks about 'rather queerly', 'And people say, Don't bother about her' and she wears 'a tall hat on the back of my head that is rather a temple' (Smith 1985: 148). Recent critics have been reading Stevie Smith's literary hats as complex political gambits, subversive of gender stereotypes, and even, in this particular poem, making a romantic claim of the sanctity of the imagination (see Sims Steward 1998 and Najarian 2003). As in the first line, the lack of regulatory punctuation and reliable rhythm seems to loosen the poem's powers of signification. Is it the speaker's hat she claims as a temple, or her head? Does 'rather' indicate it is only partially 'a temple', or a temple rather than another alternative – if so, what? There is not even a gnomic illustration to guide us, as there is with many of Stevie Smith's poems. Despite a familiar and accessible tone, its language and structure work to undo empiricism, functioning to destabilise the correlation between experience and expression. Instead, the speaker flaunts her failed scientific method, admitting that 'Although I collect facts I do not always know what they amount to.' Her finale is a parody of the 'philistine pose' adopted by Jim Dixon, as she says of her collection of facts that:

> I regard them as a contribution to almighty Truth, magna est veritas et praevalebit,
> Agreeing with that Latin writer, Great is Truth and will prevail in a bit.
> (Smith 1985: 148)

'That Latin writer' is studiedly casual, the Latin itself, 'praevalebit', comically garbled into 'prevail in a bit'. Yet this quotation is not from a Latin writer but a seventeenth-century English Puritan, Edmund Brooks, and he in turn is misquoting a Latin translation of the book of *Esdras* [*Ezra*], an apocryphal and profoundly non-canonical work of scripture. The 'original' of this contested text reads 'magna est veritas et praevalet' – 'great is truth and it prevails.' So, as Najarian puts it, 'Smith leads us on this wild goose chase to what is at most a misquotation of a translation of a translation of an obscure book of debatable authority' (Najarian 2003: 478). And part of the joke is the fact that her speaker's bungled translation of the Latin verb, 'will prevail in a bit', actually parodies Brooks's slip in altering tense, so that the magnificent confidence of truth prevailing now becomes a more modest (and more English?) prediction of its prevalence in an unspecified future. Smith's poem cannot be said merely to masquerade as light verse, as its deft comedy functions extremely well without this rather torturous footnote. Yet a level of scholarly research not dissimilar to that demanded by the poetry of, say, Ezra Pound, makes the truly subversive nature of the poem's language game apparent. Who, it implicitly asks, is less deceived – the playful, disregarded female speaker, or the men of mainstream 1950s poetry, cocksure in their ability to link language to experience?

Chapter Seven

Evil Men: Literature and Homosexuality

In 1948, the report *Sexual Behaviour in the Human Male*, better known as the Kinsey Report, revealed that, of its sample of 5,300 white US males,

> at least 37 per cent of the male population has some homosexual experience between the beginning of adolescence and old age. This is more than one male in three of the persons that one may meet as he passes along a city street. (Kinsey et al. 1948: 623)

A year later, the Mass Observation File Report 3110A, often nicknamed 'Little Kinsey', claimed a much more conservative figure for Britain: of their respondents, '12% have had homosexual relationships, and 8% admit to homosexual leanings at some time in their life.' A note added

> These last results are perhaps the most startlingly different of all from Kinsey. It may be worth noting, however, that before the survey started two independent statements were obtained by Mass-Observation, one from a Harley Street sexologist and one from a prostitute, and both said that they thought that Kinsey applied generally to Britain, except for his high incidence of homosexuality. (Mass Observation 1949: 12n)

'Little Kinsey' also documented that 60 per cent of its sample were antipathetic to homosexuality. '*It's a bit of a teaser*', a '48 year old coal depot manager' was quoted as saying. '*I shouldn't think they're human – it is done, I know – I mean animals don't do that, I shouldn't think*' (Stanley 1995: 200). A further 30 per cent claimed they did not understand what homosexuality was.

During the 1950s, this plea of ignorance would have become more and more difficult to maintain, as male homosexuality, its varying practices and diagnoses, and unwavering illegality became an increasingly prominent topic of public debate. (Lesbianism, however, was yet to become part of the discussion.) In 1954, *The Times* gave a lengthy column to 'The Problem of Homosexuality: Report by Doctors and Clergy', discussing a recent Church of England interim report which advocated the legalisation of sex between consenting men and an age of consent equal to that of heterosexual relationships. That same year saw the establishment of a Royal Commission under the chairmanship of John Wolfenden, then Vice Chancellor of Reading University. Three years later, the fifteen-strong body had heard evidence from over 200 organisations and individuals, and published the *Report of the Departmental Committee on Homosexual Offences and Prostitution* on 3 September 1957. The Wolfenden Report recommended the decriminalisation of homosexuality between consenting adults over twenty-one, and insisted that 'homosexuality cannot legitimately be regarded as a disease, because in many cases it is the only symptom and is compatible with full mental health in other respects' (Wolfenden 1957: 14). At the crux of its argument lay the claim that 'It is not, in our view, the function of the law to intervene in the private life of citizens, or to seek to enforce any particular pattern of behaviour' (10). A decade later, the committee's recommendations passed into law with the 1967 Sexual Offences Act.

Gregory Woods suggests that a consideration of gay literature in Britain and the US during the 1950s should prompt us once again to reassess the received perception of those years as 'a pinched, humourless decade', for:

> The real story of the 1950s, as well as being about censors, involves many triumphs over and circumventions of censorship. Gay writers, among others, ensured that there was an increasing amount of work for the censors to do. Indeed, you might say that, for all their reputation as a time of rigorously enforced conformity ('the tranquillised Fifties', as Robert Lowell called them), the 1950s amounted to a virtual festival of queer self-assertion. (Woods 1998: 289)

Even Jimmy Porter is uncharacteristically empathetic towards 'the Greek Chorus boys', for at least, he claims, 'they do seem to have a cause – not a particularly good one, it's true. But plenty of them do seem to have a revolutionary fire about them, which is more than you can say for the rest of us' (Osborne 1989: 35). Yet the Lord Chamberlain ensured that such fires were rarely lit onstage. Terence Rattigan's play, *The Deep Blue Sea* (1952), for example, began as the story of a homosexual relationship, but ended after censorship as the altogether more savoury scandal of a Battle of Britain hero's affair with a judge's wife. In *Separate Tables* (1955), Major Pollock's crime, originally conceived to echo John Gielgud's conviction for cruising in a public toilet in 1952, became, in the play's final version, a bemusing record of molesting women in cinema auditoriums. Other genres and media, however, were considerably less muted. Numerous discourses of (male) homosexuality competed within the public arena for dominance: state-sanctioned, sensationalist, sexological, autobiographical and literary. Yet surprisingly, though these representations of gay experience had very different cultural statuses, they tended to share a defining narrative structure.

'Evil Men', a *Sunday Pictorial* series by Douglas Warth that ran in 1952, began with the sensational claim that 'The natural British tendency to pass over anything unpleasant in scornful silence is providing cover for an unnatural sex vice which is getting a dangerous grip on this country' (Warth 1952: 12). This assertion, of course, serves its author well by casting him in the role of heroic investigator, selflessly descending into a dark underworld on his quest to increase the nation's self-knowledge. In 1954 the much publicised trial of Lord Montague of Beaulieu, Michael Pitt-Rivers and Peter Wildeblood, on charges of conspiracy to incite two other men to commit indecent acts, provided one of the showpieces of Home Secretary David Maxwell Fife's 'drive against male vice'. Like the trial of Oscar Wilde almost sixty years before it, its spectacle relied heavily upon a contrived sense of homosexual desire as something hitherto hidden, then bravely unearthed by police and prosecution. At one point in Wildeblood's cross-examination, Mr Roberts, the prosecution counsel, revealed the contents of a love letter Wildeblood had written to Edward McNally, a corporal in the RAF, pronouncing that it was 'breathing unnatural passion in almost every line' – a direct quotation from Wilde's trial (Wildeblood 1956: 72). An experienced reporter himself, Wildeblood gave his own account of his trial and subsequent imprisonment, *Against the Law* (1955), which is also driven by a narrative of revelation: 'It will be my task', he pledges at its opening, 'to turn on more lights, revealing, in place of the blurred and shadowy figure of the newspaper photographs, a man differing from other men only in one respect' (2). Chris Waters has called *Against the Law* 'a complex, unstable text. It rejected the moral outrage associated with the tabloid discourse of homosexuality, yet was inscribed within the same binary logic of secrecy and disclosure that characterised tabloid reporting' (Waters 1999: 150).

Wildeblood's quest is, to some extent, a linguistic one: an attempt, like that of the Movement poets, to re-establish an empirical relationship between language and truth. The 'Little Kinsey' Report had made the claim that 'Queers' conversation thrives on ambiguities of a sexual nature i.e. intentionally misinterpreting a harmless remark to be suggestively sexual (homosexual)' (Stanley 1995: 202). Ironically, what most enrages Wildeblood about the case is the prosecution's reliance upon bitchy innuendo, claiming that written statements of love must imply actual acts of sex: 'a nightmare edifice of snobbery, deliberate ignorance, and hypocrisy based on the proposition: There's no smoke without fire' (Wildeblood 1956: 78). By contrast, the defining battle of the trial as Wildeblood presents it is the one in which he thwarts Mr Roberts's innuendo and false logic with direct statements of truth:

> 'It is a feature, is it not, that inverts or perverts seek their love associates in a different walk of life than their own?'
> 'I cannot accept that as a deduction. I have never heard any suggestion that that is the ordinary rule.'
> 'I mean, for instance, McNally was infinitely – he is none the worse for it – but infinitely your social inferior?'
> 'That is absolute nonsense.'
> 'Well, perhaps that is not a very polite way of answering my question.' (77)

This is a moment of exact correlation between Wildeblood's testimony and his homosexual identity, between empirical, ontological and linguistic truths. His defence throughout depends upon the fact that homosexual love does not necessarily involve homosexual sex: 'I remembered my own words: "I think we ought to agree on some kind of vocabulary. If I say somebody is a homosexual I am not necessarily implying that they indulge in criminal actions"' (90). His heroism here, paradoxically, is secured by his 'straight talking', in contrast to Mr Roberts's excessive and inaccurate inferences, and fussy rebukes about politeness. Though his overt confession that he is an 'invert' is instrumental in securing his jail sentence, it also secures an on-going career in revealing the truth about gay experience. Peter Wildeblood was one of only three professed homosexuals to give evidence to the Wolfenden Committee, volunteering because, 'It was easy for me to speak for the homosexuals, because my admission that I was one of them had received the most widespread publicity; I had nothing further to lose' (174).

Like the philosophical agenda of the Movement poets, the confrontation between Wildeblood and his prosecutor quoted above has a gendered sub-text. Mr Roberts's flawed processes of deduction and schoolmarmish scolding are presented in opposition to Wildeblood's masculine linguistic and logical assertion. This gambit is indicative of a common concern in much gay British writing of the 1950s. At a time when the dominant understanding of homosexuality had shifted towards intrinsic condition, rather than mental imbalance, passing whim or the product of coercion, the dominant, and effeminate, stereotype of homosexual identity was also under investigation. Wildeblood holds that 'We do our best to look like everyone else, and we usually succeed. That is why nobody realizes how many of us there are' (7). The homosexual protagonist of the 1953 novel *The Heart in Exile*, written by Hungarian émigré Adam de Hegedus under the pseudonym Rodney Garland, is similarly at pains to distinguish his identity from the highly visible, and obviously vulnerable, 'pansies':

> I try hard to be understanding, but I shudder from them. It is not only that they give the game away, but it is my experience that such people are usually unintelligent, verbose, neurotic and generally tiresome ... They are out of their depths everywhere, except in each other's company, and they are more feminine than most women, the 'modern' woman in particular. (Garland 1966: 47)

Garland's protagonist, Anthony Page, is a psychiatrist, alerted by one of his patients to the recent suicide of an ex-lover, Julian Leclerc. The narrative is driven by Page's investigation of both Leclerc's death and his own responses to it, as the doctor is forced to move in secret social circles of postwar London that he had abandoned:

> The underground contained between a million and a half to two million males, according to the guess of the experts. It is reminiscent of the iceberg the visible shape of which looms so misleadingly small over the waves, the larger part of it being below. (79)

As Matt Houlbrook and Chris Waters put it, 'Page is, in short, Garland's cartographer of a queer city' (Houlbrook and Waters 2006: 142).

Yet as well as being a physician, a cartographer and a reporter, the aptly named Page reveals distinctly literary aspirations: 'I found myself actually enjoying my uneasiness. I was *living* a novel. All my life I had been attracted by the romantic figure of the private detective' (124). Paradoxically, to Page, the novelistic bent of this period of his life enhances the verisimilitude of his experiences: 'The fact that the novel I wished to *live* at this particular moment was a penny-dreadful, mystery story, was significant, because I always felt the penny-dreadful was the *real* novel. As a species it was immortal' (Garland 1966: 139). Yet Page's narrative seeks to deny melodrama to the homosexual experience. His assistant, Terry, asks, 'Why all plays and novels dealing with queers have an inevitably tragic end', and Page tells him that this is the only form in which 'normal society' will accept such characters: 'To be a homo is a crime, and crime mustn't go unpunished; not in books at least. Besides, I think the author himself, by giving you a tragic end, is trying to engage your sympathy: "Pity us poor buggers"'. Terry responds: 'If ever I write a book on the subject, I'd try to tell the truth. I'd write about the majority for whom it isn't really tragic' (138). This is the book that

Page (or Garland, or de Hegedus) himself produces, *The Heart in Exile*, a novel that, far from being a penny-dreadful, maintains the reasonable, confessional tone and *Bildungsroman* structure characteristic of the decade's established canon. Though Page, as a homosexual, has insider knowledge of the world he describes, his profession and his staunchly masculine, respectable demeanour position him in a space idealised by that canon – that of an emotionally invested but analytical observer; he speaks of 'the unorganized but world-wide underground society of which I myself was an associate, if not a member' (43). Rather than queering the genre, then, *The Heart in Exile* replicates it, seeking to naturalise or, rather, masculinise the homosexual experience by fashioning it to function within the generic logic of the dominant fictional form.

The novel has the conventional comedic ending of a love match, yet the tone in which Page communicates it is far from romantic: 'I now knew that I was in love with Terry or, at least, I was as near to love as I had ever been in my life. I was a psychologist: I recognised the symptoms' (214). This, of course, is the physician, diagnosing himself, and the novel regularly gives voice to contemporary medical discourses surrounding homosexuality. Pressed for an explanation of the Minister's predilection for a working-class man, Page offers this: 'My private guess on Freudian lines is that they have fewer anal fears than the upper classes, but what I think more important is that the worker gives us the impression, sometimes quite wrongly, that he's more masculine and virile than the man from the middle class' (73). 'Was Freud entirely right?' asked D. J. Enright, and Page's answer, it seems, is 'only with reference to particular classes'. Though he seems convinced of a Freudian explanation of the attraction to the lower classes, his diagnosis of the desire of working-class men to those above them in the class hierarchy is offered only vaguely: 'Possibly Ginger represented that primitive type of man which, like our ancestors, made no rigid distinction between the two sexes, but followed his instincts of lust and affection' (130).

In the Montague case, of course, the relationship between homosexual desire and class difference was a particularly highly charged issue. Prosecutor Mr Roberts's assertion that 'it is a feature . . . that inverts and perverts seek their love associates in a different walk of life than their own' (Wildeblood 1956: 77) is intended to emphasise the disreputability of homosexuality still more heavily – disruptive as it is of the very order of decent society – while maintaining a conceptual link, so vital to the Wilde case, of 'perversion' and the decadence of an idle rich. Wildeblood's vehement refutation suggests a reluctance to confront the complex dynamics of social and economic power involved in the hypergamous gay relationships of the period, casting his own attraction to McNally as a combination of romantic love and an ancient Grecian impulse to mentor. In *Thin Ice* (1956), Compton Mackenzie's narrator, George Gaymer, confused and repulsed by the homosexuality of his closest friend, Henry Fortesque, is still more agitated by the denigration of class privilege Henry's predilection for 'rent boys' allows. He professes himself horrified by 'the evil power the law placed in the hands of such creatures. That a man like Henry through a physical or mental flaw might be at the mercy of a Jack Shore seemed utterly wrong' (Mackenzie 1959: 150). In *The Heart in Exile*, Page's own romantic conclusion depends upon a love object positioned carefully outside the stark dichotomy of rich and poor, but also distinct from the doctor's own respectable middle-classness. Terry, the male nurse who acts as Page's assistant and housekeeper, is 'more at home in blue jeans, lumber-jackets, moccasins and loafers, windcheaters, cowboy shirts, in essentially masculine, revolutionary, anti-traditional, almost anti-capitalist garments. All of which, oddly enough, emanate from the most demonstratively and aggressively capitalist state in the world' (Garland 1966: 134). His modern, mid-Atlantic lifestyle, and a gay identity between tough and toff (an identity poet Thom Gunn was to adopt on his move to America), prefigures an important 'type' in later discourses of gay liberation, and it allows Page to anticipate a new and loving life outside the strictures of both the traditional class system and the 'scene'.

Telling it Straight

That Terry is 'essentially masculine' is crucial to the novel's happy ending. Page has confessed a 'shudder' in response to those homosexual men who 'are more feminine than most women' (47), and Laurie Odell, the protagonist of Mary Renault's 1953 novel *The Charioteer*, shares this revulsion towards what he calls the 'specialists' who 'had identified themselves with their limitations; they were making a career out of them' (Renault 2003: 132). At a party he meets a young flight-lieutenant, Bim, and is repulsed by the way in which 'the high girlish voice with which he greeted his friends was burlesqued and perfunctory, like a carnival vizard held with a flourish a foot away from the face. You felt, and were meant to feel, that he was playing at it' (134). Bim is later to die when he fails to bail out of his plane as it goes down over Calais: a suicide, we are encouraged to assume, due to the despair engendered by his exhaustingly performative existence. Renault's novel traces Laurie's period of convalescence at a rural veteran's hospital after an injury sustained at

Dunkirk, and the majority of its gay characters (all of them male) enact this kind of 'bad', burlesqued homosexual identity to varying degrees. At the party, Laurie is reunited with a prefect from his school, Ralph Lanyon, whose lover, Bunny, is a period archetype of the feminised queer – camp, treacherous, cruel, irrational and with an unchecked penchant for interior decoration: 'a leisured view of the room yielded so many awful little superfluities, so many whimsies and naughty-naughties, tassels and bits of chrome, that one recalled one's gaze shamefaced as if one had exposed the straits of the poor' (194). Laurie's most despised superfluity is a linguistic one – since his schooldays, he has instinctively rejected the elaborate insinuation of camp speech. His friend Carter, we are told, 'was not the only one to find Laurie's conversation disconcertingly uninhibited. The innuendo, more generally approved, was apt when it reached him to be smacked into the open with the directness of a fives ball' (18). As his attraction to Andrew, a young conscientious objector serving as hospital orderly, grows, he fantasises about the letter he really wants to write to his mother. In place of the platitudes about his progressing health, it would read: 'I have fallen in love. I now know something about myself which I have been suspecting for years, if I had had the honesty to admit it. I ought to be frightened and ashamed, but I am not' (57).

Like that of Wildeblood, Laurie's own identity, and his masculinity, are predicated upon asserting himself as a 'straight' talker, and the novel's narrative voice, focalised through him, maintains the frankness of his desire:

> Ralph was balanced on his heels, his good hand holding the edge of the bath; and it came back to Laurie that he had had beautiful hands, with which he had never made an affected or exhibiting movement; neither coarse nor overfine, full of intelligence and adaptable strength. (144)

He has only one lapse into camp expression, when, badly injured and on the verge of death, he is being evacuated from Dunkirk by ship, and wakes to find a bearded face peering at him: 'he remembered giving a wry kind of smile and saying, "Sorry, dearie. Some other time." The face had disappeared rather quickly; he couldn't remember seeing it again' (37). The face, it is eventually revealed, belongs to Ralph, and Laurie's innuendo wounds him deeply, for he reads it as an adult revulsion at the emotional and intellectual bonds they had forged at school.

The title of Renault's novel recalls an allegory from Plato's *Phaedrus*, in which a charioteer, a symbol of the intellect, drives two horses, representing positive and negative human passions. Consisting of dialogue between Phaedrus and Socrates, this is the book that Ralph gifts to

Laurie when the older boy is expelled from school, betrayed by a lover. '"Read it when you've got a minute," said Lanyon casually, "as an anti-dote to Jeepers"' (the homophobic master who has expelled him). '"It doesn't exist anywhere in real life, so don't let it give you illusions. It's just a nice idea"'(32). We might expect Laurie to have a natural affin-ity to the text, as one in which homosexual love is so directly expressed and so commonplace that it can be used as an exemplar through which to explore an ideal mode of rhetoric. Indeed, a large proportion of *The Charioteer* itself is formed by dialogues between two men (Laurie and, variously, Ralph, Andrew, Alec and Dave) attempting to forge a newly direct means of communication of the contemporary homosexual expe-rience: of a love that dare speak its name. Plato suggests that if a state or army consisted only of lovers and those they loved, their society would approach perfection, as they sought to rival each other in honour. The schoolboy Ralph rejects the possibility of this utopia – 'it's just a nice idea' (32). Yet, as Alan Sinfield has pointed out, in a novel set among the airmen of the Second World War, 'such an ideal is not irrelevant' (Sinfield 1994: 143). Laurie is seeking a homosexual identity that is naturalistic, masculine and unashamed. Of all the novel's characters, Ralph most closely approximates this state – his long experience in the Merchant Navy has allowed him happily to integrate into main-stream, 'normal' (as Wildeblood would have it) life. However progres-sive Renault's novel might seem, Alan Sinfield rejects the politics of its conclusion. Rather than enlighten Andrew as to the true nature of their mutual love, Laurie sacrifices his happiness in order that Andrew can 'remain innocent and hence untainted. Queer heroism, again, involves invalidating queerness' (Sinfield 1994: 144). Laurie's vision of a 'natural', masculine, gay sexuality does not escape the dominant, binary understandings of gender, but replicates them. Renault's attempt to 'redeem' postwar homosexuality with reference to its classical cre-dentials is a profoundly unstable one, and interestingly her next novel, *The Last of the Wine* (1956), and all subsequent work abandons the problems of the contemporary setting for a classical one.

Angus Wilson's novel, *Anglo-Saxon Attitudes* (1956), plays bril-liantly with the impulse to providing an ancient, naturalising precedent for homosexual desire. The novel opens with a spoof column in *The Times*, November 1912, regarding an archaeological dig in Melpham, England, and the unearthing of the coffin of Bishop Eorpwald (d. 695). 'The most remarkable discovery', the column proclaims, 'is undoubtedly that of a wooden fertility figure. Similar Saxon figures have been found twice before, preserved in the marshy bogs of Jutland and Friesland. But this discovery is unique in English archaeology' (Wilson 1958: ix).

The excitement generated by the pagan symbol in the Bishop's tomb is that possibility of something powerfully pagan remaining in the English tradition. Certainly this is how Gilbert Stokesay, whose father has made the excavation, boasts of it to the novel's protagonist Gerald Middleton: 'It's nice to think that the undiluted milk of the Nazarene gospel was not strong enough diet for the good old Anglo-Saxon episcopal stomach. He had to have this little wooden fellow as well, and a very priapic little fellow at that, I may tell you' (160). The 1950s society of the novel can be characterised by a distinct lack of this priapism among men (as well as a pronounced hysteria among the majority of the women); sixty years old, Gerald is described as 'sensualist who had never had the courage of his desires' (13). That these desires are homosexual, and that England's hope of an invigorating Anglo-Saxon tradition is symbolised by the motif of two men – the Bishop and fertility figure – bedded down together, is a queer and irresistible coincidence.

In 1953, W. H. Auden remarked on the publication of Wilson's earlier novel, *Hemlock and After* (1952), that American reviewers 'were horrified, not at the subject, but as his portrayal of queers as no more unhappy than anyone else' (Davenport Hines 1995: 276). His observation confirms Terry's in *The Heart in Exile* of the 'inevitably tragic end' of homosexual characters in literature (Garland 1966: 138). Much of Wilson's perceived value as a writer has been based on the way in which his novels might be thought to contribute to the Leavisite 'Great Tradition'. In their sweeping coverage of a varied cross-section of society, novels like *Hemlock and After* owe a clear debt to nineteenth-century realism (and necessitate a list of principal characters to allow readers to plot that wide sweep). However, their sociological aspects – what lecturer and anti-bomb campaigner Louie Randall identifies as 'social democratic wobbling' in the protagonist Bernard Sands's books (Wilson 1966: 75) – suggest a determinedly contemporary political agenda. Like Colin MacInnes and the folk devil of the teenager, Wilson sets out to repudiate a number of dominant discourses about homosexuality. As the grand opening of Sands's writers' retreat at Vardon Hall descends into queer bacchanalia, the vast majority of the respectable denizens of the rural community respond not with tabloid hysteria but with resolute grace; 'One solicitor's wife, having opened a bedroom door on the oddest embrace, cried loudly, "There's nothing *here*, to see anyway."'(155). The *Sunday Pictorial* series had characterised homosexuals as 'Evil Men' (Warth 1952), yet in *Hemlock and After* evil and perversion are emphatically located in Mrs Curry and Hubert Rose, as the former seeks to procure 'little Elsie Black', a working-class, fatherless child, for the latter to abuse:

'You should have heard her the other day, "I had a lot of daddies in the war,"
she told me. "A G.I. daddy and a Norsky daddy and a Polsky daddy. But
they all went away." Poor little thing, she's quite simple. Oh it *will* want a
lot of making up for.'
'We've already agreed on all that, I think,' said Hubert. (135)

It is the homosexual Bernard Sands, or, rather, his dying wishes as
executed by his wife, Ella, that initiates justice in the case of Rose; and
it is Rose, not a tragic queer, who hangs himself rather than face public
shame. Wilson's bold portrayal of heterosexual paedophilia offers a
clear challenge to the assumption that all homosexuality involves ped-
erasty, and Mrs Curry's evil business, set against Sands's staunch ethics,
anticipates the irony of the Wolfenden Committee's brief to investigate
'homosexual offences' alongside prostitution.

The Kinsey Report was definite in its assertion of sexuality as a question of a continuum rather than an exclusive binary opposition: 'The
histories which have been available in the present study make it apparent that the heterosexuality or homosexuality of many individuals is not
an all-or-none proposition' (Kinsey 1948: 638). Sands's homosexual
desires come to be exercised fairly late in his life, and that fact, together
with the existence of his wife and children, ensures he maintains a position akin to that of Anthony Page in *The Heart in Exile*: he is both inside
and outside 'the gay scene', a phrase appearing in the novel in what is
surely one of its earliest usages (Wilson 1966: 57). This dual position
of observer / participant is most clearly emphasised in Bernard's role at
society hostess Evelyn Rammage's party, shuttling between the younger,
loucher guests and their more effete elders (102). Woods notes how

> Bernard Sands' unwavering liberal sympathies make him attempt to inter-
> vene in the awkward 'borderland' between the two groups and reconcile
> them. Needless to say, in the situation that existed before law reform – as,
> to some extent, ever since – it was never going to be easy to get invisible
> homosexuals to identify readily with the more visible, and therefore more
> vulnerable and dangerous, type. (Woods 1998: 295)

Yet, unlike Wildeblood and Garland, Wilson portrays this type not as
repulsive 'pansies', easily dismissed, but as complex individuals whose
campness signifies not always weakness, but also vitality and mutuality.
The empathetic Elizabeth Sands, Bernard's daughter, is prone to a reflex
campness when attempting to jolly her profoundly withdrawn mother
into activity: '"We'll eat ourselves sick on lobster at Prunier's and
send you back complete with facial and house-gown." She had so long
pronounced these words in facetious Cockney that she could not now
say them straight' (52). Indeed, the third-person narrator, otherwise

wholly traditional, is not without moments of camp. When theatrical producer Sherman Winter and his hedonistic entourage are roaming the upper floors of Vardon Hall at the opening party, the narrator observes tartly that 'It was break-up day at St. Monica's and no punches pulled' (Wilson 1966: 154).

Battling with the legacy of parents who have always neglected her emotionally, Elizabeth embarks upon a relationship with Terence, her father's ex-lover: 'After their first night together, Terence said, "Darling Elizabeth, you can't imagine what a relief it is that sex has at last reared its ugly head," and Elizabeth agreed' (192). This plot twist allows the representation of yet more shades on the spectrum of sexuality, exploring her emotional masochism and his bisexuality. Yet their doomed relationship – the only explicitly sexual one in the novel – is effectively ghosting a real homosexual relationship. Certainly Bernard Sands's most intense emotional experience in the novel is one of selfishness rather than solidarity, as he witnesses the arrest for 'importuning' of a young man who asks him for a light in Leicester Square: 'He could only remember the intense, the violent excitement that he had felt when he saw the hopeless terror in the young man's face . . . A humanist, it would seem, was more at home with the wielders of the knout and the rubber truncheon' (107). The decline to Sands's death can be dated to this point in the narrative, and it is indicative of the warped nature of contemporary law that justice for Hubert Rose can only be initiated after that death, once Sands is immune to blackmail and exposure himself. Whether this muted and attenuated conclusion to a novel that promises such a bold examination of homosexuality is attributable to a fear of censorship, or to what Sinfield identifies as the compulsion towards 'invalidating queerness' (Sinfield 1994: 144), is unclear.

We might, perhaps, have begun this chapter with the expectation that, during the 1950s, gay men and those who represent them in British literature of the time would feel a stronger affiliation towards women than to the often-misogynistic, masculine self-assertion of the Movement poets and the Angry Young Men. Both groups were similarly confronted during the decade with journalistic images of their own lives that they found difficult to recognise; both, we might assume, had the good, brave cause of re-imagining society in their writing. Yet Bernard Sands dies unfulfilled, and even Rodney Garland's happy ending to the unashamedly gay romance *The Heart in Exile* pairs its protagonist with a man described as 'the pleasant housewife type' (Garland 1966: 32). That we end this section, 'The Less Deceived', with the same, synthetic image of the happy housewife with which we began, leads us to the conclusion that, along with their heterosexual male peers, gay writers of the 1950s were just as steady in the faith they staked so vehemently in the inevitable continuance of traditional gender roles. Testament, perhaps, to the social value of the patriarchal premium paid to British men during the 1950s (or rather, to the class of men producing these works of literature), it is the female writers who seem to produce the clearest response to the restrictive gender roles and the gendered politics of the decade. As we have seen, Elizabeth Wilson suggests that the lack of a distinct feminist agenda during the decade was due to the nature of a particularly dominant cultural discourse, that of 'a conservative society described in the rhetoric of a radical ideology. This held out in one hand the image of social revolution achieved, a political achievement, while with the other it demolished politics as a valid activity' (Wilson 1980: 6). Surprisingly, the gay writing examined here seems to provide the opposite: a vision of a (at least potentially) radical society described in the rhetoric of a conservative ideology. During the 1950s, it seems, it is women writing about women who are the least deceived.

III.

Postwar Settlements

"

Chapter Eight

Coming Home: The Literature of Immigration

The home was a powerful site of social change during the 1950s in Britain, as the private domestic space, arena of the family, leisure and consumption, was emphatically re-inscribed as a key marker of national identity. The idea of 'home', however, has a different meaning, albeit one equally invested in the concept of Britishness. As Wendy Webster puts it,

> Cultural theorists, in developing a literature concerned with notions of location and dislocation, belonging and displacement, migration and exile, have been interested in the associations of home with origins, identity, attachment and settlement, and with its common use as a metaphor for nation. (Webster 1998: ix)

These associations are, of course, heavily inflected with issues of race. In the postwar period of unfettered Commonwealth immigration bounded by the 1948 Nationality Act and the 1962 Commonwealth Immigrants Bill, Britain was alone in the world in negotiating the assimilation of those already designated as citizens (Brubaker 1989: 11). Despite an inclusive policy on nationality that allowed entrance to those from all former and current colonies, informal ideas about who should and could belong in Britain were notably racially inflected. Thus, as Kathleen Paul puts it, 'the policy-making elite perceived emigrating UK residents, immigrating continental and Irish aliens, and migrating subjects of color as belonging to different communities of Britishness' (Paul 1997: xii). Paul's *Whitewashing Britain: Race and Citizenship in the Postwar Era* traces a complex and insalubrious interplay between the thoughts and actions of this 'policy-making elite' and the propagation of allegedly 'popular' opinions of the British public and their media. Within these interdependent discourses, Paul claims, 'Differences between white and black were constructed through an opposition between an Englishness, characterized by the privacy of domestic and familial life, and "immigrants", who were characterized in terms of an incapacity for domestic and familial life, or domestic barbarism.' Cultural representations of immigrants, she suggests, 'increasingly converged on a common theme – their threat to home' (xii). (Paul's use of inverted commas around the word 'immigrants' emphasises the constructed and symbolic nature of the role.) We might add 'their threat to *the* home' too, as the enforced ghettoisation of Britain's expanding black population in cramped sub-standard urban housing stock was a defining feature of the lives of the newly arrived – and was read by the white majority to be symptomatic of a racial inability to keep house in a respectably British way.

Of course, 'black' immigration was an infinitely more nuanced phenomenon than either policy or popular opinion would allow. Indian and Pakistani immigration only became a sizeable proposition into the next decade, with a 'beat the ban' boom in response to rumours of impending restrictions: 7,500 people moved to Britain from the region in 1960, and 48,000 in 1961 (Hiro 1973: 108). For people from the sub-continent, Dilip Hiro claims, 'the economic consideration was the sole motive for migration' (107). For West Indian immigrants, motivations were more complicated. Those who had been formally educated in these island territories had received a thorough grounding in rhetoric that made Britain the 'mother country'; in Errol John's play, *Moon on a Rainbow Shawl* (1958), the precociously bright Trinidadian child Esther compulsively sings 'Land of Hope and Glory' as she goes about her housework (John 1985: 37). It was the ship *Empire Windrush* which brought the first large group of West Indians to Britain after the Second World War; docking in Essex on 22 June 1948, she carried 492 Jamaicans. Paul emphasises the dissonance between these peoples' expectations and the public reaction of those who received them:

> Though it was further away than the United States, traveling to Britain constituted something of a homeward journey. This was not the perception of those awaiting them at "home", however, who believed generally in several definitions of Britishness and specifically in a West Indian Britishness located within an exterior, political community and best maintained at the periphery of the empire, not the core. (Paul 1997: 114)

As Tornado, a Trinidadian character in George Lamming's pioneering 1954 novel *The Emigrants*, puts it to a new arrival: 'First thing the limey bastards ask you is when you goin' back home, as though they ever stay where they live . . . You ain't home, chum. You in the land o' the enemy' (Lamming 1994: 67).

The immigration policy of the 1950s in Britain (and its vital consequences for the politics of citizenship) developed between two key acts of legislation, both falling just outside the decade. The 1948 British Nationality Act established the right of any citizen of the British colonies to live and work in Britain, and it was passed in a parliamentary mood of high idealism, self-congratulation and a belief that 'To limit that right was to undermine the very foundation upon which this institution was built, and to cast a shadow on the quality of moral leadership expected of the mother country' (Hiro 1973: 190). The 1962 Commonwealth Immigrants Act centred upon the division of potential migrants into those with jobs to go to, those with skills or experience deemed useful to Britain, and unskilled labourers in search of work. By 1958 there were around 125,000 West Indians in Britain who had come over since the war. Although this number was easily absorbed by the postwar boom's demand for labour, there was a generalised shift across the decade in the nature and aspirations of the immigrants, from skilled or semi-skilled workers seeking social as well as geographical mobility, to those who were un- or semi-skilled, and driven by rural poverty (Hiro 1973: 7–8). According to the 1962 Act, it was the unskilled category only that was subject to numerical control, and in a 1961 memorandum, Home Secretary Rab Butler underlined the 'great merit' of the Act as the fact that it could be presented as entirely non-discriminatory, even though in practice 'its restrictive effect is intended to, and would in fact, operate on coloured people almost exclusively' (Paul 1997: 166). As Moses puts it in Sam Selvon's novel *The Lonely Londoners* (1956), 'the old Brit'n too diplomatic to clamp down on the boys or to do anything drastic like stop them coming to the Mother Country' (Selvon 2006: 2). Sir David Hunt, Churchill's Private Secretary, retrospectively captured the nub of the legislation, quoted in Andrew Robert's sardonically titled *Eminent Churchillians*: 'The minute we said we've got to keep these black chaps out, the whole Commonwealth lark would have blown up' (Roberts 1995: 225).

This represents an extreme and profoundly racialised shift in ideals over a mere fourteen years, and interpretations as to the motivation for this change, and the origin of the strongly influential race riots of 1958, are similarly dissonant. Some commentators blame a blind complacency in government to a rising racial unrest amongst the British populace, and a need to manage processes of assimilation better. Rose quotes Gwilym Lloyd-George, Home Secretary in 1956, as saying: 'I have no information that there is any particular problem as far as these people [the Commonwealth immigrants] are concerned' (Rose 1969: 200). Paul, however, makes a radically different claim: that, from 1954 onwards, when Lloyd-George became Home Secretary, the language and focus of much governmental activity suggests a concerted campaign by ministers and officials to prompt the public into hostility against continuing colonial migration:

> It is my contention that this campaign is the key to understanding the shift from private to public sphere and from open to closed borders. Thus, according to this interpretation, the infamous 'race riots' resulted not from a desperate *popular* hostility toward people of color but from the policy-making *elite*'s racialized understanding of the world's population and their propagation of this belief to the rest of society. (Paul 1997: 133)

Whether the culmination of an innate and increasingly visible public mood, or a covert government strategy, the riots of 1958 in Nottingham and London's North Kensington (inaccurately, but neatly, called Notting Hill by the media) were instrumental in changing Britain's immigration policy forever.

This chapter takes as its focus the turbulent West Indian experience in Britain during the 1950s as communicated in a burgeoning literature of immigration. The novel is now routinely theorised as the most reliably revealing literary document of changing social history, as well as a text that can build nation through narration (Bhabha 1990). As such, West Indian novelists provide particularly valuable insight into the re-evaluation of the concept of 'home' during the decade, from the point of view both of their own expectations of a welcome in the mother country, and of the need of a British national redefinition of belonging. Yet this insight is far from inclusive. As Bruce King notes ruefully of the decade's generation of new literary voices that included George Lamming, Edgar Mittelholzer, V. S. Naipaul, Andrew Salkey and Sam Selvon, 'It would take a while before there were women novelists' (King 2004: 41). Webster points out how the 1950s cult of the home, centred upon the white, indigenous wife and mother, excluded black women, who were deemed incapable of the kind of meaningful and dedicated motherhood newly espoused by child-care experts, while at the same time depending upon their labour as migrant workers (Webster 1998: xi). She claims that 'As black women imagined home in the 1950s, it had one dominant meaning for those who found that there were no places for them to live in Britain – back home' (xvii).

Accounts of the lives of these 'invisible women' during the decade are extremely rare. Beryl Gilroy's autobiographical *Black Teacher* was published in 1976, but provides a revealing picture of her experiences as a gifted primary school teacher from British Guyana, who arrives in London in the early 1950s to study the recent advancements in the study of child development. Her experience provides an interesting

Figure 8   West Indian immigrants arriving at Victoria Station, London, 1956.

counterpoint to E. R. Braithwaite's 1959 *To Sir With Love*. Gilroy is subject to just as much overt and polite racial abuse, and is equally undermined by the gap between the 'British Way of Life' so formative to her own education, and life in Britain as manifested around her (Braithwaite 1992: 39). Though she does not have Braithwaite's motivating resentment of war-time service to a country that now seems to despise him, Gilroy's gender brings its own particular potential for humiliation. Having come to Britain to learn about 'the new concepts of gaining the willing co-operation of children, and of trying to bring out the best in each and every child' (76), Gilroy is well schooled in the ironies of British national compassion. As a woman she is the recipient of more emotional confession from white acquaintances than Braithwaite, which she shrewdly interprets as condescension rather than compliment. When the mother of some notably deprived twins in her class confesses they are the produce of incestuous rape, Gilroy recognises that:

> She had come to me . . . for an additional reason. I was to have this happen to me over and over again. There comes a time when the terribly handicapped or grievously hurt person, with nowhere else to go, seeks the final resort of black consolation. Deep down what they're saying is, 'Now I'm on your level. When it comes to suffering and humiliation, you've been there before me. Help me, please, fellow-traveller'. (Gilroy 1976: 75)

Gilroy's autobiography lends a rare female voice to the black immigrant experience during the 1950s in Britain, but this is not to suggest that female characters do not have a vital role in negotiating the idea of 'home' in the male-authored novels that follow.

George Lamming's first novel, *In the Castle of My Skin* (1953), is an examination of the Caribbean legacy of colonialism and slavery through the life of a young boy. Arthur Calder-Marshall, reviewing it in the *Times Literary Supplement*, noted somewhat acerbically 'one is tempted to rename this book "The Portrait of the Artist as a Young Barbadian"' (Calder-Marshall 1953: 206). Lamming's characteristically oblique prose style adopted and adapted many of the stylistics of high modernism, with the disorientation of new arrivals to Britain conveyed in his next novel, *The Emigrants*, by the blaring repetition of unfamiliar and ambiguous phrases –'WILL PASSENGERS KEEP THEIR HEADS WITHIN THE TRAIN' – and fragmented apprehensions of the fast-disappearing landscape arranged in columns on the page:

> You didn't see that, partner. You see that.
> They make life there. Life. What life partner.
> Where you say they make what.
> Life partner. Read it. Hermivita gives life.

You ain't see it.
In the same direction, look, they make death
there, ol' man. Look. Dissecticide kills once
and for all. Read partner. Look what they
make.
They make everything here on this side.
All England like this. (Lamming 1994: 120)

Lamming's deliberately difficult prose is clearly at odds with the prevailing mood of 1950s British publishing, largely opposed to prewar modernism. The resistance of his work to easy reading serves to interrupt the apprehension by British readers of a habitualised, white-authored colonial narrative, which has at its core the assumption of black people, and black writers, as primitive. As J. Dillon Brown has put it,

> The category of (modernist) outsider functions to allay the threat of assimilation, while the invocation of a highly intellectualized cultural tradition (modernism) strategically disrupts, on several levels, the dismissive reduction of West Indian artists to simple, natural creatures of merely anthropological interest. (Brown 2006: 675)

If not themselves available for scrutiny, black writers within colonial culture were routinely expected, at the very least, to use fictional characters clearly to impart anthropological information to an admirably interested white readership. Published in 1958, Chinua Achebe's *Things Fall Apart* notably disrupted this assumption in its convincing depiction of the sophistication of the society of a fictional Nigerian village, presenting a life neither idyllic nor savage, but complex and dynamic. In *The Emigrants*, Lamming is similarly engaged in deconstructing the prevailing politics of anthropology, with numerous moments in the novel emphasising how the British social norms to which the West Indian immigrants are expected to assimilate are as culturally specific as those of any other tribe. Collis visits the Pearsons, a white middle-aged British couple, parents of someone he knew in Trinidad, and the narrator observes that: 'When they were together they functioned like things which worked according to the laws of their environment. Their behaviour was a device. The pattern was fixed, and they entered it, assuming the roles which such a marital relationship had assigned them' (Lamming 1994: 140). Imparting a characteristic of primitivism upon foreigners is not shown to be a racially specific tactic; a group of West Indian women at the hairdresser's are gripped with laughter at the thought of Azi, 'the African', at home: 'Why, he'd be the laughing stock of the town with all them funny marks on his face' (153).

Yet despite Lamming's chosen title for his novel, and his determination to undermine any reflex colonial identifications amongst his readers, this new body of writing in 1950s Britain is properly considered as immigration, rather than emigration, literature. It assumes an overwhelmingly white readership whose self-selection, we can surmise, marks them as intellectually engaged and, if not religiously anti-racist, at least agnostic in issues of racial discrimination. In the essay collection *The Pleasures of Exile* (1960) Lamming states that in the postwar years he had no real West Indian audience and so wrote 'always for the foreign reader' (Lamming 1995: 43). Though yet to be designated as an academic category – the notion of 'Commonwealth Literature' and its inaugural British journal ARIEL were instituted only later, in the mid-1960s – writing by authors of the former colonies (during the 1950s, most often the West Indies) – was at least a trendy literary niche. Bruce King notes how 'The end of empire resulted in new nations, new areas of interest, and made fashionable reading about decolonization and the culture of Others. There was a market for literature about this new world' (King 2004: 3). Lamming was always sceptical as to the ethics of this market. He remarked upon the role of the BBC radio programme *Caribbean Voices*, claiming the Corporation was 'taking the raw material and sending it back, almost like sugar, which is planted there in the West Indies, cut, sent abroad to be refined, and gets back in the finished form' (Andaiye 1990: 62). The benevolently bemused tone of Calder-Marshall's review of *In the Castle of My Skin* seems to confirm Lamming's suspicion that criticisms of his modernist style were underlain by what Brown calls 'ethnocultural suppositions, expressed as issues of aesthetic critique' (Brown 2006: 681).

Perhaps the most prominent difficulty of *The Emigrants* is the tendency of the text to shift suddenly between first- and third-person narration, and its determined withholding of the identity of its recurrent first-person narrator. It teases its readers with their ignorance when that narrator meets one of the leading female characters: ' "What's yer name again?" Lilian said. I answered and stepped aside to make room for a couple' (Lamming 1994: 234). These unstable subjectivities work to dramatise the conflict between individual and group that form such an important tension in the novel more generally. On Higgins's arrest for carrying drugs, a policeman comes to the barber's shop where a number of the characters habitually meet, and defends his assumption that the black community are in it together. A Jamaican responds, 'But there ain't no together . . . We ain't no more together than the Irish and the Welsh and the English, and them all look alike' (163). This sense of disjunction works to undermines the habitual racist stereotyping of all immigrants as somehow 'in league'. It also hints, however, at much more complex philosophical assumptions underpinning Lamming's theorisation of colonialism and black experience in Britain. Colonisation was, he suggested, 'simply a tradition of habits that become the normal way of seeing' (Lamming 1995: 157). As such, then, the halting, disorientated reading his style invokes can be better understood as a process of re-education through its disruption of ingrained modes of perception. Musing on a group of soldiers dozing on deck during the passage to Britain, the narrator claims that

> it seemed possible that the habit which informed a man of the objects he has been trained to encounter might be replaced by some other habit new and different in its nature, and therefore creating a new and different meaning and function for these objects. It seemed that this could happen even in a man's waking life: that change which deprived the object of its history, making it a new thing. (Lamming 1994: 82)

Yet on landing, any emigratory hope of potential newness is quickly denied by the routine, racist objectification the West Indians experience as immigrants. In London, the Barbadian teacher Dickson eagerly undresses for his landlady, thinking she has chosen him on the basis of his education and intellectual assimilation, and is confused as she re-enters the room with someone else:

> She said they only wanted to see what he *looked* like. He was lying on the divan, his clothes uncouthly thrown in one corner, and he sat up, rigid and bewildered, in his vest. The women were consumed with curiosity. They devoured his body with their eyes. It disintegrated and dissolved in their stare, gradually regaining its life through the reflection in the mirror.
>
>   me. me. me. out them all. me. (266)

At this point, like the text, Dickson's sense of himself begins to disintegrate, as his landlady's racist perception, her 'normal way of seeing', comes to disrupt and eventually destroy his identity.

It is hard to escape the perception, however, that some of the horror of this extraordinary scene, strikingly experimental in its form, and some of the responsibility for Dickson's resultant madness, lies in its perceivedly 'unnatural' power dynamic with regard to gender. In its intermittently complex and sympathetic representation of black female characters, *The Emigrants* does set a precedent rarely matched by the other texts discussed in this chapter. Lilian is presented as half of an exemplary couple of marked equality; the narrator tells us admiringly that 'reticent and gentle as she seemed most of the time, [she] showed on occasions an elemental savagery that was frightening. She and Tornado were a match in aggressiveness. They looked so strong together' (47). The vibrancy and defiance of the male scenes in the hostel and the barber's are matched by those set in Miss Dorking's hairdressers, where the West Indian women berate the oddities of the country they have settled in:

> Chil' I never know so much botheration myself. Livin' here in England is like having a job, ah mean o' job apart from your work. The things yo got to remember, and look 'bout. Ration book, National Insurance card, paper for the Ministry o' this an' the Ministry o' that, an' talking' 'bout looking for a job. The things you got to remember to answer, you tired before you start to work. (150)

Yet, like so many male-authored texts of the decade, this is a novel in which male dominance is ultimately naturalised and the much-sought liberation of selfhood clearly gendered – the narrator claims that: 'I felt this freedom. It was a private and personal acquisition, and I used it as a man uses what is private and personal, like his penis' (8).

Marcus Collins has noted a strange unity of opinion between otherwise disparate observers of West Indian men in mid-twentieth-century Britain: 'Whether bigots ranting against miscegenation, social scientists studying familial breakdown, or bohemians digging "Spades" out of sheer *nostalgie de la boue*, white commentators shared the notion that West Indian men constituted a "countertype" to that of whites' (Collins 2001: 392). A crucial element of this opposition was founded upon the perceived sexual potency and impropriety of male immigrants from the West Indies. Though his novel demonstrates an otherwise determined disruption of such prejudice, Lamming does use the sexual failure of his male characters to intensify the sense of their curtailed freedom. Azi is a notable exception, clearly possessing the phallus when it comes to virility. In one strikingly explicit scene, Azi has sex with Peggy, Frederick's wife, in front of the white man, in a ritual intended to restore Frederick's potency that is ultimately unsuccessful: 'He lay on the floor as though his energy had been stifled, locked forever in his loins. A white log shivering in the pale blue light' (223). Yet Azi, his face emblazoned with tribal scarring, is of course, African, and the West Indian men are unable to demonstrate such awesome sexual potency. The obsessively intellectual Dickson is metaphorically castrated by the white women's gaze, and the novel's only instance of miscegenation, between Julie and Phillip, ends in abortion so that Phillip's ambition of becoming a lawyer is not disrupted. One of the ways in which the British environment is oppressive to these men, Lamming suggests, is that it denies them 'natural' masculine sexual expression.

Lonely Londoners

Sam Selvon's 1956 novel *The Lonely Londoners* exercises no such denial; in fact, rather than subverting or disrupting prejudiced assumptions about the behaviour of West Indian men in Britain, it chooses rather to rebel by revelling in them. Miscegenation takes on an ironic sense of triumph, as new arrival

> Henry Oliver Esquire, alias Sir Galahad, descend on London to swell the population by one, and eight and a half months later it had a Galahad junior in Ladbroke Grove and all them English people stopping in the road and admiring the baby curly hair when the mother pushing it in the pram as she go shopping for rations. (Selvon 2006: 15)

Lewis's beating of his wife, Agnes, is treated by Moses, the lynch-pin of the novel's disparate immigrant community, as a cautionary tale against mild and amusing irrationality, rather than any kind of moral and personal failure (54–5). From a feminist perspective, the only redeeming character is Tanty, the indomitable middle-aged Jamaican aunt who is one of the few characters with an identity so strong she is able to impose it on hostile British surroundings: 'she become a familiar figure to everybody, and even the English people calling she Tanty. It was Tanty who cause the shop-keeper to give people credit' (65).

Numerous passages of *The Lonely Londoners*, such as Moses's exchange with Lewis, quoted above, and Galahad's attempt to capture a pigeon to eat (116–20), recall in tone the rueful realism of canonical Angry Young Men novels like Amis's *Lucky Jim*, albeit they are written in Selvon's own linguistically inventive register. King claims that:

> In blending Trinidadian English with other forms of black English, including phrases current in London and black American English, Selvon created the first novel of black British English ... In making novels from loosely connected amusing stories, Selvon had in mind the satiric comic narratives of the Trinidadian calypso singers as well as the British novel of social comedy which he, Salkey, Naipaul, and others inherited and mined in new ways. (King 2004: 42)

All narrative voices are on some level synthetic, of course, blending the conventions of literature with speech idiom, but that of *The Lonely Londoners* demonstrates a particularly dazzling hybridity of styles. The novel begins amidst an instantly recognisable literary landscape, a 1950s 'Waste Land':

> One grim winter evening, when it had a kind of unrealness about London, with a fog sleeping restlessly over the city and the lights showing in the blur

as if is not London at all but some strange place on another planet, Moses Aloetta hop on a number 46 bus at the corner of Chepstow Road and Westbourne Grove to go to Waterloo to meet a fellar who was coming from Trinidad on the boat-train.

When Moses sit down and pay his fare he take out a white handkerchief and blow his nose. The handkerchief turn black and Moses watch it and curse the fog. (Selvon 2006: 1)

Incorporating a calypso-like delight in the romance of place names, this opening also initiates an important symbolic motif – on Moses's hand-kerchief, the stain on a pristine background parodies white perceptions of the new black arrivals – which Galahad is later to develop into a poetic denunciation of the consequences of his colour: 'Look at you, so black and innocent, and this time so you causing misery all over the world!' (77). The most sustained, recognisably modernist section of the novel is its central interlude, a rhapsodic series of sense impressions and shifting subjective experiences of London life infused with male (hetero)sexual longing (92–102). Yet through interspersing this means of description with a more realist mode, Selvon's novel can be seen to provide a stylistic bridge between Lamming's largely uncompromising modernism and the more culturally dominant realist narratives of British fiction of the 1950s. In this way, it seems to find a solution to the relentless disorientation produced in *The Emigrants*, and could be argued that Selvon's more tactical deployment of alienation techniques has still greater impact for its readership. For example, the Labour Office, mechanism of a Welfare State still relatively novel to all of its citizens, is further defamiliarised by the disbelieving gaze of Galahad:

It ain't have no place in the world that exactly like a place where a lot of men get together to look for work and draw money from the Welfare State while they ain't working. Is a kind of place where hate and disgust and avarice and malice and sympathy and sorrow and pity all mix up. Is a place where everyone is your enemy and your friend. (27)

Colin MacInnes's novel, *City of Spades* (1957), also adopts a narrative style that blends a level of realism with lyricism and a jumble of changing impressions and allegiances. Montgomery Pew, newly appointed Assistant Welfare Officer of the Colonial Department, learns from Nigerian Johnny Fortune that 'Jumble' is immigrant slang for a member of the British native population:

'May I enquire how it is spelt?'
'J-o-h-n-b-u-l-l.'
'Ah! But pronounced as you pronounce it?'
'Yes: Jumble.'

It struck me the ancient symbol, thus distorted, was strangely appropriate to the confusion of my mind. (MacInnes 1984b: 18)

In his introduction to a 1969 edition collecting MacInnes's London novels, Francis Wyndham suggests the trilogy (also including *Absolute Beginners*, 1959, and *Mr Love and Justice*, 1960) was critically misread as a purely anthropological account during the previous decade: 'On the contrary, they are lyrical approximations to reality: highly imaginative and on occasion frankly fantastic approaches to themes of which no other contemporary novelist has yet shown himself properly aware' (vii).

MacInnes's work of the 1950s is notable for its attempts to represent current culturally suspicious experience – that of teenagers, immigrants and even pimps – in a broadly empathetic way. The narrative of *City of Spades* is balanced between the points of view of two young men, Pew and Fortune. As in *Absolute Beginners*, amidst the moral relativity of contemporary society, youth comes closest to a natural tendency to truth – both to true experience, and to reliable truth-telling about that experience. With its equilibrium between a white and a black protagonist, *City of Spades* also distinguishes itself from much colonial writing of the time, which more routinely focused upon the newly *unheimlich* nature of the former colonies from the coloniser's point of view (see, for example, Paul Scott's 1958 novel *The Alien Sky* and Anthony Burgess's *The Malayan Trilogy*, 1956–9).

Negritude, the admiration for and promotion of black experience, can be a complicated and often conflicted allegiance. In more recent, postcolonial, discourses, in its sense of a kind of collective racial consciousness of the black diaspora, it represents a powerful form of resistance to dominant white cultures. In the Britain of the 1950s, however, such a sense was yet to emerge fully, and the term is best applied to the romantic construction of blackness as 'close to nature' and naturally passionate, in a way that stands in opposition to the sensual deprivations of European rationality. Pew eulogises to his friend, Theodora, that 'Negroes' 'bring an element of joy and fantasy and violence into our cautious, ordered lives' (MacInnes 1980b: 66). In *City of Spades*, as, indeed, in Lamming's *The Emigrants*, it is African characters who are represented as possessing this naturalistic identity more strongly and confidently than West Indians. Montgomery Pew is discussing this idea with West Indian hustler Mr Tamberlaine in the 'gamble-house':

'Africans don't seem to care what anyone thinks of them. So even though they're more clannish and secretive, they're easier to talk to.'

Mr Tamberlaine considered this. 'Listen to me, man,' he said. 'If we's more sensitive like you say, there's reasons for it. Our islands is colonies of great antiquity, and our mother tongue is English, like your own, and not some dialects. So naturally we expect you treat us like we're British as yourself, and when you don't we suffer and go sour. Why should we not? But Africans – what do they care of British? For African, his passport just don't mean nothing, except for travel, but for us it's loyalty.' (157)

In *The Lonely Londoners* Selvon chooses to deal directly with dominant racial clichés about black immigrants (they are lazy, profligate, promiscuous, prone to violence) by creating a number of characters who exhibit some of these traits whilst remaining largely empathetic. MacInnes takes a different tactic, repeatedly attempting to reclaim the innocence of such traits by portraying them as charming anachronisms: Pew describes the Cosmopolitan nightclub, a hub of the black social scene, as 'an Elizabethan fragment come to life in our regimented world' (54). In *The Emigrants*, a character known only as 'the Jamaican' produces a viscerally eloquent metaphor of colonial history:

England, France, Spain, all o' them, them vomit up what them din't want, an' the vomit settle there in that Caribbean Sea. It mix up with the vomit them make Africa vomit, an' the vomit them make India vomit, an' China an' nearly every race under de sun. An' just as vomit never get back in yuh stomach, these people, most o' them, never get back where them vomit them from. Them settle right there in that Caribbean Sea, and the great nations, England, an' the rest, them went on stirring the mixture, them stir that vomit to suit themselves. (Lamming 1994: 65–6)

In contrast, in one of the chapters focalised through Johnny Fortune, MacInnes makes of this fluid metaphor a vision of liquid social and cultural nourishment, as inside the Moorhen pub,

where dark skins outnumbered white by something like twenty to one, there was a prodigious bubble and clatter of sound, and what is rare in purely English gatherings – a constant movement of person to person, and group to group, as though some great invisible spoon were perpetually stirring a hot human soup. (MacInnes 1984b: 43)

A young and bohemian employee of the BBC, Theodora functions as Pew's enlightened sounding-board throughout *City of Spades* (it might be argued that in falling in love with Johnny Fortune she acts as a respectably heterosexual double for Pew's own feelings). Towards the novel's end Pew makes an argument to Theodora that contradicts prevailing expectations that immigrants can, or should, assimilate into their host culture: 'There are entirely different moral concepts among different races: a fact which leads to endless misunderstandings on the political and social planes' (175). Yet ultimately Johnny Fortune is portrayed as wicked by the narrative, in his careless treatment of women

(Theodora in particular) and his generally profligate and perceivedly deceitful behaviour. Pew is allowed to deliver the final judgement, as he records in Johnny 'a heightened air of inwardness, of "African-ness" about him' (240). The nascent negritude which infuses the majority of the text, which, though undeniably romanticised, is none the less relatively progressive, is ultimately replaced by a more traditional, colonial configuration of regrettable black primitivism. The conclusions of MacInnes's subsequent novel, *Absolute Beginners*, however, provide a marked contrast to this regressive impulse. Amidst the chaos of the Napoli riots (MacInnes's fictional version of the Notting Hill unrest in 1958), the teenage narrator is reading a leader article by Amberley Drove (his name an intricate suggestion of aristocratic English privilege) in 'the Mrs Dale daily':

> In their own setting, coloured folk were no doubt admirable citizens, according to the standards that prevailed there. But transported unexpectedly to a culture of a higher order, serious difficulties and frustrations must inevitably arise.
>   'Must I go on reading all this balls?' I shouted. (MacInnes 1984a: 169)

His youth and open-mindedness give the narrator special insight into the hypocrisy of Drove's anti-assimilation argument, particularly when voiced by a race for which rampant colonisation has been cast as 'one of the great, splendid English things . . . Yet when a few hundred thousand come and settle among our fifty millions, we just can't take it' (173). The narrative ends on a note of fervent optimism that this young man and his peers, together with the latest arrival of African emigrants at Heathrow Airport, will forge a new, reciprocal British culture, as he approaches them in a cleansing shower of rain: 'Welcome to London! Greetings from England! Meet your first teenager! We're all going up to Napoli to have a ball!' (203).

As we have seen, Paul has cast the 1950s as a time of intense, secretive government renegotiation of ideas of citizenship and of the legal barriers to the entry of black immigrants, culminating in the 1962 Commonwealth Immigrants Bill and its heavily racialised definition of the epithet 'Commonwealth' (Paul 1997: 134). If this is the case, cracks in this conspiracy were certainly beginning to show by 1958, when, in the wake of the race riots, Tory MP Martin Lindsay claimed in the House of Commons on 5 December that: 'We all know perfectly well that the core of the problem is coloured immigration. We must ask ourselves to what extent we want Great Britain to become a multi-racial community' (quoted Foot 1965: 130). Basil Dearden's 1959 film, *Sapphire*, in its direct address of issues of multi-racialism, provides a useful point of comparison to the literary texts in this chapter, and to *City of Spades* in particular. The 'social problem' films of the 1950s (others include Dearden's *The Blue Lamp*, 1951, and his 1958 work *Violent Playground*) are predicated upon the conviction that the troubling social issues with which they deal (for example, racism, crime, teenage violence) can ultimately be solved and assimilated by an alteration of individual attitudes, rather than any fundamental refiguring of national institutions. This sense of individual responsibility for changing racial attitudes seems akin to MacInnes's argument in the majority of *City of Spades*, and certainly to the ending of *Absolute Beginners*.

Like both these novels, *Sapphire* upholds individuality with a determined attention to a range of different characters and their particular points of view. At a time when, in Britain at least, the terms of the artistic representation of racial difference are only just beginning to be scrutinised, Dearden's film shares both the good liberal intentions of *City of Spades* and many of its ethical problems in an instructive way. The film's narrative involves the investigation of the murder of a young woman, Sapphire Robbins, by Superintendent Hazard (Nigel Patrick). Sapphire is revealed to be the child of a black mother ('coloured' in the parlance of the film), who has recently been 'passing' for white amongst her white friends and the family of her fiancé, David Harris (Paul Massie). A metaphor for the film's conflicted representational politics is Hazard's determination always to proffer his hand for his black interviewees to shake. Viewers might be encouraged to read this decision as admirable, particularly in comparison to the behaviour of his colleague, Detective Inspector Learoyd (Michael Craig), a man capable of reading Sapphire's red petticoat, revealed beneath a modest brown skirt by the awkward position of her dead body, as indicative of the 'black under the white'. Sapphire's brother, Dr Robbins (Earl Cameron), confides to Hazard a boyhood experience of a white boy touching his hand and announcing, 'Look, nothing's come off on me.' 'Trouble is,' Dr Robbins continues, 'Something came off on me'. Yet barrister Paul Slade (Gordon Heath), another conspicuously professional black man, son of a Nigerian bishop and a former boyfriend of Sapphire's, condemns Hazard's observance of the gesture as patronising: 'Sanctimonious. Always *so* careful to have his hand out first.' Like *City of Spades*, *Sapphire* seeks to represent black characters and their communities as positive precisely because they retain a measure of primitive authenticity. Hazard ridicules Learoyd's idea that a person of black heritage is always 'really' black, whatever the colour of their skin, yet this idea is ultimately reinforced by a key scene in the film, set in the Tulips club.

The two policemen have gone there in an attempt to find Sapphire's dancing partner, torn from a photograph found in a locked drawer in her room that is full of exotic underwear ('I never saw Sapphire wearing anything like that,' says her shocked landlady), and are questioning Mr Tulips, the owner. A cut to Learoyd's point of view focuses upon a white woman dancing rapturously; Mr Tulips identifies her as a 'lilyskin'. After the shot has cut to reveal the woman is dancing with a black man, Mr Tulip continues, 'Your chick was a lilyskin, wasn't she? . . . Oh, you can always tell. 'Cos once they hear the beat of the bongos. Yes. No matter how fair the skin, they can't hide that swing.' Bongos are heard on the soundtrack and the camera moves to a seated white woman who begins to tap her feet, again with an ecstatic expression on her face. A rapid montage sequence from the point of view of the three men follows, cutting images of, amongst others, the female dancer and low-angle shots of her thighs and underwear, her partner, the seated white woman and the bongo drums themselves. This is clearly intended as a celebratory and liberatory moment amongst the racial strictures of the film's narrative, in the same way that Dearden repeatedly emphasises the colourful clothing of his black characters against the leached backgrounds of a wintry London. None the less, as Hill points out, the scene functions to prove that miscegenation has the inescapable consequence of inherited, 'black', primitive characteristics, and as such, is instrumental in ensuring that 'the film ends up confirming the very prejudices it would seek to subvert. For its ascription of natural qualities is, of course, not natural at all but the projection of its own culture's values, values which form part of the problem not a solution to it' (47).

In the same way that Montgomery Pew is given the final judgement on his co-protagonist in *City of Spades*, in *Sapphire* the conclusive truth is first and conclusively available to the intellect of Hazard, the white, male detective. Despite Pew's occasional deferral to the cosmopolitan experience and composure of Theodora, she is finally discredited by the irrationality of her sexual and emotional devotion to Johnny Fortune, which disrupts her characteristically measured arguments so Pew can observe how often 'she shifted, woman-like, her ground' (MacInnes 1984b: 174). Interestingly, in *Sapphire*, this configuration of blackness and femininity as unavoidably dominant in a person's character, as well as inescapably inferior to a masculine rational standard, also holds true. Sapphire is eventually revealed to have been murdered by Milly (Yvonne Mitchell), her fiancé's sister. This is a woman whose husband rarely comes home from the Merchant Navy, and who has been previously shown chastising her female twins, and working in a dairy shop so colourlessly pristine it looks to have been shot on black-and-white film stock. Sapphire, Milly relates, sat on the dairy counter, 'swinging her legs and laughing', telling her she'd 'forgotten what it was like to be wanted'. The real social problem of the film, then, is revealed to be both Sapphire's sexuality (so freely expressed it has resulted in pregnancy before marriage), and Milly's (too savagely repressed within her marriage). Rather than being reconciled, these forces of female desire, like those of the black sexuality unleashed at the Tulips club, are unsatisfactorily truncated by the trope of the detective's solution. White-authored texts of the 1950s, however well-meaning in their address of racial issues, are apparently prepared to compromise their liberalism for traditional narrative closure.

Chapter Nine

Organic Communities: Regional Literature

The on-going challenge throughout the 1950s to Britishness as a matter of racial inheritance examined in the previous chapter, together with a reaction against the kind of bellicose nationalistic discourse so necessary to war-time rhetoric, is met in numerous literary texts of the decade by a marked determination to renegotiate the scale and terms of personal and communal identification. In a 1947 essay, the Northern Irish poet John Hewitt staked out a new patch of land for the sensibilities of the postwar man:

> Regionalism is based upon the conviction that, as a man is a social being, he must, now that the nation has become an enormously complicated organisation, find some smaller unit to which to give his loyalty. This unit, since the day of the clan is over, and that of the large family is passing, must be grounded on something more than kinship. Between these limits lies the region; an area which possesses geographical and economic coherence, which has had some sort of traditional and historical identity, and which still, in some measure, demonstrates cultural and linguistic individuality. (Hewitt 1987: 122)

His definition of regionalism is a complex one, chiming closely with K. D. M. Snell's more recent taxonomy of the regional novel. In Snell's terms, regionalism is an emotional and political identification based on 'more than kinship' (implying a more active and multi-valent process). The region has 'geographical' coherence (the land has borders, as well as a distinct topography), as well as an 'economic' one (it supports a living, but in a more 'natural' way than the corporate organisation of 'nation').

Though the region might be endowed with new importance during the 1950s, its definition is rooted in a strong relationship with a past ensuring a 'traditional and historical identity' as well as its own 'cultural and linguistic individuality' (Snell 1998). Edward Said has called nationalism 'an act of geographical violence' (Said 1989: 11). After the Second World War, borders had been swiftly redrawn, and it is unsurprising that British postwar culture should register revulsion at a loyalty linked in such a raw and recent way with violence on an unprecedented global scale. This was reflected during the 1950s in a lack of overt political activism aimed at achieving independence for the individual countries of the unitary state of the United Kingdom of Great Britain and Northern Ireland. This is not to say that frictions were not palpable at a local level. In Northern Ireland, for example, the somewhat belated adoption of the new British vision of welfare and education, though socially ameliorative, did little to bridge sectarian divides or (inter)national antagonisms. F. S. L. Lyons has claimed of Ireland that these social improvements in the north 'did more to reinforce the partition of the country than perhaps any other single factor' (Lyons 1973: 741). Within 1950s Britain, however, unionism was at a striking apogee; in Scotland, the Conservative Party won an actual majority of the vote in 1955, and Labour was to abandon its aspirations to Home Rule not long after.

Hewitt's understanding of regionalism, when used as an organising principle for literature, is clearly intended to oppose the metropolitan bias of the epithet 'provincial'. His attraction to what he sees as a kind of middle ground of belonging (located between the nation and the clan) – experienced as a natural allegiance at the same time that it is intellectually coherent and fulfilling – is borne out by numerous literary texts of the 1950s. Yet these writings also point to the numerous facets of ambiguity in the definition of regionalism. Roberto M. Dainotto, working from Benedict Anderson's now a priori description of nation as an 'imagined community' (Anderson 1983), wonders,

> if nations are inventions, and their unity is, as the saying goes, 'artificial', are we to assume that regionalism could offer instead a more 'natural' collective identity than nationalism? A naïve form of regionalism relies, in fact, on the alleged 'existence of a local unitary group' – a group that can be defined clearly in terms of space, place, and region.

'The question', he goes on to claim, 'is obvious,' and it is of obvious relevance, too, to Hewitt's position: 'How is this homogenized notion of regionalism different from that of nationalism?' (Dainotto 2000: 7). In the case of the texts examined here, we might usefully begin with the assumption that it is ambiguity that makes the difference. Rather than being 'naïve', the regionalism of 1950s British literature is a revealingly contested category, riven by an anxiety over the ethics of its own construction and its relationship to national identity that invites comparison with the immigrant writing examined in the previous chapter.

Anderson's debunking of the grand narrative of nation glosses the concept of 'an imagined political community' as follows: 'It is *imagined* because the members of even the smallest nation will never know most of their fellow-members, meet them, or even hear of them, yet in the minds of each lives the image of their communion' (Anderson 1983: 15). In its representation of communities most characterised precisely by the fact that their inhabitants *do* know most of their fellow-members, the relationship between regionally focused literature and its reader is unusually dependent upon the requirement to provide admittance to the imagined rural community. This anxiety over inclusion is accentuated in the realist mode (traditionally the *modus operandi* of regional literature, and the dominant genre of 1950s writing) by a tension between the text's mimetic function and another common motivation: the didactic vision of the region as, like Hewitt's, some sort of ideal (and idealised) space. Raymond Williams, whose novel *Border Country* (1960) forms an important focus of the next chapter, is acutely aware of the spectre of nostalgia that can haunt regional literature – what he refers to as its 'fly-in-amber quality' (Williams 1991: 231). Dainotto's definition is uncompromising:

> 'Regional' is a pastoral sensibility untouched by the evils of history and sheltered from the latter within the 'boundaries of some sort' of place. To put it bluntly, regionalism is the figure of an otherness that is, essentially, otherness *from*, and against, history. (Dainotto 2000: 9)

Yet the culture of the 1950s frequently juxtaposes a modernist sense of loss with the intermittent (and usually Socialist-inflected) tendency to condone contemporary social mobility and opportunity. One of Williams's key goals in his novel (though not one he fully achieves) is to avoid the (bourgeois) isolation of the private individual by balancing a generation's loss against its social and economic gains. The regional literature of the 1950s in Britain, subject to its prevailing national climate, simply cannot allow the kind of naïve and nostalgic isolation that Dainotto attributes to traditional pastoral tendencies.

David Jones's long poem, *The Anathemata: Fragments of an Attempted Writing*, deemed by W. H. Auden to be 'one of the most important poems of our time' (Auden 1954: 67), provides an instructive opening case study, as a regionalist work riven by national, aesthetic and ideological divisions. The poem was gradually assembled and reworked between 1946 and 1951 by a writer describing himself in a Preface as 'a Londoner, of Welsh and English parentage, of Protestant upbringing, of Catholic subscription' (Jones 1952: 11). It is set amidst a mass in a Catholic church in Britain during the Second World War; prompted by the presiding sense of a contemporary cultural turn, the speaker / worshipper compiles a history of Britain that is structured by the informing mythus of Christianity. Like its obvious predecessor, the *Cantos* of Ezra

Pound, *The Anathemata* incorporates a search for an originary culture. Like Pound, Jones finds in the Anglo-Saxon a powerful presiding heritage; the poem's third section is entitled 'Angle-Land'. Unlike Pound, however, he places equal stress on the influence of cultures before this invasion, thus radically questioning a historical narrative of Britain that privileges Anglo-Saxon influences over marginalised Celtic ones:

> I speak of before the whale-roads or the keel-paths were from
> Orcades to the fjord-havens, or the greyed green wastes that
> they strictly grid. (115)

As Joe Moffett has put it, 'By pulling *The Anathemata* in two directions – between the Welsh and the Anglo-Saxon – David Jones allows himself to address the disparate parts of his own biological and cultural identities' (Moffett 2006: 16).

The poem makes the topography of the Welsh landscape in particular part of this poetic process, representing it as commemorative. In the poem's first section, 'Rite and Fore-time', a footnote informs us that the Welsh name for Snowdon's peak is Moel yr Wyddfa, which translates as 'the Hill of the Burial Mound' (Jones 1952: 68n). One translation of the Welsh name of the River Dee, Dyfrdwy, is 'divine water' (69n). Thus, as Andrew Campbell points out, the landscape 'yields the myths of the culture, both local in Arthur and more universal in Christ, and links both to the overarching symbolism of the poem, the mass, by being forms of altar and sacramental element' (Campbell 1994: 10). *The Anathemata* is cited in Rosenthal and Gall's study, *The Modern Poetic Sequence: The Genius of Modern Poetry*, as an example of what they call 'neo-regionalism', a trope involving:

> recovery of the deepest memories of a region or nation that is radically out of touch with them, and therefore out of touch with the richer experiences and values underlying its own history. Neo-regionalism may employ local color and realistic character portrayal . . . , but it is something more embattled and demanding. Its heroism resides in its refusal to yield up cultural memory to oblivion. More positively, the imaginative effort has to do with reaching a state of awareness that reaffirms a transcendent identity – the state of long continuity between the significant past and the freshest involvement in the present moment, and of one's own place in this continuity. (Rosenthal and Gall 1983: 273)

The modernist impulse of this definition is inescapable, and though Jones's poem is unarguably modernist in its fragmentary style and insistent search for origins, its determined juxtaposition of differing, but equally weighted, cultural narratives (Celtic and Anglo-Saxon in particular) to represent the story of Britain can be located at the beginning of a process that undermines the possibility of meaningful origins altogether. Moffett identifies the poem as being on the cusp of a cultural shift, noting that Jones 'paves the way for postmodern writers, like Hill and Heaney, who question English hegemony' (Moffett 2006: 17). This identification of 'neo-regionalism' as 'something more embattled and demanding' does chime with 1950s literary insecurities of belonging both to region and to nation. Jones's own task in *The Anathemata* was certainly demanding. His incorporation of the Welsh language into the poem necessitates extensive footnotes glossing both meaning and intended cadences, and his Preface sounds a clearly embattled note:

> I have given the meanings and attempted to give the *approximate* sounds in the notes. Welshmen may smile or be angered at the crudity and amateurishness of these attempts, but something of the sort was necessary, because in some cases a constituent part of the actual form – the assonance – of the writing is affected. (Jones 1952: 13)

Authenticity of voice in this work, it would seem, is equally as important as, if not more important than, an authentic (and regional) sense of place; it is ironic, then, that Jones aims to achieve this through a kind of 'synthetic Welsh' – 'real' Welsh words with lengthy English glosses. The sheer weight of the footnotes in general, which have been described as 'one of the most abashed instances of the sort that poetry affords' (Rosenthal and Gall 1983: 297), complicates for Jones's most sympathetic reader any sense of the poem's cultural identifications as organic or spiritually uplifting. Neil Corcoran concurs that 'most impartial readers do undoubtedly feel . . . the lack of a certain inwardness with his Welsh material in David Jones himself,' but convincingly interprets this lack to be 'not a mere absence, a negative point of embarrassment for the critic of the poem, but an indication at the most profound level – that is, at the level of material and language – of the poem's most central meaning' (Corcoran 1982: 17). In other words, Jones's own relationship as both outsider to and insider of Wales, its history and its myth, is indicative of that between contemporary humanity, its past, its land and its religions. With this understanding, then, we can see the anxieties of nationalism, heritage and identification that play through the regional literature of the 1950s in Britain to be more central than peripheral.

Synthetic Nations

In *Redefining British Politics* Laurence Black feels able to state of his period of focus, 1954 to 1970, that 'The evidence here is . . . of a British political culture, before British became English, Irish, Scottish and Welsh. If it is dominated by England, few signs of these devolutionary pressures were apparent' (Black 2010: 207). Tighter foci, of course, always reveal greater complexities – the Scottish Covenant, launched in October 1949, for example, would collect two million signatures in favour of a Scottish parliament – and the Conservative government were careful throughout their dominance of 1950s Westminster to appease Home Rule sentiment with a substantially expanded role for the Scottish Office, and tailored election manifestos in Scotland that denounced Labour's nationalisation policies as traditional Anglo-centralisation. Yet Scottish cultural nationalism was commonly perceived at the time as a waning force. Since the Scottish Renaissance of the early twentieth century, Hugh MacDiarmid and his followers, known collectively as the 'Lallans makars' (the makers of 'Lallans', the Lowland dialect), produced literary works in a blended form of dialectic and archaic Scots as an attempt to revive a classical Scottish heritage. In his introduction to the 1956 *New Lines* anthology, Robert Conquest named the 'Lallans-mongers' (Conquest, 1956: xii) among the 'residual nuisances' to poetry of the last decade. In 1953 Alexander Manson Kinghorn's more empathetic discussion of recent work in 'Synthetic Scots' (the term is MacDiarmid's) none the less answered the question of 'whether great literature can be produced in "Lallans"' with the judgement that 'at present . . . it probably cannot' (Kinghorn 1953: 146). This point of view was not limited to outsiders to Scotland. In *The Break-Up of Britain* in 1977, Tom Nairn posits the idea that Scottish nationalism, from the 1930s onwards, was keen to establish itself as a rational, predominantly political (parliamentary), and thus 'properly' Scottish process, in opposition to 'the giddy confusion of the cultural nationalists'. Though he acknowledges that this is, of course, a simplification, he notes how 'within a short time the serious and Scotsman-like trend was to emerge triumphant, expelling the culture-heads and *littérateurs* to a Celtic outer darkness' (Nairn 1981: 197). The irony of Robert Conquest, an advocate and participant of the Movement, itself characterised by a synthetic idiolect and a manufactured kinship, decrying another poetic for the same perceived inadequacies is, of course, to be savoured. Northern Irishman Louis MacNeice would not have been alone in celebrating a similar waning of the dominance of the Movement poets in the poetic scene: 'And behold, they go – with what docile arrogance, with what lowered but polished sights; roped together, alert for falling slates, they scale their suburban peaks' (MacNeice 1957: 55).

Kinghorn continues his critique by pointing out that 'There is, in fact, a danger that "Lallans" poetry may become more and more academic as English influences increase. In many instances the practitioners of "Synthetic Scots" could convey their meaning with far more immediacy by using standard English' (Kinghorn 1953: 146). Arguably the greatest novel of the 1950s to come from Scotland, Robin Jenkins's *The Cone-Gatherers* (1955), eschews Scots, synthetic or otherwise, for either its narrative voice or dialogue. Throughout his long writing career, Robin Jenkins refused to approach nationalist politics in anything other than a tangential way, and in *The Cone-Gatherers* he characteristically chooses not to consider nation as the organising unit of communal identification and literary evocation. Instead the novel moves from its region (a wooded Argyll estate) to argue the inextricably entwined state of all things – nature and humanity – on a global scale. It is war, of course, that most commonly functions in literature to provide this kind of vertiginous 'panning out' of priorities. Rather than being a traditional dear green place, the novel's wood does not escape the intrusions of World War Two, be this from local antagonism towards the conscientious objectors set to forestry work (as Jenkins was himself), gamekeeper Duror's violent (and Nazi) reaction to perceived human deformity, or the warship steaming down the loch at the novel's close. Yet it is a different war that disturbs the wood more immediately. Dainotto claims that '"Regions" . . . tend to solve class conflicts within their homogeneous organic identity of people and land' (Dainotto 2000: 25), but in *The Cone-Gatherers* the region is aggravated, and even defined, by issues of class and ownership, focused most directly upon the character of Lady Runcie-Campbell. In her study of visual art, Catherine Jolivette claims that 'landscape in the 1950s was as much a conceptual as a physical phenomenon and it was the very instability of landscape as a viable symbol of national, racial or gender identity during this period that charged its debates with tension' (Jolivette 2009: 2). She reads British landscape art of the decade as increasingly unable to embody the ideals of nation and property that it traditionally bore in the past, an anxiety embodied in female form in one of Jenkins's central characters.

Lady Runcie-Campbell's married name alone is telling, signifying a genealogical span from the north-east of Scotland (Runcie being an indigenous name there) to Argyll in the west (where Campbells are rife), as well evoking by the latter surname inescapable historical associations of the notorious Highland massacre at Glencoe in 1692. In contrast to the easy belonging which characterises Calum's relationship with the wood – his supervisor Mr Tulloch observes him looking 'so happy there, so oblivious, so eager, and indeed so indigenous' (Jenkins 1980: 184–5) – Lady Runcie-Campbell's identification with the landscape which surrounds her is nationally, rather than locally, inflected. The pine trees of the estate she reads as 'making against sea and sky what had always struck her as Scottish gestures, recalling the eerie tormented tragic grandeur of the old native ballads' (221–2). She feels a heightened sense of entitlement to the land she has gained by marriage that is responsible for her least likeable moments – as, for example, when she imperiously evicts the cone-gatherers Neil and Calum from the disused beach hut in which, exhausted and soaked, they are attempting to warm themselves after a downpour (159–63). The eponymous cones are being gathered in order that the wood can be replanted when its trees are harvested for the war effort. Lady Runcie-Campbell's response to this brutal destruction of the landscape is unemotional: 'It might be, she thought, that just as in the war so many lives and properties had to be destroyed to make hope struggle afresh in the wilderness, so the wood itself had to be cleared away, a necessary sacrifice' (180). Though on one level this represents a practical and resigned response to a mandatory evil, that word 'cleared' can never be innocent in the context of a Scottish forest, and it marks her role within the region she temporarily controls as outsider at the same time that she is central to its future. A good deal of the novel's emotional focalisation takes place through Lady Runcie-Campbell, and thus through a position characterised by the intense experience of social change, and a gathering resultant guilt. We might note how her marginal status as both insider and outsider itself plays out the role of the reader of regional literature.

Jenkins uses his central female character to explore what we might recognise as the more sociological (and contemporary) antagonisms of class, while his (far more numerous) male characters act within a fabular narrative driven by issues of nature and of human evil. It is the latter mode that is most critically trammelled, of course, but the former that allows us speculatively to place *The Cone-Gatherers* into a British, as well as Scottish context. We can note how the novel replicates that central dynamic of the Angry novels, as well as that of the work of Richard Hoggart and Raymond Williams: the vertiginous experience of shifting class hierarchies and social priorities. We might assume that the gendered nature of the novel's dual perspective of social commentary / fable is no more than an updated Cartesian split, in which women are associated with the more rudimentary realities of life, and men with its elevated ontology. Yet the role of Lady Runcie-Campbell has notable commonalities with that of, say, Joe Lampton in *Room at the Top*, as each character seeks to orientate herself or himself morally within hypergamous relationships and unfamiliar affluence. However, the Angry novels, and *Room at the Top* in particular, routinely figure this experience as a masculine one, set in opposition to a misogynist representation of women as fatuously enamoured of their new powers of consumership. In *The Cone-Gatherers*, this misogyny, though subverted in the emotionally complex portrayal of Lady Runcie-Campbell, resurfaces phantasmagorically in the obese form of gamekeeper Duror's wife, helpless and hysterical in their rustic forest home. Though, as Ian Crichton Smith has claimed of Duror, 'the motives given do not seem to exhaust the evil of his actions' (3), some mitigation is surely offered in the utter misery of his family situation, and twenty years of sexual privation. The interconnected nature of the gamekeeper's depraved acts and deprived life is demonstrated most powerfully at the deer drive, when Duror cuts the throat of a wounded deer cradled by the distraught and deformed Calum:

> There by the dead deer he understood for the first time why he hated the hunchback so profoundly and yet was so fascinated by him. For many years his life had been stunted, misshapen, obscene, and hideous; and this misbegotten creature was its personification. (92)

Duror slaughters the roe deer while hallucinating that it is his wife; this prompts the epiphanic realisation that his hatred of Calum, which he initially sates in starting rumours of the man's sexual perversity (52, 181–2), is itself the projected horror at what his wife has become, with her beautiful face and 'monstrously obese' body (26). *The Cone-Gatherers* thus provides us with an interesting comparative case study to the regionalism practised by the majority of the texts in this chapter, evoking as it does its sense of place and character to explore wider social influences rather than a specific national experience or clearly identifiable ideology.

The work of John Hewitt, as suggested by his assertion that began this chapter, stands in obvious contrast to Jenkins's more tangential engagement with the regional, and as such is revealing of the opposing artistic and emotional impulses at play when loyalty is pledged to the 'smaller unit' (Hewitt 1987: 122). In the novel *December Bride* (1951), Hewitt's close friend and compatriot Sam Hanna Bell is at work confronting both an Ulster region characterised by Protestant stolidity and Orange bellicosity, as well as the artistic and emotional legacy of the larger nation of which it is part. Lance Pettitt describes the latter as 'the recurrent and mutually dependent tropes of Ireland as a rural idyll, a past-centred place of escape from modernity and "originary return" or as a dark zone of historic tragedy and ancient enmities' (Pettitt 2001: 6). Bell's roots were nationally tangled: born in Glasgow, he moved to the maternal homeland of County Down aged nine, on the death of his father, and his understanding of a regional community is a dynamic, multi-faceted and conflicted one.

The extraordinary opening sentence of *December Bride* is redolent with the themes of the novel and the source of its tragedy: 'Ravara Meeting-House mouldered among its gravestones like a mother surrounded by her spinster children' (Bell 2000: 9). This complex image of fecundity, decay and faulty inheritance centred upon the dank rural church begins the story of Sarah Gomartin and her relationship with the Echlin brothers, Hamilton and Frank; she is, until the bleak ceremony brought about by the blackmail of the minister Sorleyson that is recounted at the beginning of the novel, married to neither, with a child to both. Sarah's motives for maintaining the polyandrous (yet unmarried) nature of her household at Rathard Farm are complex. Sexual desire fuelled by the mingled contempt and enthusiasm of the younger Frank is clearly an element, as is a more prosaic, but no less passionate, determination to avoid the conventional servitude of her mother's life. Her rebellion begins with a violently indignant reaction to what she considers to be the elder Sorleyson's fatuous explanation for the drowning of Andrew Echlin, father of the brothers, and the original object of her love.

Sorleyson's response (an elaborately worded version of the 'movement in mysterious ways' doctrine) interferes with her understanding of Andrew's heroic sacrifice to save both his sons and herself. Sarah is emphatically not an atheist, but rejects what she experiences as false and sanctimonious religious dogma, and her judgement is later given credence by the revelation of the minister's own lust for her (147–8). At the birth of her first child, Sorleyson tells her:

> 'There is a guidance that helps us to combat the temptations of life, and a Divine help which supports us in those evil hours that none of us can avoid. Have you availed yourself fully of that?'
> 'Here's your answer,' said the woman smiling bitterly and holding out the infant. 'And what was it ye said? To marry one of the men. To bend and contrive things so that all would be smooth from the outside, like the way a lazy workman finishes a creel.' (135)

Her evocative artisanal metaphor here emphasises her regional Ulster–Scots dialect as a flexible, eloquent and pertinent mode of expression, in contrast to Sorleyson's smooth and standard verbal ministrations. As a character, Sarah thus acts on one level to demonstrate Bell's frustration at the inability of the State, and its various institutions, to inspire and unite its subjects. Sarah's condemnation of the Sorleysons and their mode of belief is upheld elsewhere in the novel, in a pervasive sense of their religion as inorganic. Mr Sorleyson is repelled by his discovery that his parishioners, these men and women who, from childhood, had been taught to esteem right-eousness, could, without any feeling of inconsistency, show a deplorable tol-erance to things that were far from righteous or seemly. He had come to the conclusion that Nature, with her continual and invariably indiscreet fertility, was a bad example to simple folk. (144)

Sarah and her community are considered 'simple' by their ministers, and yet it is Sarah who is demanding a religious doctrine that can accommo-date her complex life experience and fierce sense of intellectual enquiry. Yet this does not prevent Sarah harbouring 'the centuries-old enmity against the papist' (184). Occasional trips to Belfast have revealed the city's sectarian feeling to be much rawer and rougher than at Rathard Farm, with the urban pubs ringing with bellicose songs, yet Bell does not flinch at suggesting that the same prejudice and cruelty are at work in the rural environment, invoking another failure on the part of Church and State. When local lad Joe Skillen is cast out of his family and their grocery business for seeking to marry Martha, her daughter, the slight again inspires Sarah to revenge, by setting the young couple up in their own business: 'Sarah's eyes closed in a cold lingering smile. "A grocer's shop. I was thinking there might be room in the townlands for two"' (284). She is swiftly punished for her vengeful motivations against the Catholic Skillen family and their sectarian rejection of their son's choice of bride by ambiguous forces of fate, accident or divinity that kill Frank with a falling rafter as he works to renovate the new shop. This complex blend of the admirable and the flawed marks Sarah out as a memorably progressive female character in the literature of the decade (particularly in the work of male authors), and her complexity is matched by Bell's nuanced exploration of the politics, personal and institutional, of the region of Ulster.

One 1950s text, perhaps more than any others, is held to be emblem-atic of a reluctance to update the English rural idyll in response to con-temporary geographical, social and political change. 'Nostalgia is sticky memory,' mused Richard Hoggart later in his life; it is 'unable to let memory stand free; emotion has overflowed' (Hoggart 2005: 126). Few texts have a stickier reputation than Laurie Lee's 1959 autobiographical work, *Cider With Rosie*, which, in its commemoration of the author's childhood in the village of Slad, Gloucestershire, is routinely read as a nostalgic representation of what F. R. Leavis and Denys Thompson identified in the 1933 *Culture and Environment* (reissued in 1950) as an 'organic community'. Set in opposition to mechanised society, such a community is one which maintains a clear sense of continuity between past and present, in which members relate to each other intuitively and individually. Raymond Williams's 1958 critique of the concept remains classic; he identified Leavis's and Thompson's envisaged idyll as 'a surrender to a characteristically industrialist, or urban, nostalgia – a late version of medievalism, with its attachments to an "adjusted" feudal society. If there is one thing certain about "the organic community", it is that it has always gone' (Williams 1971: 252). *Culture and Environment* has, in fact, much to recommend it in William's eyes; he praises Leavis's identification of the 'cheap response' of contemporary civilisation and the 'practical method of discrimination' Leavis counsels and exercises in order to negate it (250). Even Williams's chosen title for his key 1950s work, *Culture and Society*, mixes, like the text, a tribute to Leavis's ideas alongside their rebuttal. Yet Williams is, as Gary Day points out, 'responsible for the notion that *Culture and Environment* presented a mythic view of history' (Day 1996: 47), largely by his emphasis on the ideological clash between the representation of the 'organic community' and a realist account of history: 'The concept of a wholly organic and satisfying past, to be set against a disintegrated and dissatisfying present, tends in its neglect of history to a denial of real social experience' (Williams 1971: 255). So is the community presented in *Cider with Rosie* purely the stuff of myth?

Rather than a nostalgic invocation of a lost village life, Lee's text can be read as laying emphasis not just upon the idyll's irreversible pastness and unrecoverable nature, but also on its intrinsic incompleteness and anachronism. His family arrive in the village at the end of the First World War to a community that has not escaped its effects. By the end of the following decade, Lee identifies this community to be irreparably disintegrated: 'The last days of my childhood were also the last days of the village' (Lee 1984: 207). Yet the fact that the end of this way of life is coincident with the end of Laurie's childhood – the autobiography's title commemorates the tryst that leads to his loss of virginity – and that the latter is cast as a profoundly idyllic Fall, interferes with any reading of the text as purely, and provincially, nostalgic. The ambiguity of the tone of the text has been canonically underestimated; its narrative and patterns of imagery portray the inevitability of the decline of the community to be just as organic as its characteristic way of life. As Leavis (and Williams) defined it, the concept of the organic community is predicated upon a series of binary oppositions – feudal / industrial, rural / urban (or suburban), innocent / fallen, for example – with a concomitant designation of value that marks the first element in each pair as positive and potentially lost. In *Cider With Rosie*, however, we can note constantly shifting hierarchies of value across these binaries throughout the text, with Laurie's tipsy and fortunate Fall a case in point. Though the structure of the village economy might gesture towards feudality, with its Squire at the head, it is early identified to be considerably more mixed: 'The villagers themselves had three ways of living: working for the Squire, or on the farms, or down in the cloth-mills at Stroud' (36). William Empson identified the rhetorical tradition of the pastoral to be rooted in rustic depictions of 'a beautiful relation between rich and poor' (Empson 1986: 11). The relationship between the Squire and the villagers is rather characterised by Lee as one of a wry disrespect for both the gentry and its dwindled economic power; after starting their carol singing at the Big House, the children 'squatted by the cowsheds, held our lanterns over the book, and saw that he had written "Two Shillings". This was quite a good start. No one of any worth in the district would dare to give us less than the Squire' (Lee 1984: 135–6).

Rather than a rural innocence, village life is repeatedly portrayed by Lee to be one of primitivism and brutality – as in the case of Miss Flynn, who drowns herself while tormented by the spirit of her dead mother, and the returning local boy made good in New Zealand who is beaten to death for his swaggering by a gang of young men. Lee notes how 'The village in fact was like a deep-running cave still linked to its antic past, a cave whose shadows were cluttered by spirits and by laws still vaguely ancestral' (95). Even the book's eponymous encounter with a blissfully unfettered country sexuality is immediately juxtaposed with an account of the 'Brith Wood rape', ultimately aborted, but none the less enthusiastically attempted, by Laurie's peers (201). Rather than demonstrating a 'fly-in-amber quality' (Williams 1991: 231), *Cider With Rosie* is, in fact, animated by concern over the realistic representation of rural communities. While promising access to a mythic 'deep England' (a route many readers have happily followed), the text also functions to undermine the most cherished attributes of the 'organic community'.

The Welsh Regions

As we have seen, such anxiety was institutionally absent from the Festival of Britain at the beginning of the decade, which was easy in its conflation of archetypal Englishness with Britishness, in much the same vein as George Orwell's renowned essay collection *The Lion and the Unicorn* (1941), republished as a new selection, *England Your England*, in 1953. With the lion representing England and the unicorn Scotland, the symbol is originally of the Union of the Crowns. The Lion and Unicorn Pavilion at the 1951 Festival, its exhibit captioned by Lee, had skewed the symbol to suggest the character of the Briton (itself a regionalist, English, ethnic designation) tempering a (Celtic) imaginative if wayward hedonism with a grounding (and Anglicised) common sense. While rejecting its implicit hierarchy, with only a slight shift of focus, we can re-envisage this opposition as that of myth and realism, the dialectic so apparent in *The Anathemata*. Nairn's study of nationalist impulses within Britain proffers a sense of why such a dialectic might be particularly influential in the case of Wales, and so apparent in its literature, as its nationalist movement focused upon 'a battle for the defence and revival of rural-based community and traditional identity – an identity evoked overwhelmingly by literary and musical culture, and having as its mainspring the language question' (Nairn 1981: 208). Yet as poet and playwright Saunders Lewis recognised in his famous 1962 radio lecture 'Tynged yr Iaith' (The Fate of the Language), which inspired the formation of the Welsh Language Society, 'the industrial revolution which so threatened Welsh language and life also gave it a new chance of life – indeed, the only chance of surviving permanently and avoiding the fate of Cornish, Irish and Scottish Gaelic' (Nairn 1981: 198). Nowhere is the complexity of belonging so evident during the 1950s as in the literature of Wales. Or rather, in Anglo-Welsh literature of the decade: as the only texts available to this particular reader, this study must recognise the possibility that it is the language in which they are written that serves to heighten that sense of 'addressivity', or the awareness of the imposed nature of their terms of address and invited identifications (Connor 1996).

The complexity of allegiance and the spectre of the organic community figures prominently in the work of James Hanley, who lived in Wales for a number of periods during his life, and throughout the 1950s. Born of Irish parents, raised in Liverpool, with experience at sea in both war and peace time, Hanley published his regional novel, *The Welsh Sonata*, in 1958. The novel concerns the disappearance of Rhys the Wound, a wanderer living physically on the periphery of the small community of Cilgyn, but very much part of its emotional centre, with the cherished story of his tragic romantic loss and his innocent affinity for the children of the village. As a musical form, a sonata involves two voices in dialogue; Stephen Wade reads within the novel what he calls 'Hanley's subtext of making a dialectic between the Wales of myth, poetry and the aesthetic impulse and the Wales of the towns and the "English"' (Wade 2002: 124). The character who experiences this duality most intensely is Goronwy Jones, city-raised and English-speaking, who describes himself from the first as 'Policeman and retired bard'. Both vocations fuel his interest in Rhys. Three sections of the novel are formed by Jones's reports on the case of the missing person. Yet rather than being produced at work, the reports are 'written in his own time' (Hanley 1978: 7), and are infused with a poetry that exceeds the restraint of Jones's default professionalism. He describes the missing man as follows:

> Rhys the Wound, with the cloud upon his head . . .
> Roman nose.
> Musician's ears.
> Scholar's brow.
> Jim Driscoll's chin.
> Eyes Rossetti might have liked on the end of his brush.
> Light grey and the whites as clear as water. (9–10)

Jones is hopeful that he might make Rhys's case into art, then send 'it off to next year's National at Newtown, for a prize'. He rejects drama as an appropriate form: 'Then thought, "No, a long poem," remembering longer ones of his youth' (118). Jones keeps two separate books: one for these personal reports forming the basis of his prize entry, and the other a black ledger marked 'Duty' (117).

Hanley is fascinated by innocence. Rhys the Wound, though emotionally scarred by his beloved Olwen Hughes's choice of another man, was 'innocent' by a number of different scales of judgement – by virtue of his staunch religious belief, for example, and the fact that he is '"truly Welsh" because he never could speak English' (17). He also had a capacity for childlike awe that allowed him, while still at school, to locate eight of the Seven Wonders of the World in his home village of Cynant (63), and which he has maintained in adulthood. Rhys's renowned knowledge of, and dedication to, the Book is echoed by, and celebrated in, the Biblical tenor Hanley lends to his life; he is a kind of reverse Samson, growing his hair and his 'thought and word like steel' (16) when rejected by a woman, and granted eternal life through 'the living hair' still evident on his frozen body, when it is found (206). Such innocence is ultimately unavailable to Goronwy Jones, and he is mocked by Cilgyn's natives for his obsession with Rhys and with writing: '"Giving his bardic bones a last bloody shake, I suppose." "That's it. Silly. Vanity in him. Wasn't ever much at it, anyhow"' (120). Stephen Wade believes that 'the community here is poeticized in a deliberate, often uneasy prose sitting alongside a tactile realism. In this he is comparable to a particular strand of Anglo-Welsh writing that insists on mythologizing the Welsh rural communities' (Wade 2002: 126).

These concerns – of 'insiderness', national and regional identifications, the clash of myth and reality, Welsh or otherwise – have formed the focus of this chapter, and nowhere are they dramatised with more panache than in *Under Milk Wood*. Dylan Thomas's play was first broadcast posthumously on the BBC's Third Programme on 25 January

1954 (coincidentally also the publication date of Kingsley Amis's *Lucky Jim*). The audience research report conducted by the BBC notes the play received 'the exceptionally high Appreciation Index of 81'. 'True,' it added, 'there was a small minority to whom it seemed unedifying, verbose or confusing. But for most of the audience, the wit, vigour and beauty of the writing combined with a flawless production to make a memorable broadcast' (BBC 1954). Amis, out for dinner in Swansea with his wife that night to celebrate, would have missed this grand event in the career of his *bête noire*, although his evening had its own annoyances – 'Can you afford it, boy?' asked the waiter when he ordered champagne (Leader 2006: 300). Thomas's drama plays shamelessly and gloriously with Welsh cadences in its English blank verse. M. Wynn Thomas claims that:

> Dylan Thomas was deliberately brought up by his father to know little about Wales, and as a result he himself cared even less. For him the country north and west of Swansea was only Cwmdonkin Park writ large: it existed simply as an adventure playground for the imagination that his Welsh-speaking father had so lovingly anglicized, as the stuff of which hyperbole was made.

(Cwmdonkin Park lay opposite Dylan Thomas's childhood home in Swansea.) His critic adds, only marginally more charitably, 'This is not the place to ponder the genuine success that he undoubtedly made of his ignorance' (Wynn Thomas 1998: 208). One of Thomas's biographers asserts that 'The chapel influence balked at suggestions of Welsh hypocrisy and saw only malicious satire' (Lycett 2003: 377). This kind of antagonism, we can assume, would have been provoked by one character in *Under Milk Wood* in particular: that of the Reverend Eli Jenkins, Dylan Thomas's parody of the 'lone seer' and bard of his community, declaiming his amateurish tetrameters to the dawn:

> By Cader Idris, tempest-torn
> Or Moel y Wyddfa's glory,
> Carnedd Llewelyn beauty born,
> Plinlimmon old in story,
>
> By mountains where King Arthur dreams,
> By Penmaen Mawr defiant,
> *Llareggug Hill* a molehill seems,
> A pygmy to a giant. (Thomas 2000: 18)

Jenkins's poetic authority over his native landscape, with its topographical centrepiece identified later by its vicar as a 'mystic tumulus' (60), is slyly undermined by Thomas from the beginning of the play, when the first narrator urges listeners to

Stand on this hill. This is Llareggub Hill, old as the hills, high, cool, and green, and from this small circle of stones, made not by druids but by Mrs Beynon's Billy, you can see all the town below you sleeping in the first of the dawn. (16)

Yet melded within this undeniably cavalier posturing towards a particular mode of regional writing (itself a dominant national trope in Welsh writing at the time) is a concern with issues of authentic representation and of belonging. Townee Thomas, like the play's listeners ushered to the top of the hill, cannot but be aware of being outside of the community of Llareggub, and thus deprived of Jenkins's certainty of self, however misplacedly this may manifest itself in poetry. Stephen Wade notes how the vicar 'illustrates that aspect of representation in Welsh writing that exists in contradistinction to realistic modes. In other words, how does a writer dealing with a culture seen objectively, either from within or from a stranger's viewpoint, achieve the authenticity required?' (Wade 2002: 117–18) Jenkins's crass verse is certainly used to ironise the literary trope of 'mythic Wales', but he too seems aware of the incompleteness of this aestheticised response to his region, for, we are told, working 'inky in his cool front parlour or poem-room [he] tells only the truth in his Lifework: the Population, Main Industry, Shipping, History, Topography, Flora and Fauna of the town he worships in: the White Book of Llareggub' (Thomas 2000: 54). Like Goronwy Jones, he needs to write two very different kinds of books in order to represent his community.

Eli Jenkins, with his provenance of dubious propriety (his father, Esau, 'undogcollared because of his little weakness, was scythed to the bone one harvest by mistake when sleeping with his weakness in the corn'; 54) and his taste for the sustenance of his local landscape, *belongs*. He is thus well placed to be, if not a spiritual leader of his town, then at least an integral and understanding part of its community. His response to town jezebel Polly Garter's song of promiscuity and loss is a celebration of its artistic form that does not exclude awareness of its content – 'Praise the Lord! We are a musical nation' (40), and an implied refutation of the hysterical intolerance of Mrs Pugh, calling for Polly's arrest 'for having babies' (21). This point of view also forms an integral part of the play's morality: a belief in and maintenance of the possibility of innocence, and in the potential clearly to voice that innocence, as in what the vicar calls 'a greenleaved sermon on the innocence of men' (63). That the site of this innocence lies within the closed regional community of Llareggub is a source of both pathos and frustration for Thomas, a combination most explicit in the weird intervention of the voice of a guidebook, which describes the town as follows:

Though there is little to attract the hillclimber, the healthseeker, the sports-man, or the weekending motorist, the contemplative may, if sufficiently attracted to spare it some leisurely hours, find, in its cobbled streets and its little fishing harbour, in its several curious customs, and in the conversation of its local 'characters', some of that picturesque sense of the past so frequently lacking in towns and villages which have kept more abreast of the times. (17)

Heavily ironic, inescapably patronising, yet still yearning for an authen-ticity now commonly out of reach, this duality of voice forms, it would seem, the archetypal 1950s response to the pastoral, and casts us back to the consideration of David Jones's conflicted poem sequence with which we began this chapter. Once again, this role proves crucial to our under-standing of much influential writing of the 1950s, and it was another Welshman, Raymond Williams, who attempted to forge a new kind of fiction to explore it. His novel forms a key focus in the consideration of the relationship between class and community in the following chapter.

Chapter Ten

The Scholarship Class: Literature and Social Mobility

The 1950s in Britain has been routinely characterised as progressively classless, due largely to garnering private affluence during the decade, and its prevailing public rhetoric of meritocracy (rooted in the new comprehensive education system). It was this momentum that allowed Harold Macmillan, in his statement after Labour's concession in the 1959 General Election, to make the claim that the Conservative victory for a second term showed 'the class war is obsolete.' 'This seems to me', he added, 'a great gain for the future' ('Conservative Hat Trick' 1959: 6). Not everyone was in agreement. In 1954, Nancy Mitford, writing in *Encounter*, had both satirised and fetishised class differences in speech by distinctions between 'U' (upper-class) and 'Non-U' (woefully aspirational) usages (the categories were originally coined by linguist Alan Ross). Responses to her article were gathered with it in *Noblesse Oblige: An Enquiry into the Identifiable Characteristics of the English Aristocracy* (1956). Her friend, Evelyn Waugh, in 'An Open Letter to the Honble Mrs Peter Rodd (Nancy Mitford) On a Very Serious Subject', indulged in some humorous shuddering at the effects of the ignorance of proper place on literature, claiming of those who had newly profited from the increased educational opportunities instigated by R. A. Butler:

> L'École de Butler are the primal men and women of the classless society. Their novelists seem to be aware of the existence of a rather more expensive world of their own . . . – but of the ramifications of the social order which have obsessed some of the acutest minds of the last 150 years, they know less than of the castes of India. (Mitford 1960: 60)

One popular and prolific contemporary author, H. E. Bates, born in 1905, had published well over twenty novels before the 1950s began, easily escaping Waugh's degraded category of new, class-ignorant novelists. Yet, like *Cider With Rosie*, Bates's *The Darling Buds of May* (1958) has been routinely read (and frequently cherished) for the way in which it not so much ignores 'the ramifications of the social order', but reconciles them in a representation of a pastoral (and heavily nostalgic) organic community. A sense of traditional class difference is certainly important in generating much of the novel's humour, which is derived from a faintly anarchic sense of the instability of once-reliable markers of rank – Pop Larkin drives a Rolls Royce, for instance, and is better able to afford the local stately home, Bluff Court, than its impoverished aristocratic owners. Yet he is illiterate: when Mr Charlton the tax inspector mentions Larkin's need to sign a form, Mariette, the eldest of the Larkin children, tells him 'You'll have to sign it for him, . . . or Ma will. He can't write his name' (Bates 1990: 28). Pop's considerable affluence comes in part from a ready willingness to exploit new State systems of support, urging Mr Charlton, for example, to sign off sick and thereby take 'proper advantage of what he called "the National Elf lark"' (82). In this way, Pop is a very traditional comic hero. Dominic Head claims of *The Darling Buds of May* that: 'As a popular comic novel its longevity hinges on the way it taps into an enduring English enthusiasm for anti-conventionalism, which is class-based' (Head 2010: 7).

However, despite the idyllic rural environment in which the Larkins live, Bates's pastoral setting is not without a satirical edge, and their lifestyle is far from organic. The family is characterised by its unfettered, irresponsible consumption; in one of the earliest descriptions of Pop, we see that 'packets of potato crisps crackled out of his pocket, together with a bundle of pound notes, rolled up, perhaps a hundred of them, and clasped with a thick elastic band' (Bates 1990: 6). Such physical indulgence is routinely feminised through the repeated descriptions of Ma Larkin as herself both edible and excessive:

> Ma shook all over, laughing like a jelly. Little rivers of yellow, brown, and pinkish-purple cream were running down over her huge lardy hands. In her handsome big black eyes the cloudless blue May sky was reflected, making them dance as she threw out the splendid bank of her bosom, quivering under its salmon jumper. (5–6)

Television figures strongly in the novel as both another mindlessly consuming activity, an impetus to desire for more goods and indulgent experiences, and an important physical site for eating and drinking; at one point Mr Charlton has a nightmarish vision as 'In the television's flickering purplish light the young man watched the faces about the table, as they munched on fish-and-chips, ice-cream, tomato-ketchup, and jam, becoming more and more like pallid, eyeless ghouls' (16). Although undeniably funny, the critique inherent in such descriptions goes on to disrupt the novel's more simplistic pastoral, the mode which has prompted those critical accusations of Bates's alleged nostalgia. When the narrative voice silkily suggests how 'an afternoon of delicious golden content folded its transparent envelope more and more softly about the paradisiacal Larkin world, over the outlying meadow scintillating with its million buttercups and the shady fragrant walnut tree' (79), are the Larkins and their appetites being naturalised, or their appetites placed in contrast to nature? The ambiguity of that word 'content' – suggesting both a settled happiness, but also, less idyllically, 'stuff' (activity and articles for consumption) – prompts the latter interpretation. Head notes how

> The Larkins embody a hedonistic, non-judgmental *joie de vivre* that is made to correspond with the rhythms of the countryside. However, part of the comedy depends on the extent to which this correspondence is undermined—indeed, a less innocent rural economy is at work. (Head 2010: 7)

One Larkin transaction in which this denigration is clearly at work is the fast-burgeoning relationship between Mr Charlton, the tax inspector, and Mariette. Believing herself to be pregnant before his arrival at the Larkin farm, Mariette's motives for the easy rural seduction she effects are suspect, and once again their ambiguity is emphasised by that portal of corruption, the television set:

> While Mariette went upstairs to dab perfume behind her ears and in the soft hollows of her legs, Mr Charlton and Pop came in from the yard to join Montgomery, Primrose, Victoria, and the twins, who sat at the table licking thick bars of choc-ice and watching a television programme in which three men, a clergyman, and a woman were discussing prostitution and what should be done about it all. (Bates 2000: 32–3)

(Ironically, of course, it was the wild popularity of the ITV television adaptation of the Larkin novels in the early 1990s, itself legible as an exercise in naturalising and historicising the excessive consumption of the Eighties, that aggravated Bates's reputation as a nostalgic writer.) Mr Charlton, the bespectacled, serious, initially ambitious civil servant, is the archetypal scholarship boy, newly middle-class (if lower middle-class), and his body is used routinely through the novel to register a comic, class-inflected mixture of physical repulsion and attraction to the lifestyle of the Larkins. When he meets Mariette for the first time (he has previously mistaken her at a gymkhana for 'the niece of Lady Planson-Forbes', 27), 'the entire body of the young man seemed to swirl helplessly, as if half-intoxicated, out of balance, on its axis' (15).

Later in Bates's long-running and increasing dark series of Larkin novels, it is Pop's body that becomes the site of punishment for the family's consumption over the years; in *A Little of What You Fancy* (1970), Pop suffers a violent heart attack in the first chapter, and spends most of the novel recumbent, unable even to respond in a satisfactorily priapic manner to the gleamingly robust charms of Sister Trevelyan. In the final chapter, he is able tentatively to reclaim Ma from the temptations of the virile toff, Sir John Furlington-Snow, but has entirely lost his taste for alcohol. It is a muted and vanquished conclusion to the glorious Larkin saga.

Class conflict, or its obsolescence, is a rich source of humour for both Evelyn Waugh and Bates, albeit in comedy tainted by an edge of disapproval at the affluent working class's morality. For all the government rhetoric of classlessness, the persistence of traditional hierarchies within the Britain of the 1950s is in many ways counter-intuitive, given the potential of the decade's unprecedented economic and educational opportunities for a more equal society. Peter Hennessy notes:

> It is perhaps surprising that a combination of expanding education provision, the use of an ever-more professionalized and technology-based industrial culture *and* the shared Second World War experiences that fostered what McKibbin called a 'redistribution of esteem' had had such a limited effect on the factors that signalled class and cultural divisions within the British population. (Hennessy 2006: 100)

Yet it is this failure that produces what we have come to recognise throughout the course of this study so far as a key cultural and social experience of the decade (and a rich source of inspiration for its literature): that simultaneous sense of 'outsidership' resulting from the disruption of class (or racial, or national) identity, and a lingering 'insidership' that provokes a responsibility to represent empathetically the class or community to which you once fully belonged. We might term this, perhaps, a 'border country' experience.

The previous chapter suggested that, for all John Hewitt's vision of the region as a utopian 'smaller unit' of identification and loyalty (Hewitt 1987: 122), regional writing of the 1950s was inescapably burdened with the wider political and cultural issues of national society. In a 1991 essay, Raymond Williams claimed that a particular social class can 'be seen as a region: a social area inhabited by people of a certain kind, living in certain ways'. As such, it can easily, of course, be used to figure an idealistic view of an organic, self-contained community. However, Williams continues,

> a Marxist sense of class, while indeed and inevitably recognizing social regions of this kind, carries the inescapable and finally constitutive sense of

class as a formation of social relationships within a whole social order, and thus of alternative and typically conflicting (in any cases inevitably *relating*) formations. (Williams 1991: 234)

His 1960 regional novel, *Border Country*, makes this sense of class explicit in its narrative of Matthew Price, archetypal 'scholarship boy', and in its long view of its protagonist's conflicted feelings on returning to the Welsh village of his upbringing. The story is set in 1926 (the year of the General Strike), and Williams emphasises Price's experience as being part of a long revolution of class mobility and social change. The novel's (semi-)fictional examination of a rural Welsh community, like Williams's sociological work, hinges upon the conscious, even tortuous, renunciation of the safe position of the detached observer by its protagonist Matthew Price (Will to his family), whose lengthy education and job as a university lecturer prefigure the experience of the graduates of Waugh's 'École de Butler'. Williams claimed that he wrote (and rewrote) the novel during the 1950s in order to avoid the pitfalls of the regional novel, or, more precisely, that mode of regional writing which upholds the idealised self-containment of the Leavisite 'organic community':

> The truly regional novel, in this limiting sense, has initially so isolated its region, and thus projected it as internally whole – 'organic' – that it is unable to recognize the complex internal processes, including internal divisions and conflicts, which factually connect with these wider pressures. I know that I wrote *Border Country* seven times to find that alternative form in which these internal processes and division have their real weight. (Williams 1991: 231)

This 'alternative form', then, combines the recognition and analysis of wider social and historical pressures with an attention to the personal experience of those changes, or, to use a phrase coined by Williams in his 1954 text *Preface to Film*, a 'structure of feeling'. This latter, still-emergent consciousness, cannot necessarily be explicitly articulated – rather, it is best transmitted more obliquely through literature. Once again we can recognise a model of literature as a particularly privileged mode of expression of the contemporary experience, and as necessarily dual-voiced in order to convey the complexity of that experience. Just as James Hanley's *The Welsh Sonata* and Dylan Thomas's *Under Milk Wood*, for example, counselled a necessary dialectic between realism and myth, Williams's *Border Country* combines an attention both to fact and to feeling in order accurately to convey Price's gathering understanding of his adult identity and relationship with his childhood home.

Part of this relationship is with the landscape surrounding the village of Glynmawr. As in *Under Milk Wood*, we are made aware of the inappropriate nature of the voice of the guidebook that Matthew is reading on his return, with its catalogue of castles and Norman roodscreens, which he recognises as only 'the pieces of past and present that are safe to handle. Here, in this living country' (Williams 1962: 69). Matthew's own research into the economic history of the Welsh valleys has honed his skills in precisely this detached style of interpretation – in Chapter 10 of the novel he is able seamlessly to decipher the process of the Norman conquest from the signs inscribed in the terrain around the hill on which he stands. Yet, as he confesses to Morgan Rosser, his father's friend, the gradual realisation of the inadequacy of this purely academic approach has stalled any progress on his thesis on population movements during the Industrial Revolution, even before this has been underlined by his time in Glynmawr. Matthew has recognised the need for a new kind of historical writing, which can combine the analysis of facts and figures with the documentation of the period through diaries and letters, to produce 'the history of a whole people being changed'. Yet, as his discipline stands, in 1926, such a task is 'too much': 'For I saw suddenly that it wasn't a piece of research, but an emotional pattern. Emotional patterns are all very well, but they're our own business. History is public or nothing' (284). Matthew has an epiphanic realisation of the ideal combination of clarity and creativity, tradition and freedom, on witnessing the Eisteddfod, where the adult choirs provide both a vision and a chorus of unity: 'everyone singing; the faces straining and the voices rising around them, holding, moving, in the hushed silence that held all the potency of these sounds, until you listening was the singing and the border had been crossed' (207).

Sub-textually, of course, the novel asks us to recognise that it is literature, like the Eisteddfod and unlike history, that allows the melding of intellectual discipline with a structure of feeling. Yet it is difficult to conclude of *Border Country* that such a balance has been successfully achieved. It is Harry Price, Matthew's father, who is associated with the superior knowledge generated by feeling. For all the son's commendable efforts to forge a new means of expression, it is Harry's brooding inarticulacy, traditional to the romanticised working-class literary male, that draws the reader, particularly in comparison to the often-clunky earnestness shared by Matthew and the third-person narrator. As Susan Brook has noted, 'A recurrent theme of the novel is the failure of language to capture and express feeling (a failure Williams's own straining and portentous style often seems to enact)' (Brook 2007: 12). Harry's attractiveness as a literary character belies Williams's own romantic belief in the inevitable triumph of the combination of working-class intellectualism and emotional values that will signal the triumphant end of the long revolution.

Crossing Borders

Williams's 1958 *Culture and Society* was written just before the founding of the New Left, and, together with Hoggart's *The Uses of Literacy*,
had a crucial role in articulating its agenda. Dennis L. Dworkin has
summarised this as follows: 'New Left activists rejected the politics of
revisionism, but believed that its analysis of the changing society could
not be overlooked. Socialists, they argued, must acknowledge the profound impact of the new consumer society and welfare state, and create
a socialist politics founded on everyday life and experience, not outworn
myths and slogans' (Dworkin 1993: 41). This new agenda informs the
first of Arnold Wesker's trilogy of plays, *Chicken Soup with Barley*,
first performed in 1958 at the Belgrade Theatre, Coventry. It features
the young Ronnie Kahn, who is desperately, and largely unsuccessfully,
trying to articulate a new and vital Socialism relevant to the Welfare
State, and is furious at his mother, Sarah, for reiterating the sureties
of an outdated Communism. As Monty Blatt, another young activist,
remarks of her with a mixture of affection and sanctimony: 'Bless her!
Someone told her socialism was happiness so she joined the Party. You
don't find many left like Sarah Kahn' (Wesker 1964: 62).

Ronnie Kahn is an important, if absent, presence in Wesker's sequel,
Roots (1959). Like its predecessor, the play was first performed in
Coventry and then transferred to the Royal Court. At the beginning of
the play, Beatie returns from London to her family home in Norfolk,
anticipating the arrival of Ronnie, her fiancé, a week or so later. A
lively young woman, newly and unconventionally educated in Ronnie's
politics and cultural tastes, she is another character located in a kind
of 'border country': between classes, and between urban and rural
life. Wesker's 'Note to Actors and Producers' at the beginning of his
trilogy places himself in precisely this insider / outsider position, urging
casts and crews not to think of his 'people' as caricatures, for though
'The picture I have drawn is a harsh one, yet my tone is not one of
disgust – nor should it be in the presentation of the plays. I am at one
with these people: it is only that I am annoyed, with them and myself'
(Wesker 1964: 7). Taylor attributes the (still presiding) commonplace
that Wesker writes realistically about the working class to precisely this
harshness, claiming of critics that:

> The main reasons, it would seem, that Wesker's plays have impressed them as
> particularly authentic are that (*a*) they differ markedly from the conventional
> picture, and (*b*) their differences are nearly all in the direction of greater
> squalor and brutality, especially in *Roots*, which is almost a Zolaesque tract
> on the degradation of country life. (Taylor 1968: 138)

Roots is certainly an unmitigated assault on the trappings of the pastoral, and on the continuing possibility of the organic community. The play is a determined effort to show that the veneration of the rural working classes as a reliable repository of that eternal quality of 'life' is a myth; as Beatie ironically puts it in the speech that coins the play's title, 'I come from a family o' farm labourers yet I ent got no roots – just like town people – just a mass o' nothing' (Wesker 1964: 145). One of Wesker's characteristically fulsome stage directions reads:

> BEATIE *helps collect dishes from table and proceeds to help wash up. This is a silence that needs organizing. Throughout the play there is no sign of intense living from any of the characters* – BEATIE's *bursts are the exception. They continue in a routine rural manner. The day comes, one sleeps at night, there is always the winter, the spring, the autumn, and the summer – little amazes them.* (92)

For the majority of the play, even Beatie's 'bursts' are inauthentic, as no more than an uncanny ventriloquist act of Ronnie's convictions: '*when she does she imitates him so well in both manner and intonation that in fact as the play progresses we see a picture of him through her*' (88). Her words are doubly devalued by the fact that, for all Ronnie's disapproval of his mother's Communist platitudes, his own polemic is, in fact, no more than a contemporary variation on the theme of Socialism as happiness. Beatie bullies her mother into listening to Bizet's L'Arlésienne suite, intoning Ronnie's notably naïve gospel: 'This is a simple piece of music, it's not highbrow but it's full of living. And that's what he say socialism is. "Christ," he say. "Socialism isn't talking all the time, it's living, it's singing, it's dancing, it's being interested in what go on around you, it's being concerned about people and the world"' (128–9). Mrs Bryant, eventually balking at Beatie's barrage of criticism, shrewdly exposes the roots of her daughter's accusations as an act of transference of her own sense of guilt and inadequacy: 'When you tell me I was stubborn, what you mean was that *he* told you *you* was stubborn – eh? When you tell me I don't understand you mean *you* don't understand isn't it? When you tell me I don't make no effort you mean *you* don't make no effort' (145). Once again, there is the sense that Socialism, its prophets and its ideals, are detached from their source, and increasingly garbled in a game of Chinese Whispers – 'Communist Whispers', perhaps.

Yet the play is not without a final glimpse of hope for a working-class future. To Beatie, the 'workers' are responsible for their own descent into an inauthentic morass of pop and pulp culture through complicit laziness and apathy:

The slop singers and the pop writers and the film makers and women's magazines and the Sunday papers and the picture strip love stories – that's who come along, and you don't have to make no effort for them, it come easy.

Ironically, it is this diatribe against the mindless cultural consumption of her class that signals Beatie's escape into articulacy from the ventriloquism of her now ex-fiancé: 'D'you hear that? D'you hear it? Did you listen to me? I'm talking. Jenny, Frankie, Mother – I'm not quoting no more' (147–8). Beatie, she prompts us to assume, is forging a discourse of Marxism infused with her own structures of feeling. Yet any such hope in the possibility of renewed authenticity is raised by Wesker at the end of *Roots*, only to be dashed by the trilogy's final instalment, *I'm Talking About Jerusalem* (1960), in which Ronnie's sister, Ada Simmonds, and her husband, Dave, eventually call a halt in the final autumn of the 1950s to an experiment began in the first scene of the play when they move to Norfolk in 1946. The play charts the gradual failure of a conspicuously organic, William Morris-style vision of a rural family unit centred upon and supported by skilled craftsmanship.

(Sub)urban Communities

Yet, although Leavis's ideal of the 'organic community' was largely discredited in British writing of the 1950s, the desirability of a plainer, and predominantly urban, community was definitely not. In 1953, Michael Young, 'the new sociologist on the block', as David Kynaston describes him, was conducting interviews for his thesis, 'A Study of the Extended Family in East London' (Kynaston 2009: 340). His respondents were almost equally divided between inhabitants of Bethnal Green, a traditional working-class district in the East End of London, and the newly completed estate of Debden in Essex, to which many families from Bethnal Green had moved, or been moved, since the war. Young's key observation as a self-confessed 'observer from outside' was that 'Bethnal Green has a sense of community; it has a sense of history; it has a kinship system. These are independent variables, and yet in this district they are closely connected in such a way that each reinforces the other' (Kynaston 2009: 340–1). The academic debate continues today as to the precise validity of what Raymond Williams called 'that warmly persuasive word': that is, community (Williams 1976: 66). For Joanna Bourke, the concept of 'working-class community' in particular has a validity akin to that of the 'organic community' in William's critique – due, she has claimed, to the cumulative influence of 'working-class autobiographies and oral histories, where social relations are often recalled through a golden haze' (Bourke 1994: 137–8). Equally culpable, in Bourke's opinion, are generations of Socialists, for whom the concept of 'community' has 'represented the innate socialism of the workers' – in essence, she asserts, 'a rhetorical device' rather than an objective, empirical description (137). Robert Colls, by contrast, utterly refutes Bourne's thesis of community as a retrospective (and heavily nostalgic) construct, proudly grounding his argument in his personal experience of a childhood in 1950s working-class South Shields (Colls 2004).

Colls's methodology in his chapter 'When We Lived in Communities' is, of course, indebted to Raymond Williams and the argument he made for attention to a structure of feeling in both sociological and literary writing. It also invokes the work of Richard Hoggart, and another key text of the New Left which both mapped and crossed the borders of class-specific communities: the 1957 study *The Uses of Literacy: Aspects of Working-class Life with Special Reference to Publications and Entertainments*. Like *Culture and Society*, Hoggart's book was animated by changes to working-class communities brought about by contemporary social changes: increasing affluence, an accelerated consumer culture, and the way in which the welfare state apparatus had disrupted traditional associational life – reducing collective forms of economic support such as, for example, the friendly societies (Kynaston 2009: 223). These two seminal texts appeared only months apart, prompting a frequent assumption that their authors had developed their ideas in dialogue with each other – Williams was to observe that his name was so often linked with Hoggart's at the time that they sounded like a joint firm (Williams 1960: 341). Yet the argument of *The Uses of Literacy* is easily distinguished from that of Williams's 1950s texts by its pessimistic prognosis of the future of the working-class. Rather than an organic rural idyll, Hoggart's sense of loss is directed towards a tradition of urban life:

> We had been from the beginning fully of the towns, of the trams and buses, of the elaborate network of social services, of the chain-stores, the picture-palaces, the trips to the seaside. For us the country is not, after all, home; nor even the place where Father and Mother were so healthily reared. It is an occasionally remembered backcloth, a place you sometimes visit. (Hoggart 1958: 14)

Like Beatie Bryant, *The Uses of Literacy* is animated by an intense anxiety at the corruption of working-class habitat and leisure time by the vast and insistent array of garish consumer goods and vacuous entertainments now available to the masses, the relentless 'invitations to a candy-floss world' (169) issued by advertising and the mass media. More biblically, Hoggart claims that:

> One might give the title 'The Fall of the Innocents' to those activities in which working-class people, in particular, are duped, *simply because they have been approached along a line on which they are exposed* – that is, because they have been approached in a personal, friendly, and homely manner. We see this in a thousand advertisements aimed at them, in the editorial comment of some working-class papers and magazines, in the tone of the popular astrologers. (83)

The inauthenticity of this artificial culture, Hoggart worries, is corrupting, even obliterating what he considers to be the 'core of working-class attitudes', 'the sense of the personal, the concrete, the local' (33). Williams has noted the conceptual similarities of class and region: in Hoggart's text the essence of working-class identity is presented like a regional sensibility, and it is a region heavily under siege by contemporary social change.

Hoggart's claims to this core, or structure, of feeling in essential working-class experience have, unsurprisingly, prompted criticism – E. P. Thompson, another key figure in the founding of the New Left, accused his work of ahistoricism (Dworkin 1993). Yet the enduring value of *The Uses of Literacy* as both historical record and methodological exemplar is precisely the text's knowing dramatisation of the implications of the personal tendency to nostalgia. This is a tendency Hoggart reads to be as vital to the new sociology as it is to literature: 'How many major English writers are there', he asks, 'who do not, however slightly, over-emphasize the salty features of working-class life?' (Hoggart 1958: 4–5). Raymond Williams, in a 1957 review of *The Uses of Literacy*, wrote approvingly of this crossing of genres, noting how one could feel his peer 'hesitating between fiction or autobiography on the one hand, and sociology on the other' (Williams 1989: 28). F. R. Leavis was less charitable: 'He should have written a novel' (Hoggart 1996: 206). Like Bourke after him, Hoggart is suspicious of easy sentimentality: 'I avoid the word "community" at this stage because its overtones seem too simply favourable; they may lead to an under-estimation of the harsher tensions and sanctions of working-class groups' (Hoggart 1958: 60). However, like Bourke's staunch critic, Robert Colls, he sees no reason to denude his observations of the animation of personal affiliations and alienations.

On the 1976 BBC arts magazine programme *2nd House*, in an edition entitled 'Mirror on Class', Melvyn Bragg was to distinguish *The Uses of Literacy* as a 1950s 'literary breakthrough' alongside the works of Kingsley Amis, John Osborne and Arnold Wesker (Wales 2008: 103). As Tracy Hargreaves points out, '*The Uses of Literacy* itself often makes no qualitative distinction between the literary text and society. Fictional characters from the Wife of Bath to Tess of the D'Urbervilles and Jude Fawley share the same illustrative spaces as extra-textual ones' (Hargreaves 2011: 120). Yet it is Hoggart's non-fictional mode of writing that allows him explicitly to describe an authorial viewpoint that is shared, though more covertly, by many of the emerging writers covered in this study, whether or not they share Hoggart's status as 'Scholarship Boy':

> A writer who is himself from the working-classes has his own temptations to error, somewhat different from but no less than those of a writer from another class. I am from the working-classes and feel even now both close to them and apart from them. In a few more years this double relationship may not, I suppose, be so apparent to me; but it is bound to affect what I say. It may help me to come nearer to giving a felt sense of working-class life, to avoid some of an outsider's more obvious risks of misinterpretation. On the other hand, this very emotional involvement presents considerable dangers. (Hoggart 1958: 6)

As we have seen, this 'double relationship' or dual perspective in the representation of the working class by a practitioner who, by virtue of education and social mobility, stands both inside and outside the community, animates both literature and sociological commentary of the decade. Lindsay Anderson's twelve-minute documentary, *O Dreamland*, shot in Margate in 1953 (though it was not screened until 1956), is particularly striking in the ambiguity of its perspective on the working classes at their seaside leisure. Anderson claimed that

> British documentaries rarely give the impression of having been made by human beings: they seem rather the well-turned product of a highly efficient, standardised industrial process. No rough edges. 'Please one-please all.' This at least cannot (I hope) be said about *O Dreamland*. (Dupin 2007: 9)

He holds a lingering shot of a shoddy sign within the Dreamland amusement park, featuring a recumbent elf bearing the legend 'The dreams I dream are yours to see, Over There in Reality': another of Hoggart's deeply suspect 'invitations to a candy-floss world' (Hoggart 1958: 169). Anderson's attested aesthetic for documentary film, shared by other directors like Karel Reisz, was the creative use of 'actual' material (Anderson 1958). The New Wave feature films that emanated from this shared aesthetic were 'remarkable', claimed Walter Lassaly, cinematographer on *A Taste of Honey* (1961) and *The Loneliness of the Long-Distance Runner* (1962), because not only did they 'treat working-class people, working-class problems, but that they have a very poetic view of them' (Higson 1984: 2). This filmic 'poetry' is interestingly at odds with that of the Movement, with its rejection of lyrical imagery and epiphany.

Free Cinema – a small collective rebellion against documentary orthodoxy screened in a series at London's National Film Theatre between 1956 and 1959 – was precursor to and a major influence upon the subsequent New Wave films of the late 1950s and early 1960s (Dupin 2007). Anderson's film features a disorientatingly dissonant soundtrack of unsynchronised sounds that was to become one of the trademarks of the Free Cinema aesthetic. Contemporary dreamy popular hits – Frankie Lane's 'I Believe' and Muriel Smith's 'Hold Me, Thrill Me, Kiss Me' – are intercut with location recordings of bingo callers, fairground traders, and mostly harshly of all, the grating laughter of an automaton Laughing Sailor. The crowds, spilling food and spilling out of their straining summer clothes, sit staring, or wander between 'attractions' in the park: a 'Torture through the Ages' exhibit where the Rosenbergs are executed again and again, and a desolate zoo with mangy, pacing animals. A stall selling balloon hats offers one which reads 'My resistance is low.' Gavin Lambert's 1956 review is certain that in *O Dreamland* and other Free Cinema works he is witnessing the zeitgeist:

> In seizing upon these aspects – the anonymity of urban life, the aimless lonely figures swallowed up in the greater loneliness of the crowd, the pleasures hideous and mechanical or imaginatively aspiring – these film-makers compel above all the shock of recognition. How is it these images, so redolent of the times, have hardly appeared on our screen before?

The expressionless faces of the elderly, children, young women all dolled up are juxtaposed with those of the fairground's garish automata: are these people shamefully complicit or piteously trapped? The film's conclusion refuses an answer; in a virtuoso shot, the camera soars vertiginously into the night sky to a view of the shimmering and blaring park like, Lambert claims, 'a plea for release'. Certainly the film's relentless emotional ambiguity inspires such a plea in its audience; if there is compassion here, Lambert suggests, 'it is the most rigorous, difficult and austere kind of compassion: not for the moment or the particular situation, but a kind of permanent temperamental heartache for the world and the people apparently lost in it' (Lambert 1956: n.p.).

One such lost soul is Joe Lampton, protagonist of John Braine's first novel, *Room at the Top* (1957). The narrative begins in 1946 with Joe moving both literally and metaphorically up in the world, from Dufton, a mill town huddled in a valley, to graciously appointed lodgings in suburban (or, perhaps more accurately in the text's topography, super-urban) Warley, right at T'Top of the town (Braine 1959: 9). Lampton is a grammar-school boy (148), a position Frank Musgrove's study, *Youth and the Social Order*, identifies to be 'at the point of maximum tension', because his 'role-conception is remote from the perceived role-expectations of adults and friends' (Musgrove 1964: 120). Although we are not told of a scholarship, we can further position Lampton as part of the 'larger group' of 'The Uprooted and the Anxious' whom Hoggart describes with a line from Matthew Arnold: caught 'between two worlds, one dead, the other powerless to be born' (Hoggart 1958: 249). Elsewhere, that same year, Lindsay Anderson has used the same line to describe the contemporary position of Socialists in *Declaration* (Anderson 1957: 164).

A similarly anxious sense of duality is generated within the novel by Joe's angstfully retrospective narration that recalls his younger self from 1956, a decade on:

> I look back at that raw young man sitting miserable in the pub with a feeling of genuine regret; I wouldn't, even if I could, change places with him, but he was indisputably a better person than the smooth character I am now, after ten years of getting almost everything that I ever wanted. I know the name he'd give me: the Successful Zombie. (Braine 1959: 123)

After a job as accountant at the town hall, Joe's social and economic aspiration drives him, by the novel's conclusion, to a forthcoming marriage to the glossy Susan Brown and a lucrative job with her father, Warley's richest entrepreneur. It also results in the moral degradation registered by the older, richer, zombified Joe, and his resignation that he 'cannot go back; with one part of himself he does not want to go back to a homeliness which was often narrow: with another part he longs for the membership he has lost' (Hoggart 1958: 250). The uprooted Joe's home is figured as nostalgically working-class, his thoroughly decent parents – his father with staunch Labour convictions, his mother charmingly garrulous – gathered together at their hearth every evening. It is also forever unavailable to him, lost in a 1941 bombing raid while Joe served as a 'Sergeant-Observer' in the RAF, spending the last two years of the war in Stalag 100, studying for his accountancy exams (Braine 1959: 148). The hearth, significantly, survives the bomb untouched (93). The settled fidelity of his parents' marriage is very far from the licentiousness of Warley's middle-class set, and from Joe's tawdrily priapic behaviour upon joining its amateur dramatics society. His moral decline is measured through his relationship with two women he meets there: beautiful and privileged Susan and older woman Alice Aisgill, unhappily married and as rootless and anxious as Joe himself.

It is not simply Joe Lampton's morality that has become corrupted in the decade between action and narration – the very language of the narrative itself has been taken over by the new climate of affluence and acquisition, as Joe calibrates everyone and everything according to the fetishistic standards of 'admass', or advertising-driven consumerism. Joe is attracted to Susan because, he says, she is 'conventionally pretty', and the source of these conventions is immediately revealed: 'she was like the girl in the American advertisements who is always being given a Hamilton watch or Cannon Percle (whatever that is) Sheets or Nash Airflyte Eight' (36). To say that Joe acquires Susan like just another consumer status symbol would be to belie the fraught and degrading nature of their 'courtship' (the inequality and inauthenticity of their relationship chafes against the term), which reaches a nadir in her rape and subsequent ecstatic celebration: 'Oh Joe, I love you with all of me now, every little bit of me is yours!' (199). Susan's triumphalism stems from her belief that her eventual surrender to Joe's attritional 'seduction' will secure her victory over the Other Woman. The honesty and equality of Joe's intellectual and physical relationship with Alice is reinforced by that fact that, during the central section of the novel when their love for each other is deepening, his relentless reference to the language of commodity capitalism is greatly diminished (Ferrebe 2005: 53). As a partner for Joe, and as a textual symbol, Alice is Susan's opposite, but this is no neat whore / Madonna dichotomy. Her unfettered sexuality throws Susan's faked and manipulative primness into relief, and, despite an 'angular fashion plate figure', the conspicuous and viscerally described imperfection of Alice's body with its big, sagging breasts is very far from Susan's poster-girl perkiness (Braine 1959: 48). Unlike most of the conspicuously middle-class consumers in Joe's new circle, Alice's own class background is more shady – she has what she calls 'low tastes' for '*real* beer' and salted crisps (55, 52). (Christine in *Lucky Jim* pours ketchup all over her cooked breakfast, signifying for Jim a similar authenticity of self; Amis 1976: 67). In other words, for Joe, Alice represents a return to origins, a figure of what Brook has called a 'turn to feeling as a way of combating the social and cultural effects of late capitalism' (Brook 2007: 8). 'As long as Alice was there,' Joe realises in a post-coital flush, 'I wouldn't die, it was like having my father and mother alive again, it was the end of being afraid and alone' (Braine 1959: 180).

Alice dies in a sensational car crash at the end of the novel, drunk and despairing after Joe has broken off their relationship in order to marry Susan. Market economics – Susan's glossy middle-class magazine aesthetic, her father's wealth and the crass narrative conclusions of pulp fiction – win out over the alternative system of mutual exchange glimpsed in Alice and Joe's affair. Hargreaves points out how many of the novel's citations of desirable consumer goods are anachronistic to the novel's setting but contemporary to its narration and publication. This makes Alice's car, Susan's watch, for instance:

> Easy to register for a culture that supposedly celebrates novelty and youth as the very index of contemporaneity, as Hoggart suggests in *The Uses of Literacy* ... Nobody has to try too hard to understand how modish this car is, how sexy or expensive this watch is, ... gratifyingly, it is all there for immediate consumption. *Room at the Top* is, then, a text that, like *The Uses of Literacy*, realizes and recognizes the new texture and material fabric of the 1950s. (Hargreaves 2011: 113)

The novel's representation of the end-stage of capitalism exhibits a kind of 'flatness' of history that parallels both the envisaged non-hierarchical classlessness of the consumer market and the stalled personal development of the monster it has created, Joe Lampton, 'Successful Zombie' (Braine 1959: 123). As well as its ahistoricity, and despite its closely documented Midlands setting, Stephen Wade considers *Room at the Top* to be 'anti-regional', 'concerned with insisting that the definable area has gone, and a featureless waste-land has stepped in' (Wade 2002: 137). The novel carries the logic of the consumer market that so infiltrates the language of its narration through to structure the narrative itself. *Room at the Top* ends with an epiphanic moment for Joe, distraught by Alice's death:

> 'Oh, God,' I said, 'I did kill her. I wasn't there, but I killed her.'
> Eva drew my head on to her breast. 'Poor darling, you mustn't take on so. You don't see it now, but it was all for the best. She'd have ruined your whole life. Nobody blames you, love. Nobody blames you.'
> I pulled myself away from her sharply. 'Oh my God,' I said, 'that's the trouble.' (Braine 1959: 235)

Yet the potential of Joe's realisation to effect change has already been negated by the resignation of his older, narrating self, rendering his identity as featureless as the landscape that Wade describes. In *The Writer and Commitment*, John Mander takes angry issue with this moral and chronological flatness as signifying its author's failure:

> We do not know where we are with Joe Lampton: is it the present Joe Lampton speaking or the Joe of the first months in Warley? The dialectical conflict between past action and present reflection might have been used to comment on Joe's character and on his actions in the novel. (Mander 1961: 193)

Yet it is precisely this lack of comment that makes Braine's political point about his hero. By losing his working-class roots and the woman who reconnected him to them, and entering a new society devoid of moral foundation, Joe Lampton ends the novel as he began it, trapped 'between two worlds, one dead, the other powerless to be born'.

Changing One's Voice

D. J. Taylor's assertion in 2008 that Alan Sillitoe was 'almost single-handedly responsible for a shift in the way working-class characters found themselves represented in literature' was echoed across the writer's obituaries in 2010. In a review article in the *Guardian*, Taylor argued that it was Arthur Seaton, hero of Sillitoe's novel, *Saturday Night and Sunday Morning* (1958) and its subsequent 1960 film version, who caused the shift away from presiding literary models of the working class. These ranged, he suggested, from 'the decently downtrodden house painters' of Robert Tressell's *The Ragged-Trousered Philanthropists* (first published in 1914 but first unabridged in 1955), through the heroic but cowed unemployed factory workers of Walter Greenwood's *Love on the Dole* (1933), to George Orwell's vision amidst the determinedly realist documentary of the 1937 *The Road to Wigan Pier* of 'the perfect symmetry' of a back-street life in which 'Father, in shirt sleeves, sits in the rocking chair at one side of the fire reading the racing finals, and Mother sits on the other side with her sewing' (Orwell 2001: 108). (We might also add the first half of D. H. Lawrence's *Sons and Lovers*.) 'Set against these "good" working-class characters, whether actively virtuous, patiently resigned or indifferently ground-down,' Taylor claims, 'Arthur Seaton is a horribly ambiguous figure' (Taylor 2008: 21).

As Hoggart's study, and the debate around it that still rages today (see Bailey 2011, Hanley 2009, Owen 2008) attest, this idea of representing a class, and the working one in particular, is a complex and deeply felt one. Nigel Gray is vitriolic about what he reads as Sillitoe's cowardice and cliché in creating the character of Arthur, whose much-touted rebelliousness amounts to no more than the verbal abuse of the ruling class while he proffers his labour, rent and taxes. 'That's what Sillitoe calls class cunning,' Gray complains. 'Doing what you're told'; and he pronounces the author to be 'too much taken with the working-class hero cult' (Gray 1973: 129, 113). Ritchie reads this ultimate conformity as the point behind the character's presentation, conveying as it does 'the constant swaggering and the fantasies of destructive protest of someone whose main concern is always to come out on top but who knows he is ruled by "Them" in authority' (Ritchie 1988: 191). Certainly, Arthur's success as the hero of the novel relies upon his readers' judgement that, for all his violence, selfishness and misogyny, he is, in Joe Lampton's parlance, 'indisputably a better person' on some fundamental level than those around him (Braine 1959: 123). For the reviewer of the *Manchester Guardian*, the book has 'a glow about it as though he had plugged in to some basic source of the working-class spirit' (Perrott 1958: 4). Arthur's own value system functions in exactly the same way:

> Arthur did not assess men on their knowledge or achievement, but by a blind and passionate method that weighed their more basic worth. It was an emotional gauge, always accurate when set by him, and those to whom it was applied either passed or did not pass the test. (Sillitoe 1960: 34)

Leaving these emotive issues aside, the textual structure and voice of *Saturday Night and Sunday Morning*, and the ambiguity that they inarguably display, provide a synthesis of the class and aesthetic conflicts of 1950s writing that have been raised in this chapter. Though written predominantly in the third person and focalised through Arthur, the novel's narration comprises two very different registers. One of Arthur's numerous affairs is with Brenda, and when she asks him for an excuse to feed to her husband to disguise their illicit time together, he promptly provides one. We are told, 'It was simple and explicit, because he had not thought about it. If he gave things too much thought they did not turn out so well' (45). This sentiment, and the simple terms in which it is couched, aptly describe one narrative mode, which, in giving vent to Arthur's atavistic anger and desires, garners much of the novel's fabled (and frequently misogynistic) energy: 'Dave got a woman into trouble who had turned out to be the worst kind of tart, a thin, vicious, rat-face whore who tried to skin him for every penny he'd got' (65). The other mode is a more traditionally controlling narrative voice, that can interpret a drunk throwing a beer mug through the window of an undertakers in these eloquently apocalyptic terms: 'Arthur was stirred by the sound of breaking glass: it synthesised all the anarchism within him, was the most perfect and suitable noise to accompany the end of the world and himself' (93). Sillitoe suggested in interview that the keenest problem facing him in writing the novel was 'how to write a book about a man who hadn't read a book' (Allsop 1965: 60) – he himself, he claimed, had 'read nothing that was adult till I was twenty' (Ritchie 1988: 185). It is the dual narration, and the kind of 'double relationship' it generates between hero and reader, that address this problem directly.

By the fifteenth chapter of the novel, the rumbustious and promiscuous events that characterise Arthur's Saturday nights are left behind for the relative calm of a Sunday morning. The chapter opens with a few rare paragraphs in which Arthur's voice reaches his reader without the mediation of the third-person narrative. Tellingly, this is the most-cited part of the book, conforming as it does to the idea of a new, angry voice in 1950s British fiction: 'Once a rebel, always a rebel. You can't help being one. You can't deny that. And it's best to be a rebel so as to show 'em it don't pay to do you down' (176). Arthur's 'you' idiom, however, is used regularly throughout the novel, working to persuade the reader of a shared understanding (Ferrebe 2005: 30), and this passage of direct address by the working-class hero is immediately followed by one from his narrator, who reworks Arthur's sentiments into more traditionally literary language:

> If he was not pursuing his rebellion against the rules of love, or distilling them with rules of war, there was still the vast crushing power of government against which to lean his white-skinned bony shoulder, a thousand of its laws to be ignored and therefore broken. (Sillitoe 1960: 177)

This is not to criticise Sillitoe for 'selling out' (as Gray so determinedly does), but rather to recognise his technique to be not just an engagement with the personal, ethical dilemmas explored above by Williams, Hoggart, Wesker, Anderson and Braine, but a creative response to a literary establishment staffed and patronised almost exclusively by the middle classes. In other words, Sillitoe's problem was not just that of 'how to write a book about a man who hadn't read a book', but how to write that book in order for it to be read by men (sic) who had read many others. In Chapter 8 we noted how George Lamming's work – Sam Selvon's too, to a lesser extent – might best be classified as 'immigrant', rather than 'emigrant' literature, written as it necessarily was for a white middle-class readership. The pronounced modernist tendencies of *The Emigrants*, as well, of course, as the colour of Lamming's skin, excluded him from all but the most niche of literary markets during this decade. Yet Sillitoe and Braine, through their responsiveness to the nature of the market available for their work, and the double relationship they attended to in their narratives (together with, it must be admitted, the success of the film versions), ensured the voices of their heroes were widely heard. That, as Harry Ritchie points out, the literary sensation surrounding Alan Sillitoe took longer to accrue due to the inherent class bias of the critical establishment (Ritchie 1988: 197–8) only reinforces the significance of his achievement.

It was linguist Alan S. C. Ross who coined the idea of 'U' and 'Non-U' usage in 1954. Writing on the subject of '*Changing one's voice*', he asserted confidently that

In England today – just as much as in the England of many years ago – the question 'Can a non-U speaker become a U-speaker?' is one noticeably of paramount importance for many Englishmen (and for some of their wives). The answer is that an adult can never attain complete success. (Ross 1960: 28–9)

This finality over the impossibility of voices crossing classes, and the inherent assumption of the expressive inferiority of lower-class speech, flattered the snobberies of the likes of Waugh and Mitford, as we have seen. Yet the new registers forged to express working- and middle-class experience and the vertiginousness of affluence and social mobility during the 1950s confounded such hide-bound certainties. *Saturday Night and Sunday Morning* and *Room at the Top* were novels that changed the voice of literature in Britain forever.

IV.

Other Uses of Literacy

Chapter Eleven

Criticism Under Scrutiny

American poet Randall Jarrell, himself a dauntingly acerbic literary critic, claimed in 1955 to be writing during 'The Age of Criticism'. 'There has never been an age', he asserted with characteristic humour, 'in which so much good criticism has been written – or so *much* bad; and both of them have become, among "serious readers", astonishingly or appallingly influential.' Across the pond in Britain, this zeitgeist certainly holds true for a decade in which the debate surrounding the position of literary criticism within the wider culture had become a territorial skirmish among those Jarrell called 'our most conscious and, perhaps, most troubled readers . . . cultivated or academic folk, intellectuals' (Jarrell 1973: 72). Several different factions of these 'serious readers' were in the fight. Each upheld criticism as an essentially public discourse but inflected this idea of 'public' in different ways. One considered it a role for an inherently intelligent elite, whose intellectual discernment in matters literary set them apart from the labile masses. For another, the powerful cultural position of critic was hard-won and formally professionalised, as the ranks of scholarship boys (for they were, in the main, male) rose, according to merit, to their proper places in the newly expanded university system and an increasingly buoyant literary market. 'It takes a long time to learn to become a critic, and I have only been at it for ten years,' wrote John Wain in 1957 (Wain 1957c: x). To their detractors, this group displayed 'the dull managerial qualities of the State bureaucracy which had supposedly supervised the ascent of the group' (Ritchie 1988: 116–17). Allsop wrote of Wain that he was 'undoubtedly the most over-rated writer of the Fifties, and stands as a lesson in present-day careerism – how, if he is aggressive enough about it, a writer can get himself accepted at his own evaluation, irrespective of talent' (Allsop 1968: 68). For yet another faction, prestige was still harder won outside the Academy by a new generation of journalists and other media types writing against what they considered to be the high cultural consensus perpetrated by the first, and older, group. We might, as a very broad sketch, think of these competing factions as upholding an agenda for criticism characterised by, respectively, intellectualism, professionalism and commercialism. A glance at just one of the combatants, John Wain (he whom Allsop so decried) – born in Stoke-on-Trent, Oxford-educated, teacher at the University of Reading and a prolific journalist, as well as a novelist and poet – already suggests the divisions to be irreparably, but revealingly, porous. None the less, this chapter attempts to confine itself to the territory of those first two groupings, while the next chapter addresses the last grouping.

Under the definition of the term established since (and we might debate this if space allowed), criticism in the 1950s in Britain was pre-theoretical. Yet its discussions were punctuated with reference to a variety of book-length manifestos for critical thinking, some but not all published during the decade itself. George Orwell's writing provided many writers with an exemplar of plain speaking / writing, but this was the 'straight' documentary Orwell of *The Road to Wigan Pier* (1937), rather than the more symbolic social science fiction of *Nineteen Eighty-Four* (1949). As we have seen in a previous chapter, A. J. Ayer's *Language, Truth and Logic* (1936), with its championing of an empirical language rooted in real experience, was also an important influence. William Empson's *Seven Types of Ambiguity* (1930), with its celebration of the ambiguity inherent in English literary language, and the resultant cherished irony available to those witty enough to unpick it, influenced the Movement in particular in both its poetry and prose. In 'Ambiguous Gifts', a 1950 essay in (the last) *Penguin New Writing*, Wain claimed fulsomely that 'The plain fact is that many of the reputations which to-day occupy the poetic limelight are such as would crumble immediately if poetry such as Empson's, with its passion, logic, and formal beauty, were to become widely known' (Wain 1950: 127). In his study, *The Movement*, Blake Morrison notes a sharpish turn against Empson from the mid-1950s onwards; D. J. Enright's introduction to *Poets of the 1950s* criticises Empson's 'cold-bloodedly mathematical' approach (Empson's first undergraduate degree, from Cambridge, was in mathematics). He suggests that 'the fallacy of "Empsonianism"' was its 'assumption that triviality or banality, if expressed ambiguously, changes into significant profundity' (Enright 1955: 7). Yet it was the work of F. R. Leavis that forms the fulcrum of debate surrounding the role of criticism in Britain during the 1950s.

Certainly the idealisation of a small, young(ish), academic, sympathetic audience by the Movement poets chimes with a Leavisite ideal. Reading Donald Davie's poetic manifesto, *Purity of Diction in English*

Verse (1952), one would be forgiven for thinking that the Movement writers approached Leavis's work with an unqualified obsequiousness. Davie references Leavis only ever to agree with him, his only challenge a coy one of covert comedy in the metaphors Leavis uses to describe Dr Johnson: 'Must I think that Dr. Leavis is being impish?' (Davie 1952: 38n). Yet Leavis's kinship with the generation of critics following him was as complicated as his relationship with the group of older intellectuals of which he was nominally a part. From the mid-1930s to the early 1950s, while teaching at Downing College, Cambridge, Frank Raymond Leavis had produced a series of essays re-mapping English Literature from Shakespeare and Donne to the Victorian era, and he and his wife, Queenie Roth, had founded the literary journal, *Scrutiny*. This quarterly ran until 1953, and its limited circulation (rising to only 1,500 copies in its 1950s heyday) belied its enormous influence on teaching and thinking about literature in universities during the period. Leavis published *The Common Pursuit*, a manifesto of the critic's proper task of 'the common pursuit of true judgment', in T. S. Eliot's phrase, that same year, and *D. H. Lawrence: Novelist* in 1955, thereafter making the public lecture and published letter his favoured platform. This new means of expression was to culminate in a notorious 1962 lecture replying (albeit rather belatedly) to C. P. Snow's 1959 warning of a dangerous gulf between the 'two cultures' of the arts and sciences, in which Leavis berated the novelist and government adviser on science as a figurehead of the demise of contemporary society. 'The intellectual nullity', he claimed with awesome rudeness, 'is what constitutes any difficulty there may be in dealing with Snow's panoptic pseudo-cogencies, his parade of a thesis: a mind to be argued with—that is not there; what we have is something other.' He then went on to demolish any literary pretensions Snow, author of the lengthy and still expanding *Strangers and Brothers* sequence, might have: 'As a novelist he doesn't exist; he doesn't begin to exist. He can't be said to know what a novel is' (Leavis 1972: 44, 45).

The quite breathtaking intellectualist snobbery evidenced in Leavis's treatment of Snow, however, came in spite, or perhaps because, of a problematic place within the ivory tower he so viciously defended. Between 1931 and 1936 he was passed over several times at Cambridge for appointment to a lectureship; when this did come about in 1936, it was on a part-time basis only until 1946. It took until 1959 for Leavis to be promoted to Reader, a position that, within university hierarchies, went only some way towards recognising the international reputation he had accrued, however belligerent it might be. When *Scrutiny* closed in 1953, Leavis blamed it on his 'utter defeat at Cambridge' (quoted in Jameson 1970: 297). His withering critique of Snow's writing has been regularly matched by critics of his own notoriously indirect style, crammed as it is with parentheses and sub-clauses. As Frances Mulhern puts it, 'Leavis writes badly. That objection was made by his earliest reviewers and it has been repeated a thousand times since. His prose is gnarled, jagged, convoluted, a danger to itself at times – in short, not well written' (Mulhern 1995: 80). Ironically, too, in the light of his later critique of Snow, Leavis relies almost as much on economic metaphors as he does on those of battle. These seem to capture one of the key contradictions of Leavis's thought (as well, perhaps, of that of a capitalist society *per se*) – the idea that money corrupts the sense of value co-existing with an impulse towards rationalisation in order to secure 'true' value (for money). As Gary Day puts it, 'Leavis may have associated literature with "life", with what cannot be measured or precisely defined, but his logic belongs to that of scientific management which disregards human significance in the interests of what can be quantified' (Day 1996: xiii).

That 'life' belongs to another value set of vocabulary for Leavis – alongside words such as 'real' and 'there' (or, in the case of his judgement on Snow, 'not there') – it is loaded with a significance that is never fully explained. It is these plain terms, of course, that pepper the expositions of both the conflicted empiricism of Movement writers, in Conquest's introduction to *New Lines*, for example, and the (occasionally mystic) realism of Hoggart and Williams: two key sections of *The Uses of Literacy* are entitled 'The "Real" World of People' and 'The Full Rich Life' (Hoggart 1958: xii). Though it saw the death of *Scrutiny* (and before that, the end of *Penguin New Writing* and Cyril Connolly's *Horizon*, both in 1950), the Age of Criticism was driven by debates surrounding a number of new journals. *Encounter*, which began in 1953, while nominally upholding a need for plain speaking, did so in a tone that was markedly declamatory and self-consciously intellectual. Its first editorial, 'After the Apocalypse', by Stephen Spender and Irving Kristol, proclaimed:

> Now, perhaps, words will again mean what they say, and we shall be spared the tedious sophistry by which despotism could pose as a higher form of freedom, murder as a supreme humanism. Now, perhaps, we shall no longer be plagued by the rhetoric of a messianic arrogance of the spirit which has blithely perpetrated so many hideous crimes against the flesh. (Spender and Kristol 1953: 1)

Its initial inclusion of contributions from, amongst others, Virginia Woolf, Cecil Day Lewis and Edith Sitwell made it difficult to recognise as the fresh intellectual beginning it claimed for itself, as did the proclamation in the second, November, issue, of its policy *not* to publish any of the young contributors to John Wain's new literary radio show, *First Reading*. Spender's article 'On Literary Movements' castigates the members of what he calls 'a rebellion of the Lower Middle Brows' for their embarrassment at the title of 'don', which, as lecturers, many of them could claim: 'This capacity for being amusingly embarrassed evidently derives from Cambridge – from Dr. F. R. Leavis's anti-university Cambridge where the Leavisites devote some of their critical faculties to being embarrassed much as the Quakers did to quaking' (Spender 1953: 66, 67). (*Encounter*'s moral authority was rather diminished when it was later revealed to be funded in large part by the United States Central Intelligence Agency, albeit without the knowledge of the editorial team.) *Essays in Criticism*, which began in 1951, presented itself as a more 'scholarly' (read 'professionalised') version of *Scrutiny*, while *Critical Quarterly* (from 1959) was more straightforwardly intended as its successor, and included in its first volume a symposium on 'Our Debt to Dr Leavis'. Raymond Williams opened his contribution with 'We must try to pay our debt to F. R. Leavis, whether or not he will acknowledge us as debtors' (Williams 1959: 245).

Williams's somewhat hangdog demeanour here provides a telling indicator of the profoundly conflicted attitude to Leavis's influence on the new cultural initiatives of the 1950s, and one which is at odds with that oft-cited vision of an army of Leavisites marshalling the expansion of education through into the Sixties. We might pinpoint the centre of this conflict as being at one debate in particular: that of the role of context within literary criticism. Leavis had a different term for it; in his preface to *The Common Pursuit*, he bemoaned the fact that

> No one seriously interested can have failed to perceive that, where the critical function is concerned, what peculiarly characterizes our time in England is the almost complete triumph of the 'social' (or the 'associational') values over those which are the business of the critic. (Leavis 1962: vi)

Later in the volume, in the essay 'Sociology and Literature', he contests that

> No 'sociology of literature' and no attempt to relate literary studies with sociological will yield much profit unless informed and controlled by a real and intelligent interest – a first-hand critical interest – in literature. That is, no use of literature is of any use unless it is a real use. (198)

A metaphor combining the martial with the economic ('yield much profit') and that plain but emphatic 'real use' mark this as a particularly vital issue. Yet though Leavis has often been read as denying any role for contextual information in literary interpretations, he is explicit in this essay in his refutation of the idea that

> a serious interest in literature can confine itself to the kind of intensive local analysis associated with 'practical criticism' – to the scrutiny of the 'words on the page' in their minute relations, their effects of imagery, and so on: a real literary interest is an interest in man, society and civilization, and its boundaries cannot be drawn. (200)

Storer argues that

> The reason he is not usually credited with an interest in context is because Eliot's essay [that is, 'Tradition and the Individual Talent'] allowed him to conceptualise context – the 'social' – in terms different from those which critics usually have in mind when they insist on context. He did not conceptualise it in political terms (that is, in terms of the distribution of economic power between different social groups at a particular moment in history) but more in terms of what Eliot called an 'ideal order'. (Storer 2009: 59)

Leavis's idealised conception of the social and its relationship to literature certainly jarred with that of F. W. Bateson, editor of *Essays in Criticism*, who initiated perhaps the most striking example of this debate surrounding context during the 1950s. Bateson was a friend of John Wain's, an early publisher of Davie's poetry in his journal, and had supervised Kingsley Amis's B.Litt at Oxford. He later described his book *English Poetry* (1950) as the 'by-product of the tutorials and weekly seminars I held with that idealistic first post-war generation' (Bateson 1966: ix) – such an ascendancy is apparent in its assertion of the primacy of clarity and intelligibility within poetry. In the 1953 editorial essay 'The Function of Criticism at the Present Time', Bateson set out to delineate what he called 'the English-speaking critic's business today, here and now, in the 1950s' (Bateson 1953: 1). This was, he claimed, by no means the same business as that of 'such men as T. S. Eliot, J. Middleton Murry, I. A. Richards, John Crowe Ransom, Kenneth Burke, F. R. Leavis, C. S. Lewis, G. Wilson Knight, William Empson and Yvor Winters', who, though they represented 'probably the best of the older critics', were all culpable of 'critical defects' that 'can be summed up in the one word *irresponsibility*' (3). 'In so far as Messrs. Richards, Lewis, Empson and Ransom are chargeable with irresponsibility,' Bateson continues, 'it follows that they are, as professing critics, implicitly abusing their social function' (12). In the spring edition of the still-existent *Scrutiny*, Leavis was quick to take up the cudgels against *Essays in Criticism* and what he called 'the long statement of position and elaboration of programme contributed to the issue for January this year by the Editor' (Leavis 1953: 162). Seizing upon Bateson's contextualised reading of Pope's *Dunciad*, Leavis spits that 'It is impossible not to comment severely on the gratuitousness, the flimsy and fanciful arbitrariness, of what Mr. Bateson then offers us as summaries of the implicit "social contexts" (and his "social" is a term we need to note)' (172–3). Though he reiterates an earlier claim that 'the study of literature should be associated with extra-literary studies' (174), Leavis emphasises that criticism should never become dependent upon the context of literature, and he goes on to claim that '"social" is an insidious word' (176) – almost as insidious, we might suspect, as Leavis's term 'organic community' becomes to Williams and Hoggart, in the vanguard of a new critical discipline altogether.

Richard Storer suggests that 'Leavis's main contribution to "Cultural Studies" . . . is probably the negative one of giving "Cultural Studies" something to define itself against' (Storer 2009: 44): namely, a particular, and high, conception of what culture is. Yet, as is so often the case when we confront the wide and frequently contradictory sweep of Leavisite thinking, this is something of a false dichotomy. During the 1950s in particular, what is more noteworthy is the way in which Leavis's greatest younger champions, the Movement set, became so swiftly some of his greatest detractors – 'for me, as for many of my generation, Leavis is the god that failed,' wrote Donald Davie twenty or so years on (Davie 1976: 1233). However, it is in the work of his staunchest younger critics – Raymond Williams in particular, whose utter refutation of the idea of the concept of the organic community we considered in Chapter 9 – that some of Leavis's most fundamental principles of the role of literature and criticism within society are upheld. Hoggart and Williams certainly had a wider conception of what constituted cultural forms than Leavis, but there is no easy continuum here from a traditional Leavis to the radical pair of 'scholarship boys'; just as Leavis's thought could be radical, so both Hoggart and Williams harbour a strong streak of cultural conservatism. We began this chapter with a division of the interests surrounding literary criticism in the 1950s into intellectual, professional and commercial. As Storer suggests, 'Leavis believed . . . that criticism should be located between the academic and the journalistic, and that to speak in that space was the most important modern function of the university' (Storer 2009: 4).

Chapter Twelve

The Dedicated Man: Publishing, Media and Reviewing

In an interview entitled 'My Genius', Colin Wilson contended that 'Any man of real genius must be prepared to take on the most difficult forms of self-expression, such as the newspapers' (Farson 1957: 24). Around 28 May 1956, the publication date of his first book, *The Outsider*, assertions of Wilson's intellectual superiority sounded loudly in his cacophonous rise to fame. By the autumn of the following year, however, such claims had a profoundly vainglorious ring. As Allsop put it, 'Wilson's parabola, 1956–7, was spectacular,' and, as such, it provides an instructive study in the role of journalism in literary criticism during the 1950s (Allsop 1958:148–9). Born in Leicester in 1931, Wilson was a scholarship boy, but his commitment dwindled at the Gateway Secondary Technical School, and he left at 16 to work in various factories and conduct his own, eclectic, education. *The Outsider*, first product of this autodidacticism, was a farrago of literary interpretations, hero worship, wild philosophical deductions, potted biographies and pop-psychological analyses of selective life events from some ostentatiously selected lives. The critics (or a specific section of them – those with the refined sensibilities dubbed 'Mandarin' after the upper echelons of Imperial China) *loved* it. The cover of the first edition was lavished with the commendation of Mandarin doyenne Edith Sitwell, who had read the book in proof, pronouncing it 'astonishing' and Wilson 'a truly great writer'. Philip Toynbee, reviewing for the *Observer*, called it 'an exhaustive and luminously intelligent study of a representative theme of our time, and what makes the book truly astounding is that its alarmingly well-read author is only twenty-four years old' (Toynbee 1956: 14). That 'representative theme', or Wilson's take on it, stood in direct opposition to the positivist plain speaking of the Movement (Jim Dixon would have pulled his Edith Sitwell face in response to it):

The problem for the 'civilization' is the adoption of a religious attitude that can be assimilated as *objectively* as the headlines of last Sunday's newspapers. But the problem for the individual always will be the opposite of this, the conscious striving *not* to limit the amount of experience seen and touched; the intolerable struggle to expose the sensitive areas of being to what may possibly hurt them; the attempt to see as a whole ... The individual begins that long effort as an Outsider; he may finish it as a saint. (Wilson 1957: 281)

A. J. Ayer, who had popularised the 'principle of verification', or the idea that a sentence had meaning only if it was either analytic or empirically verifiable, unsurprisingly reviled the book. Taking issue with the swathes of reviews hymning Wilson's precocity, his own, in *Encounter*, began with the assertion that 'His book is not very good, but it is serious; and it deserves to be assessed on its own merits. I assume Mr. Wilson would himself prefer this to receiving compliments upon his youth' (Ayer 1956: 75). Ayer takes serious issue with Wilson's methods – with his plethora of sources, which make 'his concept of the Outsider annoyingly protean', and with his lack of evidence:

Though Mr. Wilson assumes, apparently on *a priori* grounds, that the great mass of people, the despised *bourgeoisie*, who work at regular jobs, are living the lives of automata, I have no doubt that if one could undertake the research one would find that it was not at all uncommon for them to be interested in the question of how they should live. (75)

In *Language, Truth and Logic*, the work he was later to call 'in every sense a young man's book' (Ayer 1967: 5), Ayer had stated that 'the assertion that there is a god is nonsensical' (115). By 1956 he had mellowed a little, saying of Wilson's religious aspirations that 'I am sure that mystical experiences are very well worth having, but so are many other things.' But speaking of *The Outsider*, he continues that 'What is quite unwarranted is the assumption, which Mr. Wilson is disposed to make, that the world that the mystic inhabits is somehow objectively more "real" than the world of common sense' (Ayer 1956: 76). He ends dolefully, 'I hope ... he does not think that there is anything exceptionally meritorious in constantly brooding over the state of one's own soul' (77) – redundantly, too, for Wilson and his many supporters so clearly did. Yet such nay-saying did little to halt sales, even if, as Allsop suggests, 'a large proportion were "furniture sales", copies bought for casual, conspicuous display in the current gamesmanship stakes' (Allsop 1958: 150). The 5,000–copy initial print run sold out on the day of publication, the second impression within three days of that. By October, when Ayer's review came out, 20,000 copies had been sold in hardback, and *The Outsider* continued to sell at a high rate well into the following year (Ritchie 1988: 144, 146). Ritchie is decisive on the driving force of Wilson's extraordinary debut: 'Wilson owed his success to the Mandarins and for two main reasons: first, they were obviously susceptible to the *sort* of nonsense he wrote, and second, he seemed to offer the kind of young talent they desperately wanted to find' (175).

Yet a substantial and increasing portion of Wilson's fame was not under the beneficent control of the literary Establishment, buffing their own figurehead of youth. Initially the press had bought and were selling the scruffy romance of the book's genesis; written during the day in the British Museum Reading Room, while its author slept at night in a sleeping bag on Hampstead Heath – it is a blurb that endures into Wilson's introduction to its reissue in 2001 (Wilson 2001: 1). Yet by the end of the year, popular press had turned bad. Wilson had confessed *The Outsider* to be a fraud (*Daily Express*, 5 December); he had abandoned his wife and 5–year-old son without a share of his new-found wealth (*Sunday Pictorial*, 16 December); and the parents of his girlfriend, Joy Stewart, had stormed Wilson's flat to save their daughter from the pornographic clutches of the monster revealed in the diaries of his they had read (*Daily Express, Evening Standard* and *Daily Mail*, 20 February 1957). Presumably in the name of his fearless quest for honesty, Wilson handed his diaries over to the *Daily Mail*, who mockingly published a selection of self-aggrandising extracts three days later. In tandem with this souring of his celebrity, Wilson was also undergoing a backlash against his scholasticism. Critic John Carswell wrote to the editor of the *Times Literary Supplement* on 14 December 1956, having examined a sample of forty-six quotations in *The Outsider* to find 82 major and 203 minor errors of citation. Carswell's letter dismisses Wilson himself as wholly unimportant, arguing that:

> What does matter is that such a gallimaufry of misquotation and the standards it implies should have been passed into edition after edition (I used the fourth) by a reputable publisher; and greeted with enthusiasm by many (you, Sir, were not among them) whose business it is to guide the public taste. (Carswell 1956: 749)

Wilson's sequel, entitled *Religion and the Rebel*, met with universal critical condemnation only a year after the parabola of his fame had begun.

Carswell is not alone, in the alleged Age of Criticism, in bemoaning the state of that criticism. Randall Jarrell, who coined the phrase, complained that a great deal of criticism 'might just as well have been written by a syndicate of encyclopedias for an audience of International Business Machines' (Jarrell 1973: 73), while in his survey, *The Modern*

Writer and His World, G. S. Fraser noted how current 'little magazines' reflect

> the workings of a kind of intellectual stock exchange: month by month one discovers that Existentialism is flagging, that Freud is steady but Jung is rising, that there are few buyers of Marx, but that some hardy spirits are risking a belated flutter in Surrealism. (Fraser 1953: 338)

Corrupted by the pseudo-critical work of the popular press, criticism has become a different industry for these commentators, or rather, as their commercial metaphors signal, the fact that it is an industry at all is a cause of anxiety. In the previous chapter we noted the importance of book-length critical and philosophical manifestos in the shaping of British criticism during the early 1950s. Towards the end of the decade this situation is markedly different, with Tom Maschler's edited collection, *Declaration* (1957), a case in point. Intended as a crescendo to the angry social protest of a new generation, the essays are instead mismatched ineffectual rants on topics as diverse and tepid as the over-privilege of monarchy (Osborne) and the Will to Power (Stuart Holroyd). In his contribution, 'Beyond the Outsider', Wilson begins by stating how 'the idea of writing a credo seemed unreasonable,' but attempts it all the same, with a rehashing of his two books (Maschler 1957: 31). Ritchie calls the collection 'the ill-fated climax of the AYM's contentious reputation as social rebels and protesters', and it is inarguably proof of his thesis that any intellectual cohesion of the Angry literary phenomenon was to a large extent the product of media hype (Ritchie 1988: 42).

Yet, in 1950s terms, *Declaration* was still a publishing success. Published in August, it had sold 25,000 by the end of the year, and sales picked up again when the BBC's new television arts programme, *Monitor*, included a discussion of the book on 16 February 1958. A key contribution to the Angry hype, and one that demonstrates the increasingly porous division between academic criticism and journalism, was Philip Oakes's 1956 *Observer* article, 'A New Style in Heroes', in which he claimed that the new 'movement' in writing was more widespread than was usually believed, extending it to include 'Theatre, film and television critics, mostly around thirty' (Oakes 1956: 8). With its inclusion of essays by theatre critic and script advisor Tynan and film critic and maker of film and television programmes Lindsay Anderson (the biographical notes emphasise these credentials), *Declaration* embodies Oakes's point. Its immediate outdatedness as a statement of the zeitgeist also signals the way in which the 1950s marked a distinct acceleration in the pace of cultural debate. Criticism, and publishing more generally, had become a multi-media experience.

Initially, of course, radio was the dominant means of promoting literary writing outside the print media. Wain's *First Reading*, first broadcast on the Third Programme on 26 April 1953, played a key role in forming the sense of a Movement amongst emerging writers, and began with a long extract from the still-unpublished *Lucky Jim*, featuring the hungover Dixon accidentally burning his host's guest bed. The only professional affirmation that Alan Sillitoe had seen for a long time, despite moving to Majorca to dedicate himself to writing from the beginning of 1952, was 'Kedah Peak' being accepted as a radio talk. What Ritchie identifies as Sillitoe's 'first notable success' was finally broadcast on the Home Service in April 1957, once its author had eventually saved his passage home in order to record it (Ritchie 1988: 186). As the decade progressed, it was television that became increasingly important as an opinion prompter on matters literary. Colin Wilson first appeared on television in interview with Daniel Farson for ITV's *This Week* on 17 August 1956, and the BBC invited him to contribute a series of radio talks, beginning on 30 September of that year with *What I Believe*. On 18 June 1956, Brendan Behan appeared on *Panorama* to discuss his play *The Quare Fellow*. Despite a BBC spokesperson's later efforts to convince reporters that he was 'extremely nervous', rather delectably from the point of view of his bad boy image (at sixteen, IRA member Behan had spent three years in Borstal for attempting to blow up Liverpool's docks), it was apparent to viewers that he was very drunk. John Braine appeared in a more coherent form with Woodrow Wyatt on *Panorama* on 8 April 1957, and 12,000 copies of *Room at the Top* were reputedly sold as a direct result (Ritchie 1988: 37).

Yet the big screen trumped even the selling power of television. An inauspicious start to the films-of-the-books of the 1950s was *Lucky Jim*, which came out in 1957. Patrick Campbell's screenplay managed to reduce Amis's novel to a witless farce, from its opening snide screen reading: 'A REDBRICK UNIVERSITY IN BRITAIN'S NEW ELIZABETHAN AGE: HERE ARE MOULDED THE INTELLECTUAL DRAKES AND RALEIGHS OF TOMORROW – FEARLESS, INDEPENDENT – [next screen] – 'AND STATE SUPPORTED.' However, 1959 saw the release of *Room at the Top*, and Shelagh Delaney receiving the then dizzying sum of £20,000 for the film rights to *A Taste of Honey*, which was produced by John Osborne's new company, Woodfall Productions, in 1961, and released on the back of their success with the Sillitoe-scripted film of *Saturday Night and Sunday Morning* (1960). Lindsay Anderson's *Declaration* essay, 'Get Out and Push!', included a spoof composite of Jack Warner's most famous leading film roles during the Forties (in *Holiday Camp* and *The*

Blue Lamp), whose muted emotional responses, he raged, were greeted by 'Polite critical applause for another piece of truly British understatement. English film makers, to quote Roy Campbell, use the snaffle and the bit all right – but where's the bloody horse?' (Anderson 1957: 158).[1] The cinematic New Wave that was cresting at the end of the 1950s, though short-lived, broke all such taboos, and revolutionised the British industry.

Braine's *Room at the Top* had received a notable boost in sales from rave reviews in 'capitalism's dedicated publicists', the *Daily* and *Sunday Express*; released in March 1957, it was serialised in the daily paper from 22 April (Ritchie 1988: 37). Yet, however sensationalist this publicity, it could not match that generated by the film release. Penguin published the novel in paperback the month after the premiere in January 1959, in what now seems a distinctly understated copy featuring a bland black-and-white picture of Laurence Harvey as Joe Lampton between the already classic orange cover bands. Resultant sales, however, were far from restrained: 300,000 copies within three months of publication (62). Braine's novel in hardback, however, had already been a (relative) best-seller (40,000 copies in the preceding two years), while Alan Sillitoe's *Saturday Night and Sunday Morning* was one of the first British novels to gain an enduring reputation through its filmic, rather than printed, version. Despite solidly approving reviews, the hardback had sold only 8,000 copies in two years, but Pan printed 150,000 paperback copies to coincide with the film's release in November. Three months later, 750,000 copies had been sold, and within a year of the Pan imprint, Arthur Seaton's story became one of the first five-million-selling paperbacks in Britain. Not only did the novel achieve its richly deserved (and rather delayed) fame by being one of the first books-of-the-film-of-the-book, but Sillitoe was the beneficiary of a vital new development in British publishing during the 1950s which cut the time lag between publications in hard and soft covers from at least five years to less than two. *Lucky Jim*, for example, published in hardback in 1954, waited six years for its paperback edition. Pan published Sillitoe's short story collection, *The Loneliness of the Long-Distance Runner*, in October 1960, just thirteen months after the hardback (189). The increasing dominance of newspaper criticism over and above journals on the literary debate during the decade can be most accurately attributed to this speeding up of British culture.

Literary texts are always presented with certain 'accompanying productions' – their titles, their covers, the author's name, for example – and it is this framing paraphernalia that Gérard Genette has termed 'the paratext' (Genette 1997). Ian Brookes has explored the revealing dissonance between the genteel dust jacket of the first, hardback, edition of *Saturday Night and Sunday Morning*, with its muted watercolour by Mona Moore, and the cover of the 1960 Pan paperback, with a dramatic graphic design referencing the American crime fiction so popular in Britain through the 1940s and 1950s (Brookes 2009). Pan, who had been publishing the James Bond series since 1955, knew how to present a book as if it were pulp, drawing in a completely new readership from that of W. H. Allen's self-consciously literary jacket. Putting the meek and monochrome image of Laurence Harvey as Joe Lampton to shame, Albert Finney bestrides Pan's paper cover in a challenging pose; as Brookes suggests, 'About to light a cigarette, the figure appears inflamed, an incendiary figure' (Brookes 2009: 23). The back cover is no less fiery: a still from the film of Finney in bed with Rachel Roberts as Brenda, who is clipped to show only her naked back and a camisole, strap artfully askew. A glorious review quotation on the front harnesses the reputation of *Room at the Top* ('a savage story of lust and ambition' ran the X-certificated film's tag-line) only to trump it: '*A novel of today with a freshness and raw fury that "makes ROOM AT THE TOP look like a vicarage tea-party" DAILY TELEGRAPH*' (Sillitoe 1960). These cross-media, cannily exploited paratexts – which also include another review quote referencing 'Lawrence country' and *Lady Chatterley's Lover* (Sillitoe was Nottingham-born), and even the phallic figure of Pan himself on the publisher's colophon – combine to produce a lucrative phenomenon akin to the dual narration of Sillitoe's novel examined in Chapter 10. As Brookes concludes: 'the demographic expansion of audiences for *Saturday Night and Sunday Morning* was achieved through the strategy of generic hybridity' (Brookes 2009: 30). Though retaining some blurb from the first, self-consciously literary edition, and emphasising the Lawrence connection, Pan's cover marketed the book to its new film audience with panache.

Albert Finney as Arthur Seaton seems to be the result of a peculiarly apt piece of casting in order to achieve the dual perspective that so distinguishes the novel. Born in Salford, Finney the understudy had replaced Laurence Olivier as Coriolanus at the Royal Shakespeare Theatre in Stratford-upon-Avon in 1959 to enormous acclaim. In interviews around the release of *Saturday Night and Sunday Morning* he was noticeably keen to re-establish the authenticity of his working-class background: 'I know how Arthur Seaton . . . feels and the way he thinks', he claimed, 'because I have known blokes like him' (Finney 1960: n.p.). This close identification between actor and hero is mirrored by another characteristic of 1950s criticism – the regular conflation of writer and hero. (Colin Wilson's story was predicated upon a similar

Figure 9   The 1960 Pan paperback edition of Alan Sillitoe's novel *Saturday Night and Sunday Morning*, with its tie-in to the film of the same year.

gambit to market him as an outsider.) Disregarding Sillitoe's carefully wrought solution to the problem of 'how to write a book about a man who hadn't read a book', which produces the primal thrill of a new working-class voice with a framing, traditionally literary narration, the sparse reviews on the novel's release focused, admiringly but exclusively, upon the unmediated authenticity of the working-class experience that the text supposedly transmitted (Allsop 1965: 60). This was prompted to a large extent by the well-publicised paratext of Sillitoe's biography, leaving school at fourteen for a series of factory jobs, one on a capstan-lathe: 'I know nothing about the interior life of a typical lathe operator', wrote Wain in the *Observer*, 'and not very much about his exterior life; but I felt confident, reading Mr. Sillitoe's book, that I was getting a truthful account' (Wain 1958: 20). The avid identification of author and hero had obvious benefits to those in search of more sensational journalism, not least the addition of salacious gossip and eye-catching photographs to what were, nominally, the 'book pages'. Such a 'method' of reading (Mandarin critics would balk at the term) was the thick end of the wedge of the revitalised emphasis upon context examined in the previous chapter; author's lives, like their work, were mined for con-temporary social significances. Of course, this stood at odds with the methods of both New and Practical Criticism, which read, or assumed to be able to read, the text in isolation from any literary, historical or biographical background, and which held sway in both British and American universities during the decade. Mander was to note the way in which contemporary conditions made such exclusive focus very difficult:

> The Biographical Fallacy is not a new phenomenon. Mass publicity, however, is; and in consequence biography, which has always been popular as a sub-stitute for criticism, now threatens to replace it entirely. So far, we have not encountered this difficulty in an acute form. (Mander 1961: 181)

It was now so acute, however, that the Fallacy, if so it can reasonably be called, spread beyond authors to the literary critics themselves.

The 'dedicated man'

The connection between the beginning of the paperback boom during the 1950s and a concurrent, anti-elitist and more robust (some would have it, American) style of reviewing and criticism is an irresistible one. As with so many literary developments during the decade, the shift in cultures is markedly generational. Physicist / novelist C. P. Snow had been appointed as a lead reviewer for the *Sunday Times* at the end of

1948, and his vigorous style at the decade's turn anticipates the vocabulary of the New Left, examined in the next chapter. Of James Hanley's novel, *Winter Song*, for example, he claimed, 'For sustained energy of *feeling*, for the heart-beat in every human moment, there is no one in the last twenty years to surpass Mr. Hanley, perhaps no one to equal him' (Snow 1950: 3). Also writing for the paper during the decade were Mandarin literary stalwarts of the calibre of Edith Sitwell. Her technique is markedly different: reviewing John Malcolm's *Dylan Thomas in America*, she begins, 'I will speak of Dylan Thomas as I knew him … He was one of the most endearing people I have ever known. It would be impossible for anyone who knew him well not to love him' (Sitwell 1956: 5). Unlike Snow, who frequently used a statement of personal investment to open his literary discussion, Sitwell's closes it to all but those with privileged access to the truth. Though he was almost exactly of an age with Snow, another *Sunday Times* lead reviewer, Cyril Connolly (editor of the by then defunct *Horizon*), tends towards the Sitwell technique. Here, he is celebrating the demise in prominence of the work of romantic novelist Marie Corelli with an evident distaste for popular culture that, one suspects, extends to Snow's own novels:

> Writers like Marie Corelli make one believe in progress; it is almost unthinkable that anyone so dreadful should have such a success today. She was both unbearable and unreadable, and her little stupid face, like a bulldog in ectoplasm, would hardly be televised. (Connolly 1956: 5)

From 1953 Amis and Wain were principal book reviewers at the *Spectator*, at the behest of editor Anthony Hartley, a strong supporter of the *New Lines* poets. For all their plain speaking, as we have seen, the Movement writers (if we can abuse the term once again) were adamant about their own professionalism. In a 1955 *Spectator* review of a collection of critical essays by Lionel Trilling, Wain delineated the main faults of contemporary criticism as follows:

> First, lack of information. It is a widespread belief that anyone can criticise a book, so long as he has read it. He need not have read anything else. Thus it is quite common to find a person in a fair position of authority, able to influence people's taste, who would be floored by the simplest question about any writer who lived more than fifty years ago. The second fault is lack of attention to the theoretical basis of what they are doing; the failure to ask themselves, for instance, whether they are producing a relevant criticism of the book, or merely making a statement about themselves. (Wain 1955a: 171)

As he writes this, Wain is on the point of resigning his lectureship in English at Reading University, and just after he does so, he pointedly fashions a contrary definition of criticism which excludes the academic, and includes – in fact, demands – the kind of plainly voiced literary discussion that characterises his own reviewing practice. Lecturers, he claims, by virtue of their positioning as experts, cannot perform as critics, for 'Literary criticism is the discussion, between equals, of works of literature, with a view to establishing common ground on which judgements of value can be based' (Wain 1956b: 143). These mutually reached, or at least recognised, values ensure that 'everything is *not* just a matter of individual "taste"' (144). Wain provides a brief but instructive case study of the debates surrounding the literary critical industry during the 1950s, as his career bridges so many of its factions – he was at various points an academic, critic, reviewer, broadcaster, poet and novelist, as well as a particularly determined, and obstreperous, crusader for his own vision of what criticism should be. Wain was never one to let a slight go by. Reviewing Leavis's *D. H. Lawrence, Novelist*, Wain defends both Leavis and himself against a recent letter to the *London Magazine*, which made a claim familiar from the previous chapter, that 'Dr. Leavis's adherents are largely state-aided young men who cannot afford a claret and Peacock approach to literature. They come from poor homes where books are luxury and must be taken seriously.' 'If the justification of great literature is not, in the end, a *moral* justification,' as Leavis believes, Wain demands, 'then what is it? And if it is moral, then where has Leavis gone wrong? *That* is the issue, and no amount of whiffling about claret can obscure it, except for readers who want it obscured' (Wain 1955b: 458).

In 1956 Wain left the *Spectator* for the *Observer*, offended by a pseudonymous parody piece printed at the end of the previous year. Wain's upholding of a professionalised accountability in his writing might alone have made him balk at Dr Aloysius C. Pepper's pointed critique, but its sarcastic humour is clearly directed at him personally. 'Pepper' meets a character called Ercole, who is fashioning himself at the cutting edge of literary modishness: 'Now', he tells the doctor, 'the ideal is the provincial-academic':

> Pedantry's the thing now – good, solid, didactic dullness; sound, flat, dreary moralising in 'creation' and pedagogic impertinence in 'criticism'. I trust that you read the American reviews?'
>   I made a grimace of distaste. (Pepper 1955: 887)

At the *Observer* Wain was immediately to provoke the disdain of a Pepper-like spectator of contemporary mores. Reviewing P. G. Wodehouse's *French Leave*, Wain is on bold form, smartly rebutting criticism of the sociological bent of his own first novel in his response to Wodehouse's hero: 'His name is Jeff. Jeff! Do you remember the time when all Wodehouse heroes were called Bertie, or Claude, or Algy? I recommend this new hero for sociological study.' He concludes the piece:

> I enjoyed this book, as everyone will; Mr. Wodehouse is probably the most endearing author in the world. But I cannot quite get rid of the feeling that the needle is scratching rather badly and that sooner or letter the record will have to be taken off. (Wain 1956a: 9)

Back at the *Spectator*, Evelyn Waugh has stirred at Wain's treatment of 'a master I have all my life revered, Mr P. G. Wodehouse, CMG, D.Lit'. He objects, quite simply, he writes,

> to Mr Wain's manners. That he does not deign to notice. Integrity is all. Considerations of common decency must not stand between the young critic and his high purpose. I had come up against that redoubtable person, the 'dedicated man'. It is rather alarming to one trained in a laxer school. (Waugh 1956: 243)

If Wain wrote one, the *Spectator* printed no response to Waugh. Yet in a letter published the following year he gets some small revenge. In a continued public debate with D. J. Enright about the function of contemporary criticism, he emphasises a lack of connection between serious criticism of 'classical English literature' and 'the day-to-day work of reviewing'. The latter is no more than 'a chorus of "smart" frivolities, written for the most part by petty Narcissists whose concern is to leave the reader with an impression of their own personalities' (Wain 1957b: 55). By way of example, he cites a recent review by Iain Hamilton, his former literary editor at the *Spectator*, which decries the philistinism of Bloomsbury detractors:

> It's all so easy. Anyone who doesn't accept Virginia Woolf as a major novelist, Strachey as a great biographer, and the Bloomsbury *ethos* as a workable view of human life, can be got rid of simply by calling him a lout and talking about his big black boots. (56–7)

Making Culture Popular

From the relentless and claustrophobic nature of these exchanges, Wain's concerns seem much more personal than political. He is walking a difficult line through his own propaganda, between the personality, or at least the persona, which exudes from his own critical / reviewing work (and which is relied upon as an important method of reader identification and consensus) and his condemnation of those 'whose concern is to leave the reader with an impression of their own personalities'

(55). Certainly in 'Get Out and Push!', Lindsay Anderson can distinguish no difference. As a Scot, he is already understandably chafed by Wain's substitution of 'English' for 'British' in the recent article in *The Twentieth Century*, 'How it Strikes a Contemporary: A Young Man who is not Angry' (Anderson 1957: 167). He takes further issue with the reasoning processes behind Wain's supposedly reasonable tone: 'Like Amis, Wain writes with a pretence of logical argument, but in fact he is doing little more than stating his preferences. They are conservative' (168). He concludes of the pair and their ilk that 'This kind of liberal will commit himself to nothing more specific, or more dynamic, than a vague notion of "decency" . . . He opposes the death penalty; he disapproves of our action in Suez. But his reactions are all *against*: his faiths are all negative' (169). 'Where (again)', demands Anderson, 'is the bloody horse?' (170).

Yet as all these examples indicate, something has changed in the tone of critical debate between the two generations of critics of the 1950s, and it pertains not just to a heightened defensiveness, but also to an issue of deference. Kenneth Tynan, whose reviews have been discussed in Chapter 4, was driven out of his post at the *Evening Standard* in 1953 by a barrage of complaints at his attacks on untouchables within the theatrical establishment (Kynaston 2009: 308). The young were both demanding and initiating a new kind of journalistic commentary. Onstage in *Look Back in Anger*, Jimmy Porter wonders of the *New Statesman and Nation* why he spends 'ninepence on that damned paper every week' just to read another piece by J. B. Priestley 'casting well-fed glances back to the Edwardian twilight from his comfortable, disenfranchised wilderness' (Osborne 1989: 15–16). In his autobiography, a less reactionary George Scott regrets that Priestley, 'one of our most talented and voluble fireside doctors', assumes in his column

> the role of the man who is always misunderstood. This is a pity. Although he can always turn his petulance and grievance into good copy and remain highly readable even when he is behaving most like some irrity old aunt, it distracts him from concentrating upon analysis of the problems of our time. (Scott 1956: 208)

He later quotes Priestley's irritable complaint about finding himself in 'the new age of snap personal judgments – *I like this, I don't like that*' (218). He is implying, of course, that this is a fault of the young, yet the opening chapter to Evelyn Waugh's 1957 'Conversation Piece', *The Ordeal of Gilbert Pinfold*, establishes its eponymous hero by means of a list of what he does not like: 'He abhorred plastics, Picasso, sunbathing and jazz – everything in fact that had happened in his own lifetime'

(Waugh 1957: 7). There is a weird echo here, surely coincidental, of the first editorial of a new magazine that epitomises precisely the carelessly consumerist culture that Priestley despises – Hugh Hefner claims of the *Playboy* type: 'We enjoy mixing up cocktails and an *hors d'œuvre* or two, putting a little mood music on the phonograph, and inviting a female acquaintance for a quiet discussion on Picasso, Nietzsche, jazz, sex' (Hefner 1953: 3).

The irony for Priestley is that Waugh's list immediately and succinctly locates Penfold's cultural position for a contemporary readership. Dick Hebdige provides a precise decoding: '*plastic* (i.e., festival of Britain / "inauthentic" mass culture); *Picasso* (Continental modern art / subversive high culture); *sun-bathing* (increased leisure / national inertia / a "soft" obsession with cosmetics . . .) and *jazz* (American negro / subversive "low" culture)' (Hebdige 1988: 50). In other words, the consumerist ethos is already legible through all levels of the newly affluent 1950s culture; this, according to Hebdige, is 'what we call "popular culture"'(47). Wain's upholding of the critical practice of his generation, heavily dependent upon a common sense / man persona, as opposed to the personality-based judgements of his elders, is certainly problematic. Yet his determination that practices of traditional criticism and those of journalistic reviewing should be in conversation is symptomatic of a period in which impassioned literary debate was taking place both inside and outside universities. Whether this represented a sullying of high culture, or its just democratisation depended very much on whether, in the terms of Mitford and Waugh, one was 'U' or 'non-U'. For F. R. Leavis, who, as we have seen, provided a moral compass (albeit an occasionally unreliable one) for Wain's intellectual generation, it had been a long-held ambition. In a morose and belated farewell to *Scrutiny*, Leavis maintains that his time in academia was far from academic, where that pejorative term suggests thinking confined to issues of method and theory:

> Where the Idea of a University was in question, we were concerned to demonstrate that Cambridge need not be academic – that the essential Cambridge *was* not. Our special business was literary criticism but we saw nothing arbitrary in our taking the creative process of criticism – that interplay of personal judgements in which values are established and a world created that is neither public in a sense congenial to science nor merely private – as representative and type of the process in which the human world is created and renewed and kept living. (Leavis 1963: 5–6)

The 1950s saw the broadening of criticism among a greater readership and a wider band of practitioners, shaping the Humanities as we know (and must defend) them today.

Note

1. Anderson is referring to a poem by South African poet Roy Campbell, 'On Some South African Novelists', which runs:

   You praise the firm restraint with which they write –
   I'm with you there, of course:
   They use the snaffle and the curb all right,
   But where's the bloody horse? (Campbell 1949: 198)

Chapter Thirteen

Where East Meets West: Literature, the New Left and the Cold War

In their political history of postwar Britain, Sked and Cook note how Labour's run of nationalisation at the end of the 1940s (the Bank of England in 1946; the coal industry in 1947; railways in 1948; and iron and steel in 1949) signified:

> No new beginning for Labour. No transformation of its relationship with capital occurred. In practice all that happened was that the state bought out the former owners and allowed the former management to remain. Labour was accorded no greater say in industrial decision-making, and since it shared in no profits it gained no economic benefit either. The Labour government had approached the question with no imagination whatsoever. (Sked and Cook 1993: 31)

Anthony Crosland was thirty-eight when his book, *The Future of Socialism*, the key British political text of the 1950s, was published in 1956. He had lost his ministerial seat of South Gloucestershire the year before, and he was determined that, for a struggling party in a new political climate, 'the much-thumbed guidebooks of the past must now be thrown away' (Crosland 2006: 51). His book, he was careful to assert, would 'say nothing of the long pre-capitalist tradition of "communism", stretching all the way from the early Christians to the Levellers, since modern socialism is concerned with an industrial society, and the doctrinal formulations of purely agrarian societies can have little relevance' (52–3). He calls the Fabians 'instinctive gradualists and permeators' (56), and the label seems an appropriate one for Crosland, himself prominent in the Fabian Society and offering, as he does, precisely that re-imagining of the relationship with capital (and capitalism) that Sked and Cook diagnose the postwar Labour Party as lacking. Crosland quotes another Fabian, political theorist G. D. H. Cole, saying that, before the Second World War, 'The will to Socialism is based on a lively sense of wrongs crying for redress.' 'When the wrongs were so manifest', Crosland suggests,

> We all knew what to do, and where the enemy was, and what was the order
> of battle; it was exhilarating to fight for such clear-cut and obviously right-
> eous aims. But now the certainty and simplicity are gone, and everything has
> become complicated and ambiguous. (Crosland 2006: 73)

Crosland's own guidebook to these ambiguous times embraces the
new affluence with an optimistic view of the extent to which it will
percolate through all levels of society. This will prove to be excessive.
Yet throughout his economic argument he proclaims the continuance
of 'the underlying moral values' that 'embody the only logically and
historically permissible meaning of the word socialism' (77): that is, the
belief in equality of rights and opportunity; a concern for wider 'social
welfare'; an ideal of co-operation and fraternity; and continued protest
against the inefficiencies of capitalism, the poverty it still creates, and its
tendency to mass unemployment. He found these values to be realised
most convincingly, if still patchily, in Sweden, and, controversially for
many Socialists, in the USA. His rejection of the ownership of the means
of production as always desirable and inherently Socialist was another,
and abiding, source of controversy.

The Future of Socialism, however, was largely received positively
across political divides. An advertisement for the book in the *Economist*
prominently flaunts the praise of Graham Hatton of the reliably right-
wing *Spectator*: 'Mr. Crosland has principles, conviction and courage
... he has *élan* without *hubris*; realism without cynicism; intellect
without frigidity; and warmth without sentimentality' (10 November
1956, 19). Unsurprisingly, perhaps, stauncher criticism came from
the Left. Hugh Dalton, who had served as Chancellor from 1945 to
1947, wrote to Crosland attacking his use of what he called 'Teutonic-
American-Sociological-Psycho-Analytico-Pathologico' jargon (Dalton
1956). As Dalton had presided over the nationalisation of the Bank of
England, this might well have been prompted by what he perceived as
personal criticism in Crosland's critique of outdated Labour doctrine,
or he may just have been riled by Crosland's inscription in his gift copy:
'so that he may know what to say when instructing the young' (Barnes
1981: 10).

The People is Me

In his introduction to the 2006 anniversary re-issue of *The Future
of Socialism*, Crosland's friend and Private Secretary, Dick Leonard,
claimed that 'the only hostile reviews' came from what he called 'the

far Left, particularly the recent ex-Communists associated with the *Universities and Left Review*' (xv). The *ULR*, edited by Stuart Hall, Gabriel Pearson, Raphael Samuel and Charles Taylor, and the *New Reasoner*, edited by historians John Saville and E. P. Thompson, both began in 1957, and were merged to form the *New Left Review* at the turn of the new decade. Contrary to Leonard's assertion, it was the *New Reasoner* that attracted dissident Communists and disaffected Labour supporters despairing over Suez and disgusted by the Soviet invasion of Hungary and the brutal suppression of an uprising that began with a student demonstration. The Communist Party of Great Britain offered unequivocal support to the USSR, and 7,000 people left the party in 1956, almost one-fifth of its total membership (Rebellato 1999: 18–20). The *ULR*, whose editors' average age was 24, appealed rather to a younger crowd of students and creative types hopeful of reinvigorating socialist theory and practice, and less reluctant to articulate their political commitment explicitly.

Lindsay Anderson wrote in his contribution to *Declaration*:

> When the *Universities and Left Review* appeared, in the spring of 1957, it was reviewed neither in the *New Statesman*, the *Observer*, the *Sunday Times*, nor *The Times*. Yet it sold out its first edition, reprinted, and sold out again. I take this as a portent. Perhaps people are beginning to understand that we can no longer afford the luxury of skepticism, and that we must start again believing in belief. (Anderson 1957: 176)

The New Left was a heterogeneous group, determined to create a democratic politics that was rooted in national tradition without being reified by the orthodoxies of the past. *The Uses of Literacy* and *Culture and Society* were written just after its foundation, but both texts had an important role in consolidating an agenda. Crosland's 'revisionist' way, an American-style liberalism, was not the way of the New Left, though they acknowledged the validity of its analysis of a postwar consumer society. The conclusion of *The Future of Socialism*, though it predates the term, is greatly concerned with an equality in 'quality of life'. The New Left emphasis was a heavier one on the transformative power of culture. Thirty years later, Stuart Hall was to explain its importance as follows:

> First, because it was in the ideological and cultural domain that social change seemed to be making itself most dramatically visible. Second, because the cultural dimension seemed to us not a secondary, but a constitutive dimension of society . . . Third, because the discourse of culture seemed to us fundamentally necessary to any language in which socialism could be redescribed. (Hall 1989: 25–6)

As Crosland had put it, 'now the certainty and simplicity are gone, and everything has become complicated and ambiguous' (Crosland 2006: 73). The cultural and political project of the New Left was certainly both, as its various voices upheld traditional working-class values and the aspiration to classlessness, jazz and the rejection of mass cultural forms, and the aesthetics of modern pluralism alongside those of an organic Englishness (Brook 2007: 21). The expression of the New Left ethos in literature was similarly diverse. Kingsley Amis's first novel reputedly sold 250,000 copies in Russian translation to a Soviet Union keen to read the Angry phenomenon as indicative of a long-awaited English revolution (Sutherland 2000: 33). If this is true, it was thwarted. Jim Dixon does little explicitly to express his political position beyond a half-hearted assertion that 'If one man's got ten buns and another's got two, and a bun has got to be given up by one of them, then surely you take it from the man with ten buns' (Amis 1976: 51); and Joe Lampton, bewitched by the privileged Susan Brown chattering about her foreign holidays, offers only one jokily radical solution: 'I've often thought that if I wanted to put paid to Communism once and for all I'd have a hundred girls like Susan ride on buses the length and breadth of Great Britain' (Braine 1959: 133). Doris Lessing negotiates the contemporary challenges to Socialism with far more earnestness and finesse in her novels of the 1950s. Just as Mary Turner in *The Grass is Singing* (1950) comes to realise the uselessness of doctrinal 'isms' when confronting poverty on a Rhodesian settler farm, so Martha Quest, the eponymous heroine of Lessing's 1952 novel, is failed by those 'much-thumbed guidebooks of the past' (Crosland 2006: 51). Martha, we are told, 'began to read, hungrily, for some kind of balance. And more and more, what she read seemed remote; or rather, it seemed that through reading she created a self-contained world which had nothing to do with what lay around her' (Lessing 1982: 90). Lessing's essay, 'The Small Personal Voice', was the first, and the most measured, contribution to *Declaration*, and in it she opposes the detached nature of traditional political doctrine ('the people', she notes succinctly, 'is me'). She goes on to bemoan what she perceives to be the increasingly removed positions of those presiding over the testing of Britain's hydrogen bomb: 'Of the men who took the decision I am sure there is not one who says: Because of me thousands of children will be born crippled, blind, deaf, mad. They are members of a committee. They have no responsibility as individuals' (Lessing 1957: 19). In this, at least, her opinion chimes with Crosland's, who notes how, in contemporary business, 'more and more influence passes to the technical experts and specialists – the new "organisation men" with the "long-haired know-how", to use the current American slang' (Crosland 2006: 16).

C. P. Snow, himself a physicist, provided an early warning of this widening divide between those with the scientific know-how (although, this being Britain, they are all respectably crew-cut) and those making the decisions. *The New Men* (1954) is set between 1939 and 1945 during the birth pangs of the British nuclear industry, and is one of the *Strangers and Brothers* series, a ranging fictional study of the British professions published between 1940 and 1974. Civil servant Lewis Eliot, the quasi-autobiographical narrator who endures throughout the eleven-novel sequence, places his younger brother Martin in the fission programme, and their difficult relationship forms a means of examining the intellectual gulf between scientists and non-scientists. The narrative is fairly even-handed with its attribution of blame for this divide. Lewis admits that, when the process of fission is explained to him, 'the words and symbols might as well have been in Hittite' (Snow 1954: 16), while an applicant to the nuclear programme is asked at interview:

'Do you read anything?'
'I haven't had much time.'
The scientists smiled. These non-technical questions and answers were per-functory on both sides of the table. Anything outside science was a frippery. That was all. (82)

Yet by the time of 'The Two Cultures', the Rede lecture in 1959 that so enraged Leavis, Snow's judgement has changed to accuse intellectuals, 'in particular literary intellectuals' of being 'natural Luddites' (Snow 1969: 22). While they stew 'complacent in one's unique tragedy', he claimed, scientists 'are inclined to be impatient to see if something can be done: and inclined to think that it can be done, until it's proved other-wise. That is their real optimism, and it's an optimism that the rest of us badly need' (7). For many observers, Luddite or otherwise, such a rheto-ric of scientific advancement was difficult to square with an industry that seemed to be working towards the annihilation of the human race.

Cosy Catastrophes

The Cold War had developed dramatically in 1948 and 1949 with the Berlin blockade and airlift, and international tension increased when the Soviet Union undertook its first atomic bomb test in August 1949. October 1952 saw the first successful test of a British atomic (fission) bomb, *Hurricane*, in October, in the north-west corner of Australia and notably not in the US testing grounds, a reluctant gesture of independ-ence. Before the explosion, Churchill had drafted two telegrams to the atomic scientist who headed the development team – 'Thank you, Dr Penney' and 'Well done, Sir William' (Hennessy 2006: 182). He sent the latter. The test of the first (albeit undeployable) US thermonuclear (or hydrogen) device went ahead the following month. It produced a yield of 10.4 megatons, or the equivalent of twice the amount of *all* the explosives, atom bombs included, used in the Second World War (165). As is often the case with destruction on so large a scale, it was a relatively small incident that crystallised a shift in public thinking away from pride in Britain's third place in this new arms race. In 1954 the *Bravo* H-bomb, exploded by the Americans off the Marshall Islands, contaminated the Japanese crew of the fishing boat Lucky Dragon, bobbing eighty-five miles away and outside the exclusion zone, and thus putting paid to the arguments that an increase in the strength of a bomb did not result in increased radiation. Britain's atomic partnership with the US had been ended by the 1946 US Atomic Energy Act (the McMahon Act), which made it illegal to pass restricted atomic information to another country. Through the 1950s there was a dawning realisation of the vulnerability of Britain's situation – her American air bases and relative proximity made her a likely first target for the Soviets, yet she had no agreement for consultation with the US before a launch. An April 1957 Defence White Paper was brutal in its honesty: 'It must be frankly recognized that there is at present no means of providing adequate protection for the people of this country against the consequences of attack with nuclear weapons' (Montgomery 1965: 348).

Yet even this stark appraisal of Britain's position in the Cold War suggests that such a thing as 'adequate protection' might exist in the event of a nuclear attack. In 'The Small Personal Voice', Lessing is keen to stress the magnitude of the consequences unleashed when humanity 'assaulted that colossal citadel of power, the tiny unit of the substance of the universe' (Lessing 1957: 16), and she finds that ultimate horror in the minutiae of the everyday:

> We think: the tiny units of the matter of my hand, my flesh, are shared with walls, tables, pavements, trees, flowers, soil . . . and suddenly, and at any moment, a madman may throw a switch, and flesh and soil and leaves may begin to dance together in a flame of destruction. (Lessing 1957: 18)

The British cultural response to the Bomb was a dislocated one. Catherine Jolivette has noted how artist Graham Sutherland's

> mutant chimeras, suggestive of horrific transformation, gave tangible form to what, until the early 1950s, were largely indescribable fears – fears overlaid . . . with such public displays of national assurance as the Festival of Britain and the Coronation. Sutherland's new landscapes reconfigured the earth as

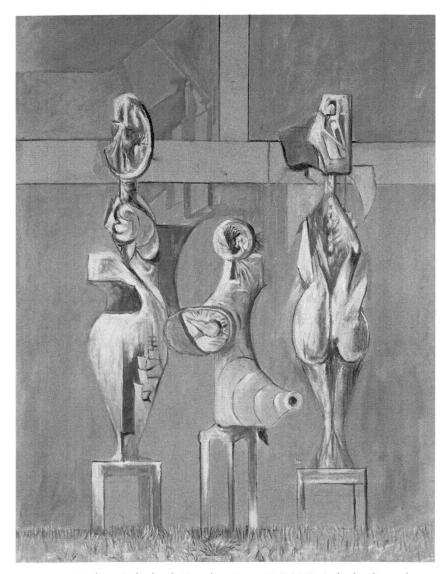

Figure 10   Graham Sutherland, 'Standing Forms II' (1952). Sutherland's work was exhibited at the Festival of Britain, but its mutant humanoid forms suggested a much darker approach to the legacies and realities of nation.

a site for anxiety, rather than a reassuring haven, a place where nature was no refuge and could even turn against man in acts of malevolence. (Jolivette 2009: 34) [Figure 10]

Astounding, the American science fiction magazine that regularly featured the work of British writers, was full of stories of an Earth ridden with the effects of radiation (Aldiss 1973: 246). In the mainstream, television adaptations of Nigel Kneale's *Quatermass* trilogy were broadcast live between 1953 and 1958, and offered viewers a disturbing blend of the consequences of nuclear rockets, manned space flight and alien organic mutations into what a reviewer of the film adaptation called, with relish, 'a huge crawling mass of cactoid pulp', which 'calls to mind a particular *Thorn Head* by Graham Sutherland' (Sylvester 1956: 69, 71). Kneale adapted *Nineteen Eighty-Four* for a notorious television screening as the Sunday play on 12 December 1954; two days later the *Daily Express* reported that a forty-year-old mother of two had collapsed and died after witnessing the post-nuclear future portrayed in the 'TV horror play' (quoted Rodden 1989: 275). Kneale was later to say of the 1950s:

> that decade has sometimes been called one of paranoia, which means abnormal, sick attitudes and irrational fears. I don't think it was irrational to be fearful at that time; there was a lot to be frightened of and stories like mine were a sort of controlled paranoia, inoculation against the real horrors. (Kneale 1996)

Producer / director of both *Quatermass* and *Nineteen Eighty-Four*, the Austrian Rudolph Cartier had a rather less cathartic take on the effect of these nuclear fables on their mass audience, claiming that *The Quatermass Experiment* was more successful on television than its 1956 film remake 'because of the "hypnotic" power emanating from the T.V. screen to the viewer, sitting isolated in his darkened room. There is nothing to distract him' (Cartier 1958: 10). In other media, Adam Piette has made a persuasive case for Ted Hughes as a nuclear poet:

> The predatory creatures encountered in Hughes' poems are mutants of the imagination, dark and deadly recessive forces triggered in the genes by the radioactive dangers of space. These radioactive dangers had become spectrally systemic to the imagination of the human species at least since the disastrous Castle / BRAVO atmospheric tests [of 1954]. (Piette 2009: 123)

As for novels, Paul Brians claims of British nuclear war fiction that its output

> remained for many years spasmodic and idiosyncratic. It did not sort itself readily into identifiable genres, as did that of the Americans, and it did not form a tradition, so that each author seems to be unaware that he or she has any predecessors. (Brians 1987: 17)

Science fiction might seem an obvious place to seek such a tradition, but at the beginning of the decade at least the field was largely dismissed as a literary genre; as science-fiction writer Brian Aldiss has put it, 'Pornography got a better press' (Aldiss 1973: 251–2). Yet Aldiss is quick to dismiss the writer whose novels during the 1950s went some way towards establishing a wider market for science-fiction writing. He dubs John Wyndham 'master of the cosy catastrophe', and claims of hugely popular *The Day of the Triffids* (1951) and *The Kraken Wakes* (1953), 'Both novels were totally devoid of ideas but read smoothly, and thus reached a maximum audience, who enjoyed cosy disasters.' Wyndham's 'best novel', Aldiss claims, is the 1955 *The Chrysalids*, set in New England after nuclear war (Aldiss 1973: 293, 294). Though the inhabitants of Waknuk have numerous horrors to negotiate – chief among them a genetic mutation that has left half the population infertile – the strictures of the British class system that so antagonise Aldiss are not among them. Yet in spite, or perhaps because, of its eminently respectable middle-class tone, *The Day of the Triffids* is notable for its early anticipation of many of the cultural anxieties examined in this volume as characteristic of the 1950s in Britain, as well as an instructively ambiguous response to the implications of the newly atomic age.

The novel is narrated by Bill Masen, one of the minority of British people who have not been blinded by the sight of a mysterious meteor shower. He is thus one of the few able to form a defence against the triffids, deadly plants (Aldiss calls them 'huge perambulating vegetables with poisonous flails') developed by science, which have escaped secure cultivation and are colonising the world (293). The novel tells the story of his developing romance with novelist Josella Playton, and their attempt to find a place in a colony that can continue the struggle against the triffids. So what is the utopian social organisation for this dystopian future? A number of models are offered – Christian; in a snobby joke, a series of 'tribal communities' in South Wales, focused upon the pits; and 'a kind of – feudal seigneury' with blind women as incubators to replenish the human race (Wyndham 1973: 256, 266). A key concern of the novel is that of gender politics, and there is a perceptible level of glee that global catastrophe has forced the modern woman to re-assess her role in relation to child-bearing. Josella Playton, best-selling author of *Sex is My Adventure*, ends the novel with a proper devotion to motherhood and to Masen, while still retaining the intelligence and forthright desire that sets her apart from purely docile 'breeders' like Mary Brent.

Mary and her husband, Dennis, own Shirning, a refurbished farmhouse on the South Downs with its surrounding lands boasting 'a suburban rather than a rural tidiness and had for years known no form of animal life rougher than a few riding horses and ponies' (218). For a few months, this forms a fleetingly idyllic environment for Bill and Josella, but is ultimately unsustainable due to the narrowness of the small group's skills and the shallowness of its breeding pool. A colony on the Isle of Wight is the (relatively) 'happy ending' for the couple, with a motivating purpose of a search for a genetic means to massacre the triffids. The deadly plants are eventually revealed to have been created by a humanity who is able neither to understand nor to control them; the parallel with atomic energy is unavoidable. As one character puts it, 'Triffids, huh! Nasty damn things, I reckon. Not natcheral as you might say' (131), yet the novel's distaste for their mutation is matched by one for unruly nature itself. Strolling by the sea, Josella notes how quickly a row of bungalows has been reclaimed. 'The countryside is having its revenge, all right,' Bill responds. 'Nature seemed about finished then – "who would have thought the old man had so much blood in him"?' (242). Shakespeare's play with the walking wood is, of course, appropriate to their plight, but this reference to Lady Macbeth's disgust signals a revulsion at that which is natural, as well as 'not natcheral'. It is Shirning's suburban air, in the heart of London's commuter belt, that makes it such an idyll: a resolutely inorganic community.

Such ambiguity extends from the novel's local to its global politics. Wyndham's imagined future has a clearly Cold War cast, with the freedom to travel 'over five-sixths of the globe – though the remaining sixth was something different again' (27). That remaining sixth is the USSR but, surprisingly, the triffid threat does not seem to have emanated from here; the 'inventor' (or introducer, or stooge) of the triffids is Umberto Christoforo Palanguez, 'of assorted Latin descent, and something South American by nationality' (32, 29). After the 'meteor shower' (later in the novel it is suggested this was actually a malfunctioning governmental weapons system), many of the small groups that Masen encounters on a helicopter survey of the South of England are simply waiting

> for the arrival of the Americans who were bound to find a way. There seemed to be a widespread and fixed idea about this. Our suggestions that any surviving Americans would be likely to have their hands more than full at home was received as so much wet-blanketry. (201–2)

The American threat, or rather the threatening consequences of British over-reliance upon the USA, trumps that of the USSR in practical terms. The real trigger of the triffids' dominance over Britain is revealed to be Western culture's eager embrace of the plants as charming horticultural curiosities, and amusing playthings for the kids, their deadly stings neutered by an annual pruning. The real triffid invasion, the novel suggests, was an easy, invidious and purely domestic one.

The staying power of normality is identified as the source of the

nation's downfall, both in its casual assimilation of a highly dangerous organism and its passive, and doomed, anticipation of inevitable
American rescue from adversity. Paradoxically, however, *The Day of
the Triffids* sustains that belief in normality at its conclusion. Early in
the narrative, in a newly blind London, Masen mocks his own tendency
towards 'a feeling that as long as I remained *my* normal self, things
might even yet in some inconceivable way return to *their* normal ...
Such a foolish niceness of sensibility in a stricken world! (53). Yet
despite a retrospective narrative and the assertion that 'It is not easy
to think oneself back to the outlook of those days' (16), the novel ends
with the hero and his woman setting out for the Isle of Wight, so the
post-post-apocalyptic world which rejects such 'niceness of sensibility'
for a more ruthless survival strategy is never imaginatively created or
offered to us as readers. This, then, is why Wyndham's catastrophe,
to return to Aldiss's accusation, remains cosy. In Wyndham's defence,
it is exactly this unswerving belief in the maintenance of a very white,
English, middle-class normality after the apocalypse that gives the novel
its effectively eerie tone.

Frank Parkin has documented the specific characteristics of middle-
class radicalism, which he distinguishes from a working-class radicalism
geared mostly to reforms of an economic or material kind:

> The radicalism of the middle class is directed mainly to social reforms which
> are basically moral in content ... [and it] envisages no rewards which will
> accrue to the middle class specifically, but only to society at large, or to some
> underprivileged groups. (Parkin 1968: 2)

The focus of such expressive, rather than instrumental, politics in 1950s
Britain was the Campaign for Nuclear Disarmament (CND), which
included in its diverse but overwhelmingly middle-class membership
a number of prominent cultural figures and writers, including E. M.
Forster, Victor Gollancz, Doris Lessing, Compton Mackenzie and E. P.
Thompson, with philosopher, historian and critic Bertrand Russell as
President. Its formation in 1958 was spurred by the testing of Britain's
first H-bomb on Christmas Island on 15 May 1957. This was followed
by the clarion call of J. B. Priestley's article, 'Britain and the Nuclear
Bombs', in the *New Statesman* on 2 November, which posed the question, 'When and where have these preparations for nuclear warfare ever
been put to the test of public opinion?', and posited the idea of an independent action by Britain to ban nuclear bombs, for though this 'would
involve our foreign minister in many difficulties, most of us would rather
have a bewildered and overworked foreign office than a country about
to be turned into a radio-active cemetery' (Priestley 1957: 554).

That same year, 1957, also saw publication of Nevil Shute's novel, *On the Beach*, the horror of which is derived from the relentless progress south of the zone of radioactivity after bombs have been dropped across the Northern Hemisphere. The novel has been credited with rousing many to take part in the first CND protest march from London to Aldermaston, the site of the Atomic Weapons Research Establishment, built on a former RAF airfield, in Easter 1958. (The march, like other of CND's tactics – the rally, the sit-in – tapped into a radical political tradition unsullied by Stalinism and clearly in contrast to the consensus-building that dominated parliamentary activity during the decade.) Nevil Shute, a British engineer, had emigrated to Australia in 1950, and his tale is set in Melbourne, as the community attempts to maintain a fairly normal routine whilst awaiting its death. Like Wyndham's, Shute's tone has been roundly criticised, this time for its weird reticence – Anthony Burgess thought it 'so impersonal, some dimwitted archangel's chronicle' (Burgess 1983: 256). British writers had often envisaged the human race's post-apocalypse future as antipodean; *On the Beach* put paid to any sense that life (expatriate or otherwise) would carry on after the Bomb. As Brians puts it:

> What makes *On the Beach* nevertheless one of the most compelling accounts of nuclear war ever written is its almost unique insistence that everyone – without exception – is going to die. Shute directly addresses the most primal fears of the human race, which has spent most of its history denying or compensating for the fact of personal death, and does so with a relentlessness which the complex technique of a more sophisticated writer might have muted. (Brians 1987: 20)

Bertrand Russell made the same point as Shute with no little eloquence:

> As things are now and as statesmen go, it is an even chance whether any human being will exist forty years hence . . . I do not care to owe a few years of precarious liberty to an ability to participate as an accomplice in a crime which has no parallel in human history. (quoted Montgomery 1965: 348)

CND served to consolidate the heterogeneous New Left in the late 1950s with an ability to consolidate expressive political feeling that endures to the present day; Brians attributes the organisation's 'high survival value' to its ability to shift emphasis from one set of political concerns to another, 'because political activity in support of the values it upholds can be claimed to be beneficial in and of itself' (Brians 1987: 39), and by the mid-1960s its focus was on the injustices of the Vietnam War.

The early 1950s saw a resurgence in popular writing about the Second World War, with Paul Brickhill's *The Dambusters* (1951), P. H. Reid's *The Colditz Story* (1952) and Dudley Pope's *The Battle of the*

River Plate (1956). Nicholas Monsarrat's *The Cruel Sea* (1951) was the decade's blockbuster of the genre, at least by the standards of the day, in selling over one million copies, although some of its popularity might be attributed to subject matter beyond that of traditional military heroism – Sutherland claims that 'For much of the narrative, VD is more of an enemy than the U-boat' (Sutherland 2000: 29). As we have seen, more traditionally 'literary' British fiction dealing with the new climate of the Cold War tended towards a tangential approach, but one strand of popular fiction was well placed to deal with more direct political antinomies, as well as to cash in on a building public fascination generated by the disappearance of British diplomats Guy Burgess and Donald Maclean from the Washington Embassy in 1951. Michael Denning has claimed that 'the spy novel is in a sense the war novel of the Cold War, the cover story of an era of decolonization and, particularly after the debacle at Suez in 1956, the definitive loss of Britain's role as a world power' (Denning 1987: 92). The definitive secret agent series, Ian Fleming's James Bond, began with *Casino Royale* in 1953, but the Bond moment does not really begin until the novel's paperback publication in 1956, the year that Burgess and Maclean finally issued a statement confirming their status as KGB spies during the war. It was 1957 that saw the serialisation of the fifth Bond novel, *From Russia, With Love*, in the *Daily Express*, after which sales of the Bond books really began to build: ironically, as that novel ends with the apparent death of Bond, whose creator, in a letter to Raymond Chandler, his close friend and admirer, had cited his 'waning enthusiasm for this cardboard booby' (Pearson 1966: 284). Filmic versions of Fleming's novels, launched by *Dr No* (1962), were to make the series apparently indestructibly perennial.

Denning suggests that 'No formal account of the genre's progress explains the Bond books and their enormous popularity' (Denning 1987: 93). In his slavishly admiring 1965 analysis, *A James Bond Dossier*, Kingsley Amis attempts to attribute much of this success to what he calls the 'Fleming effect', or the way in which the fantastic elements of the Bond tales are 'bolted down' to intensely realistic detail (Amis 1966: 112). In the earlier novels, these details pertain to a Soviet enemy, an organisation called SMERSH (a contraction of the Russian '*Smiert Spionam*', or 'Death to Spies'), but this direct Cold War scenario is only just to last the decade, before the novel *Thunderball* (1961) introduces a new antagonist in the form of SPECTRE, or the Special Executive for Counter-intelligence, Terrorism, Revenge and Extortion, a freelance group motivated not by ideology but by the acquisition of wealth and power. Brian Aldiss was to note of the sub-genre of 'cosy catastrophe' that its essence was 'that the hero should have a pretty good time (a girl, free suites at the Savoy, automobiles for the taking) while everyone else is dying off' (Aldiss 1973: 294). The Bond books exhibit this kind of acquisition *par excellence*; in fact, they work to make continuous consumption a heroic act in itself. Fleming demonstrated a masterly exploitation of the gamut of codes that were coming to characterise mass culture – sensationalism, escapism, voyeurism, pornography – together with a lifestyle that allowed the identification of author and hero we found to be a feature of the publicity surrounding the Angry Young Men.

In 'Sex, Snobbery and Sadism', a 1958 article in the *New Statesman*, Paul Johnson is enraged to the point of an ending attributing all global ills to the cruel culture *Dr No* represents:

> Recently I read Henri Alleg's horrifying account of his tortures in an Algiers prison; and I have on my desk a documented study of how we treat our prisoners in Cyprus. I am no longer astonished that these things can happen. Indeed, after reflecting on the Fleming phenomenon, they seem to me almost inevitable. (Johnson 1958: 432)

Hebdige claims the negative consensus that united critics as diverse as George Orwell, Evelyn Waugh and Richard Hoggart in revulsion at contemporary culture had begun, by the later 1950s, 'to settle around a single term; Americanisation' (Hebdige 1988: 52). In the early Bond books, the narrative stance on the US tends towards the gentle patronisation of a culture infinitely less refined than the British. However, the insecurity underlying such superiority is revealed by a telling moment when Bond, gambling against Le Chiffre in an attempt to bankrupt him of money belonging to SMERSH, loses all the money provided by MI6. The relaxed and admiring CIA agent Felix Leiter gets an envelope to him at the gaming table: 'There was one line of writing in ink: "Marshall Aid. Thirty-two million francs. With the compliments of the U.S.A."' (Fleming 2004: 79). Leiter's pleasant demeanour, and indeed Bond's own urbane mode of operation, are a tribute to what Anthony Crosland identified as 'One of the strong attractions of . . . American society: the extraordinary social freedom, the relaxed, informal atmosphere, the easier contacts, the natural assumption of equality, the total absence of deference' (Crosland 2006: 165).

Yet Crosland's admiration for American culture was so counter to the British zeitgeist that, according to Leonard, his close friend, Michael Young, tried to persuade him to tone down his enthusiasm in a letter responding to an early draft of the book (xiii). Meanwhile, the fear of the unknown in political dealings with Russia was gradually diminishing. Early in 1956 it had become apparent that Nikita Khrushchev was the new strong man of the USSR, and on 25 February he addressed the twentieth congress of his nation's Communist Party with a tirade against the 'crimes of Stalin' and the cult of personality (Montgomery 1965: 358). The speech was given in secret, but leaked out. Two months later, Khrushchev paid a ten-day official visit to London – and two years later he was joking with Richard Nixon in a model American kitchen. Though the mid-1950s saw Eisenhower's relaxed and consensual style finally eclipsing McCarthyite hysteria in the US, American cultural annexation posed a threat that seemed more immediately pressing than that of the Soviet Union. As Hebdige puts it, 'Although during the Cold War the *prospect* of Soviet Territorial ambitions could provoke similar indignation and dread, American *cultural* imperialism demanded a more immediate interpretive response' (Hebdige 1988: 52). Published in 1962, Francis Williams's *The American Invasion* announced itself as 'an intelligence report on an invasion. No doubt the invasion is benevolent. But that does not make it less threatening. There are few things so menacing as wholesale benevolence' (Williams 1962: 13). Williams notes that American investment in Britain had risen by an average of 13.6 per cent each year between 1954 and 1959 to an amount estimated by the US Department of Commerce to be around a billion pounds (16). Yet his argument is less troubled by economic realities than by cultural ethics – by an 'American admass that threatens us with its concern to turn ideas into no more than handmaidens of commerce' (39) – and he is appalled less by McCarthy's wickedness than by 'the supineness of the society in which he operated' (122). It is a similar supineness, recreated in a British context, upon which Wyndham places the blame for the triumph of the triffids.

John Brunner's 1959 nuclear war novel, *The Brink*, opens with a prologue tracing the path of an unidentified missile:

> It rose into the sky of a world whose nerves were strained to breaking point. It flew very high, and very fast . . . nothing could hinder its passage as it shrieked and thundered downward, towards the United States, towards the state of Nebraska, towards its fiery and devastating end. (Brunner 1959: 7)

The object is eventually revealed to be a manned Soviet satellite, whose pilot has steered it to the outskirts of Woodlawn, Nebraska, so as to destroy only one family home out of a population of 41,453. The car of Edward Carter, a journalist returning to his home town, is struck by part of the satellite's third-stage rocket; as a result, of all the town's inhabitants, only he is privy to classified military information, largely due to a quickly established rapport with the disillusioned Major Gotobed. Through him, he learns that Ben Goldwater, US Air Force colonel, acting on instinct, cancelled the retaliatory nuclear strike automatically launched when the US defence network has been compromised. Goldwater's reward for saving the human race by disobeying military orders is his immediate disappearance for court martial or worse, and the suppression of the truth about his actions. As the Major puts it, should the story get out,

> You'd get the people who think like that saying, 'That's what comes of putting a bastard kike in a responsible post!' They'd call him a traitor and a crypto-Red, and say he'd lost us a priceless opportunity to wipe Russia off the map when she was unprepared for it. (119)

As such dialogue might suggest, Brunner's novel is no forgotten classic; it 'proves' Carter's liberal credentials by his ability to lust after Goldwater's black girlfriend Miriam, and ends in his rush to publish the truth through the only reliable outlet – a British newspaper. Yet it does distinguish itself amongst the disparate British nuclear literature of the 1950s by its determination to interrogate the American political psyche and confront the question of whether national pride is more valuable within 'the American small town *gestalt*' than global survival. Carter wrestles with questions that suggest the greatest potential for cruelty within the Cold War confrontation lies paradoxically within the supposedly easy-going 'ordinary American': 'Suppose these people knew how narrowly they had escaped being a pyre of dead bodies? Would they be grateful to Ben Goldwater? Or would they be sorry that a few millions of other men, women and children had not promptly been dispatched to another world?' (41).

One of Richard Hoggart's most arresting images in *The Uses of Literacy* is that of the juke-box boys, ghoulishly pale in the harsh lights of the new milk bars, feeding their meagre copper coins into the record machine and staring 'as desperately as Humphrey Bogart across the tubular chairs' as another American pop song blares out. They are living, Hoggart suggests, 'to a large extent in a myth-world compounded of a few simple elements which they take to be those of American life' (Hoggart 1958: 204). Brunner's *The Brink* prompts its British readership towards the realisation that beneath the 'huge and centralized palliness' of American culture noted by Hoggart lies a dark, discriminatory and profoundly illiberal edge (283). Though the distant threat of Soviet belligerence was felt throughout the 1950s, so too was a realisation that the 'myth-world' of America had its own potential for malign influence on British culture.

Chapter Fourteen

Conclusions: Decade Talk

'That we talk as if the *Zeitgeist* shed its skin every ten years is a vice of the English language,' wrote Rayner Heppenstall in the 1956 article 'Decade Talk' (Heppenstall 1956: 377). And the zeitgeist is a tricky reptile, much easier to invoke than to define. As Alexander Galloway has put it:

> Periodization theory is a loose art at best and must take into account that, when history changes, it changes slowly and in an overlapping, multilayered way, such that one historical moment may well extend well into another, or two moments may happily coexist for decades or longer. (Galloway 2006: 27)

Yet during the 1950s, British writers seemed unusually keen on pinning down a characterisation of their decade. Kenneth Allsop's premature but none the less perceptive 1958 summary was called *The Angry Decade*. The *Spectator* leader that coined that over-reaching term 'the Movement' identified the poetic zeitgeist as 'part of that tide which is pulling us through the Fifties and towards the Sixties' (Scott 1954: 1). Donald Davie's 1959 article, 'Remembering the Movement' (for it was by then already over), shows him thinking how 'poetic production becomes meaningful as it enters into narratives of literary "history", into periods which thereby contain it' (Tuma 1998: 95).

Davie's title is ironising his own poem, 'Remembering the Thirties', which is also about intellectual traditions, or, more accurately, the rejection of one in particular. Leslie Paul's autobiography, *Angry Young Man* (1951), the title that was to spawn a hundred 1950s headline clichés, told the story of the author's struggle to overcome the deprivations of the 1920s and 1930s. 'What the intellectuals of the Thirties had', claimed George Scott in his own autobiography, was

> a Cause to live for. They sustained devotion to that Cause in the face of the kind of formidable evidence of infidelity that would make any other man,

normally equipped with ears, eyes and his ration of common sense, sue for divorce. But these men were seemingly not so equipped. They erected a barrier between themselves and the truth, aided ... by the crudities of anti-Communist propaganda – crudities, it may be said, worthy of *Pravda* and *Izvestia* at the height of the cold war. (Scott 1956: 76–7)

Politics and the position of government had, of course, changed considerably since the 1930s, in response to a fundamental postwar shift in public attitudes towards full employment and social welfare. Yet the reaction against the 1930s reverberated not just in the politics of the New Left when it emerged, but also a much more widespread sense of language, literacy and their uses. Scott continues: 'As Stephen Spender said in his letter to *Truth* ... the one thing the writers of today might learn from those of the Thirties "is to relate themselves to a particular time and a particular place, though of course both time and place are different"' (81).

As we have seen, for all its leanings towards realism, writing in the 1950s across the genres is shot through with a deep-seated concern over the authenticity of the existing means of responding to and recording reality. For all its enduring image as dull, settled and insular, the decade apprehended itself most often as a time of vertiginous change, of true transition. No wonder, then, that the definitive position of its writers has emerged here as that of the involved observer, who harbours simultaneously a sense of exclusion resulting from the disruption of national, or class, or racial identity, and a lingering belonging that provokes a responsibility to represent a particular community, time and place empathetically. It is no coincidence that this split decade – a time of faltering national confidence, of looking inward and looking back, and finding wanting – was a period during which the voices of the true outsiders to literature – the working class, the young and the immigrants (though mostly male) – began to emerge.

Once we know this, the more radical and historically prominent politics of the 1960s can be understood not as revolution, but as the development and extension of the various existing cultural currents. As Hewison puts it, 'Many of the conditions which now prevail in British cultural life are the result of what happened in the 1950s' (Hewison 1981: ix). The decade saw an unmistakable loosening of licence as to what constituted acceptable, moral, even British behaviour. In February 1956 (that year again), the death penalty was abolished; the campaign that achieved this had gathered much support during the winter of 1952, when Derek Bentley, 'an illiterate and Grade IV mental defective', was hanged for being present when Christopher Craig shot and killed a policeman (Montgomery 1965: 109). Craig was under eighteen and so could not be hanged. The real rush of liberalising legislation was not to come until the next decade, beginning with the Obscene Publications Act of 1960, outcome of the notorious Chatterley trial. The belated decriminalisation of (male) homosexuality in 1967 was the direct result of the recommendations of the 1957 Wolfenden Report.

Yet for all the continuity with its more glamorous successor in the decades of the twentieth century, and with the culture and society of the twenty-first, 1950s Britain was still a foreign country and they did things differently there. John Wolfenden's recommendations regarding the rights and treatment of homosexuals and prostitutes were submitted substituting the code words 'Huntleys' and 'Palmers' (Huntley and Palmers being a well-known brand of biscuit) for the groups in question, so as not to offend the typists (Shellard et al. 2004: 157). Anthony Crosland's ideal for the future of his country moved beyond public statutes to the very stuff of life – what Hoggart called 'the sense of the personal, the concrete, the local' – and to aspirations we now take for granted (Hoggart 1958: 33). In *The Future of Socialism* Crosland proclaimed 'I should like to see action taken both to widen opportunities for enjoyment and relaxation, and to diminish existing restrictions on personal freedom':

> Much could be done to make Britain a more colourful and civilised country to live in. We need not only higher exports and old-age pensions, but more open-air cafés, brighter and gayer streets at night, later closing hours for public houses, more local repertory theatres, better and more hospitable hoteliers and restaurateurs, brighter and cleaner eating-houses, more riverside cafés, more pleasure-gardens on the Battersea model, more murals and pictures in public places, better designs for furniture and pottery and women's clothes, statues in the centre of new housing-estates, better-designed street-lamps and telephone kiosks, and so on ad *infinitum*.

This, he suggested, was where Britain should begin, and then the nation would have no option but to address the 'socially-imposed restrictions on the individual's private life and liberty', such as 'the divorce laws, licensing laws, prehistoric (and flagrantly unfair) abortion laws, obsolete penalties for sexual abnormality, the illiterate censorship of books and plays and remaining restrictions on the equal rights of women'. He concludes his book: 'We do not want to enter the age of abundance, only to find that we have lost the values which might teach us how to enjoy it' (Crosland 2006: 402–3, 409). His words serve as a reminder to our own Age of Abundance of some of the best, bravest causes of all.

Works Cited

Abrams, Mark (1961) *Teenage Consumer Spending in 1959 (PART II)*, London: London Press Exchange.

Achebe, Chinua (1958) *Things Fall Apart*, London: Heinemann.

Aldiss, Brian W. (1973) *Billion Year Spree: The History of Science Fiction*, London: Weidenfeld & Nicolson.

'All this, and Everest too!' (1953) *Daily Express*, 2 June, p. 1.

Allen, E. L. (1953) *Existentialism from Within*, London: Routledge & Kegan Paul.

Allsop, Kenneth (1958) *The Angry Decade*, London: Peter Owen.

—(1965) *Scan*, London: Hodder & Stoughton.

Amis, Kingsley (1956) 'Art and Craft', review of *The Craft of Letters in England*, ed. John Lehmann, *Spectator*, 13 July, p. 69.

—(1966) *The James Bond Dossier*, London: Pan.

—(1976) [1954] *Lucky Jim*, Harmondsworth: Penguin.

Andaiye and Richard Drayton, eds (1990) *Conversations: George Lamming: Essays, Addresses and Interviews 1953–1990*, London: Karia.

Anderson, Benedict (1983) *Imagined Communities*, London: Verso.

Anderson, Lindsay (1957) 'Get Out and Push!', *Declaration*, ed. Tom Maschler, London: MacGibbon & Kee, pp. 153–78.

—(1958) 'Free Cinema', *Universities and Left Review*, Vol. 1, No. 2, pp. 51–2.

—(1981) [1957] 'Vital Theatre?', *New Theatre Voices of the Fifties and Sixties: Selections from Encore Magazine, 1956–1963*, ed. Charles Marowitz, Tom Milne and Owen Hale, London: Eyre Methuen, pp. 41–7.

Arden, John (1987) 'Introduction', *Serjeant Musgrave's Dance, Plays: One*, London: Methuen, pp. 11–13.

Auden, W. H. (1954) 'A Contemporary Epic?', *Encounter*, Vol. 2, No. 2 (February), pp. 67–71.

Ayer, A. J. (1956) 'Mr. Wilson's Outsider', *Encounter*, Vol. VII, No. 3 (September), pp. 75–7.

—(1967) [1936] *Language, Truth and Logic*, London: Victor Gollancz.

Bailey, Michael and Mary Eagleton, eds (2011) *Richard Hoggart: Culture and Critique*, Nottingham: Critical, Cultural and Communications Press.

Banham, M. and B. Hillier (1976) *A Tonic to the Nation: The Festival of Britain 1951*, London: Thames & Hudson.

Barnes, Michael (1981) 'Pig in the Middle', *The Times*, 15 January, p. 10.

Bates, H. E. (1990) [1958] *The Darling Buds of May*, Harmondsworth: Penguin.

—(1991) [1970] *A Little of What You Fancy, The Pop Larkin Chronicles*, London: Michael Joseph.

Bateson, F. W. (1953) 'The Function of Criticism at the Present Time', *Essays in Criticism*, Vol. III, No. 1 (January), pp. 1–27.

—(1966) [1950] *English Poetry*, London: Longman.

Behan, Brendan (1956) 'Theatre Workshop: "The Quare Fellow"', anonymous review, *The Times*, 25 May, p. 3.

—(1967) [1958] *Borstal Boy*, London: Hutchinson.

Bell, Robert (1998) 'Introduction: Kingsley Amis in the Great Tradition and In Our Time', *Critical Essays on Kingsley Amis*, ed. Robert Bell, New York: G. K. Hall, pp. 1–19.

Bell, Sam Hanna (2000) [1951] *December Bride*, Belfast: Blackstaff.

Bergonzi, Bernard (1971) *The Situation of the Novel*, London: Macmillan.

Beveridge, William Henry (1997) [1942] 'Social Insurance and Allied Services' ('The Beveridge Report'), *Internet Modern History Sourcebook*, ed. Paul Halsall, Fordham University, New York <http://www.fordham.edu/halsall/mod/1942beveridge.html>, accessed 7 April 2011.

Bhabha, Homi K., ed. (1990) *Nation and Narration*, London: Routledge.

—(2005) 'Adagio', *Critical Inquiry*, 31 (Winter), pp. 371–80.

Birmingham Feminist History Group (2005) [1979] 'Feminism as Femininity in the Nineteen-fifties?', reprinted *Feminist Review*, No. 80, pp. 6–23.

Black, Laurence (2010) *Redefining British Politics: Culture, Consumerism and Participation, 1954–70*, Houndmills: Palgrave Macmillan.

Bloom, Harold (1999) 'Introduction', *Critical Interpretations: William Golding's Lord of the Flies*, Philadelphia: Chelsea House, pp. 1–2.

The Blue Lamp (1949), film, dir. Basil Dearden, UK: Ealing Studios.

Blyton, Enid (1949) *Noddy Goes to Toyland*, London: Sampson Low, Marston.

Bond, Michael (1958) *A Bear Called Paddington*, London: Collins.

Booth, James (1992) *Philip Larkin, Writer*, Hemel Hempstead: Harvester.

Bosco, Mark (2005) *Graham Greene's Catholic Imagination*, Oxford: Oxford University Press.

Bourke, Joanna (1994) *Working-Class Cultures in Britain, 1890–1960*, London: Routledge.

Bowen, Elizabeth (1955) *A World of Love*, Oxford: Alden.

Bowlby, John (1966) [1953] *Child Care and the Growth of Love*, Harmondsworth: Penguin.

Bradbury, Malcolm (1969) 'Introduction', *Scenes from Provincial Life*, William Cooper, Houndmills: Macmillan, pp. i–xiv.

Bradford, Richard (1998) *Kingsley Amis*, Plymouth: Northcote House.

Braine, John (1959) [1957] *Room at the Top*, Harmondsworth: Penguin.

Braithwaite, E. R. (1992) [1959] *To Sir With Love*, Sevenoaks: Hodder & Stoughton.

Brannigan, John (2003) *Orwell to the Present: Literature in England, 1945–2000*, Houndmills: Palgrave Macmillan.

Brecht, Bertholt (1957) *Two Plays by Bertolt Brecht: The Good Woman of Setzuan and the Caucasian Chalk Circle, Original English Version by Eric Bentley and Maja Apelman*, New York: Grove.

Brians, Paul (1987) *Nuclear Holocausts: Atomic War in Fiction, 1895–1984*, Kent, OH: Kent State University Press.

Brickhill, Paul (1951) *The Dambusters*, London: Evans Bros.

Brief City (1951), film, dirs Maurice Harvey, Jacques B. Brunius, UK: Massingham Productions, <http://www.nationalarchives.gov.uk/films/1945 to1951/filmpage_bc.htm>, accessed 8 July 2011.

Brien, Alan (1958) Review of *A Taste of Honey*, *Spectator*, 6 June, p. 728.

British Broadcasting Corporation (1954) *Under Milk Wood*, Audience Research Report, BBC WA, R9/74/1, March, no pagination.

Brittain, Vera (1953) *Lady into Woman*, London: Andrew Dakers.

Brook, Peter (1981) [1959] 'Oh for Empty Seats!', *New Theatre Voices of the Fifties and Sixties: Selections from Encore Magazine, 1956–1963*, ed. Charles Marowitz, Tom Milne and Owen Hale, London: Eyre Methuen, pp. 68–74.

Brook, Susan (2007) *Literature and Cultural Criticism in the 1950s: The Feeling Male Body*, Houndmills: Palgrave Macmillan.

Brookes, Ian (2009) '"All the rest is propaganda": Reading the Paratexts of *Saturday Night and Sunday Morning*', *Adaptation*, Vol. 2, No. 1, pp. 17–33.

Brown, Ivor (1950) 'Handling the Text', *Observer*, 19 February, p. 6.

Brown, J. Dillon (2006) 'Exile and Cunning: The Tactical Difficulties of George Lamming', *Contemporary Literature*, Vol. 47, No. 4 (Winter), pp. 669–94.

Brubaker, William R., ed. (1989) *Immigration and the Politics of Citizenship in Europe and North America*, Lanham, MD: University Press of America.

Brunner, John (1959) *The Brink*, London: Victor Gollancz.

Burgess, Anthony (1962) *A Clockwork Orange*, London: Heinemann.

—(1979) [1956–9] *The Malayan Trilogy*, Harmondsworth: Penguin.

—(1983) 'The Apocalypse and After', *Times Literary Supplement*, 18 March, p. 256.

Burnett, Frances Hodgson (1911) *The Secret Garden*, London: Heinemann.

Burton, Richard D. E. (1997) *Afro-Creole Power, Opposition and Play in the Caribbean*, London: Cornell University Press.

Calder-Marshall, Arthur (1953) 'Youth in Barbados', review of *In the Castle of My Skin*, George Lamming, *Times Literary Supplement*, 27 March, p. 206.

Campbell, Andrew (1994) 'Strata and Bedrock in David Jones' *Anathemata*', *Renascence: Essays on Values in Literature*, Vol. 46, Issue 2 (1 December), p. 10.

Campbell, Olwen W. (1952) *The Report of a Conference on the Feminine Point of View*, London: Williams & Norgate.

Campbell, Roy (1949) 'On Some South African Novelists', *Collected Poems*, Vol. 1, London: Bodley Head, p. 198.

Camus, Albert (1942) *The Outsider* [*L'Étranger*], trans. Stuart Gilbert, Harmondsworth: Penguin.

Carswell, John (1956) 'The Outsider', *Times Literary Supplement*, 'Letters to the Editor', 14 December, p. 749.

Cartier, Rudolph (1958) 'A Foot in Both Camps', *Films and Filming*, Vol. 4, No. 12, p. 10.

Clark, S. H. (1994) *Sordid Images: The Poetry of Masculine Desire*, London: Routledge.

Clarke, Peter (1996) *Hope and Glory: Britain 1900–1990*, London: Allen Lane.

A Clockwork Orange (1971), film, dir. Stanley Kubrick, UK: Warner Bros.

Collini, Stefan (2008) *Common Reading: Critics, Historians, Publics*, Oxford: Oxford University Press.

Collins, Marcus (2001) 'Pride and Prejudice: West Indian Men in Mid-Twentieth-Century Britain', *Journal of British Studies*, Vol. 40, No. 3 (July), pp. 391–418.

Colls, Robert (2004) 'When We Lived in Communities: Working-class Culture and its Critics', *Cities of Ideas: Civil Society and Urban Governance in Britain 1800–2000*, ed. Robert Colls and Richard Rodger, Aldershot: Ashgate, pp. 283–307.

Conekin, Becky, Frank Mort and Chris Waters, eds (1999) 'Introduction', *Moments of Modernity: Reconstructing Britain 1945–1964*, London: Rivers Oram, pp. 1–21.

Connolly, Cyril (1956) 'A Forgettable Favourite', *Sunday Times*, 1 January, p. 5.

Connor, Steven (1996) *The English Novel in History: 1950–1995*, London: Routledge.

Conquest, Robert, ed. (1956) *New Lines*, London: Macmillan.

'Conservative's Hat Trick' (1959) *The Times*, 10 October, p. 6.

Cooper, William (1969) [1950] *Scenes from Provincial Life*, London: Macmillan.

Corcoran, Neil (1982) *The Song of Deeds: A Study of The Anathemata of David Jones*, Cardiff: University of Wales Press.

Cosh Boy (1953), film, dir. Lewis Gilbert, UK: Daniel Angel Films.

Croft, Michael (1954) *Spare the Rod*, London: Longmans.

Crosland, Anthony (1956) Advertisement for *The Future of Socialism*, *Economist*, 10 November, p. 19.

—(2006) [1956] *The Future of Socialism*, London: Constable.

Crouch, Marcus (1962) *Treasure Seekers and Borrowers: Children's Books in Britain 1900–1960*, London: Library Association.

Crozier, Andrew (1983) 'Thrills and Frills: Poetry as Figures of Empirical Lyricism', *Society and Literature 1945–1970*, ed. Alan Sinfield, New York: Holmes & Meier, pp. 199–234.

Dainotto, Roberto M. (2000) *Place in Literature: Regions, Cultures, Communities*, Ithaca, NY: Cornell University Press.

Dalton, Hugh (1956) Letter to C. A. R. Crosland, British Library of Political and Economic Science, Crosland Papers 13/8, quoted Martin Francis (1999) 'The Labour Party: Modernisation and the Politics of Restraint', *Moments of Modernity: Reconstructing Britain 1945–1964*, ed. Becky Conekin, Frank Mort and Chris Waters, London: Rivers Oram, p. 162.

The Darling Buds of May (1991–3), TV programme, ITV, UK: Yorkshire Television.

Davenport Hines, R. (1995) *Auden*, London: Heinemann.

Davie, Donald (1952) *Purity of Diction in English Verse*, London: Chatto & Windus.

—(1976) 'A Voice in the Desert', *Times Literary Supplement*, 1 October, p. 1233.

Davis, John (1990) *Youth and the Condition of Britain: Images of Adolescent Conflict*, London: Athlone.

Day, Gary (1996) *Rereading Leavis*, Houndmills: Macmillan.

Delaney, Shelagh (1982) [1956] *A Taste of Honey*, London: Methuen.
Demastes, William W. (1997) 'Osborne on the Fault Line: Jimmy Porter on the Postmodern Verge', *John Osborne: A Casebook*, ed. Patricia D. Denison, New York: Garland, pp. 62–9.
Denning, Michael (1987) *Cover Stories: Narrative and Ideology in the British Spy Thriller*, London: Routledge & Kegan Paul.
Dennis, Nigel (1999) [1955] *Cards of Identity*, London: Penguin.
—(1958) *Two Plays and a Preface*, London: Weidenfeld & Nicolson.
Department of Education and Science (1956) *The Handbook of Health Education*, London: HMSO.
Devine, George (1957) 'The Royal Court Theatre: Phase One', *International Theatre Annual*, No. 2, pp. 152–62.
—(1962) 'The Birth of the English Stage Company', *Prompt*, No. 1 (Summer), pp. 6–13.
—(1981) [1956] 'The Berliner Ensemble', *New Theatre Voices of the Fifties and Sixties: Selections from Encore Magazine, 1956–1963*, ed. Charles Marowitz, Tom Milne and Owen Hale, London: Eyre Methuen, pp. 14–18.
Dickens, Monica (1956) Column in *Woman's Own*, 8 March, p. 28.
Dowson, Jane and Alice Entwhistle (2005) *A History of Twentieth-Century British Women's Poetry*, London: Cambridge University Press.
Dr No (1962), film, dir. Terence Young, UK: Eon Productions.
Dupin, Christoph (2007) *Free Cinema* [Booklet accompanying DVD], British Film Institute.
Dworkin, Dennis L. (1993) 'Cultural Studies and the Crisis in British Radical Thought', *Views Beyond the Border Country: Raymond Williams and Cultural Politics*, ed. Dennis L. Dworkin and Leslie G. Roman, New York: Routledge, pp. 38–54.
Dyson, A. E. (1983) 'General Editor's Comments', *Look Back in Anger: A Casebook*, ed. John Russell Taylor, London: Macmillan, pp. 22–31.
Eagleton, Terry (1996) *The Illusions of Postmodernism*, Oxford: Blackwell.
Empson, William (1986) [1935] *Some Versions of Pastoral*, London: Hogarth.
Enright, D. J. (1955) 'Poetry in England Today: An Introduction', *Poets of the 1950s: An Anthology of New English Verse*, Tokyo: Kenkyusha, pp. 1–15.
Erikson, E. H. (1950) *Childhood and Society*, New York: Norton.
'Escapers' Club' (1956) *The Times*, 27 August, p. 9.
Ezekiel, Nissim (1989) *Collected Poems*, Delhi: Oxford University Press.
Family Portrait: A Film on the Theme of the Festival of Britain, 1951 (1950), film, dir. Humphrey Jennings, UK: Central Office of Information.
Farson, Daniel (1957) 'My Genius', interview with Colin Wilson, *Books and Bookmen*, October, pp. 24–5.
Ferrebe, Alice (2005) *Masculinity in Male-Authored Fiction 1950–2000: Keeping It Up*, Houndmills: Palgrave Macmillan.
—(2011) 'Excursions into the "Baroque": Hoggart, *Angel* and the Uses of Romance', *Richard Hoggart: Culture and Critique*, ed. Michael Bailey and Mary Eagleton, Nottingham: Critical, Cultural and Communications Press, pp. 95–107.
Festival in London (1951), film, dir. Philip Leacock, UK: Central Office for Information for Commonwealth Relations Office, <http://www.national archives.gov.uk/films/1945to1951/filmpage_fil.htm>, accessed 8 July 2011.

Finney, Albert (1960) Interview in 'Albert Finney Rides In On the New Wave', Press Book: Saturday Night and Sunday Morning BFI Information File.

Fleming, Ian (1957) *From Russia, With Love*, London: Jonathan Cape.

—(1958) *Dr No*, London: Jonathan Cape.

—(1961) *Thunderball*, London: Book Club.

—(2004) [1953] *Casino Royale*, Harmondsworth: Penguin.

Floud, Roderick (1956) *Social Class and Educational Opportunity*, London: Heinemann.

Foot, Paul (1965) *Immigration and Race in British Politics*, Harmondsworth: Penguin.

Francis, Martin (1999) 'The Labour Party: Modernisation and the Politics of Restraint', *Moments of Modernity: Reconstructing Britain 1945–1964*, ed. Becky Conekin, Frank Mort and Chris Waters, London: Rivers Oram, pp. 152–70.

Fraser, G. S. (1953) *The Modern Writer and His World*, London: Derek Verschoyle.

Frayn, Michael (1963) 'Festival', *Age of Austerity 1945–1951*, ed. Michael Sissons and Philip French, London: Hodder & Stoughton, pp. 319–38.

Free Cinema (2007), film, various directors, UK: British Film Institute.

Freeland, Richard M. (1972) *The Truman Doctrine and the Origins of McCarthyism*, New York: Knopf.

Fyvel, T. R. (1963) [1961] *The Insecure Offenders: Rebellious Youth in the Welfare State*, Harmondsworth: Penguin.

Galef, David (1997) 'Beyond Anger: Osborne's Wrestle with Language and Meaning', *John Osborne: A Casebook*, ed. Patricia D. Denison, New York: Garland, pp. 21–33.

Galloway, Alexander (2006) *Protocol: How Control Exists After Decentralization*, Cambridge, MA: MIT Press.

Gandhi, Leela (1989) 'Preface to Ezekiel', *Collected Poems*, Nissim Ezekiel, Delhi: Oxford University Press.

Garland, R. (1966) [1953] *The Heart in Exile*, New York: Pyramid.

Geertz, Clifford (1973) 'Deep Play: Notes on the Balinese Cockfight', *The Interpretation of Cultures*, New York: Basic, pp. 412–53.

Genette, Gérard (1997) [1987] *Paratexts: Thresholds of Interpretation*, trans. Jane E. Lewin, Cambridge: Cambridge University Press.

Gilleman, Luc (2008) 'From Coward and Rattigan to Osborne: Or the Enduring Importance of *Look Back in Anger*', *Modern Drama*, Vol. 51, No. 1 (Spring), pp. 104–25.

Gilroy, Beryl (1976) *Black Teacher*, London: Cassell.

Goffman, Erving (1990) [1959] *The Presentation of the Self in Everyday Life*, Harmondsworth: Penguin.

Golding, William (1988) [1956] *Pincher Martin*, London: Faber & Faber.

—(1996a) [1954] *Lord of the Flies*, London: Faber & Faber.

—(1996b) [1965] 'Fable', *Lord of the Flies*, London: Faber & Faber, pp. 249–71.

The Gorbals Story (1950), film, dir. David MacKane, UK: New World Pictures.

Gray, Nigel (1973) *The Silent Majority: A Study of the Working Class in Post-War British Fiction*, London: Vision.

Greene, Graham (1955) *The Quiet American*, London: William Heinemann.

—(1970) [1951] *The End of the Affair*, Harmondsworth: Penguin.

—(1971) [1938] *Brighton Rock*, Harmondsworth: Penguin.

Greenwood, Walter (1933) *Love on the Dole: A Tale of Two Cities*, London: Cape.

Gross, Robert F. (1990) 'Benign Descent in Terence Rattigan', *Modern Drama*, Vol. 33, No. 3 (September), pp. 394–408.

Gunn, Thom (1962) [1954] *Fighting Terms*, London: Faber & Faber.

—(1982) 'Cambridge in the Fifties', *The Occasions of Poetry*, ed. Clare Wilmer, New York: Farrar, Straus & Giroux, pp. 157–68.

Hall, Stuart (1989) 'The "First" New Left', *Out of Apathy: The Voices of the New Left Thirty Years On*, ed. Robin Archer, Diemet Bubeck and Hanjo Glock, London: Verso, pp. 11–38.

Hanley, James (1978) [1958] *The Welsh Sonata*, London: André Deutsch.

Hanley, Lynsey (2009) 'Introduction', *The Uses of Literacy: Aspects of Working-Class Life*, London: Penguin, pp. ix–xxiv.

Hare, David (2011) 'Terence Rattigan and a Theatre of Cultural Reaction', *Guardian*, 1 June, p. 28.

Hargreaves, Tracy (2011) '"Caught between two worlds": *The Uses of Literacy*, the "Angry Young Men" and British New Wave', *Richard Hoggart: Culture and Critique*, ed. Michael Bailey and Mary Eagleton, Nottingham: Critical, Cultural and Communications Press, pp. 108–22.

Hartley, Anthony (1963) *A State of England*, London: Hutchinson.

Hartley, L. P. (1961) [1953] *The Go-Between*, Harmondsworth: Penguin.

Hayman, Ronald, ed. (1977) *My Cambridge*, London: Robson.

Head, Dominic (2010) 'Writing Against the Nostalgic Grain: H. E. Bates in the 1950s', *Literature and History*, Vol. 19, No. 1, pp. 4–15.

Heaney, Seamus (1983) 'Hughes and England', *The Achievement of Ted Hughes*, ed. Keith Sagar, Manchester: Manchester University Press, p. 15.

Hebdige, Dick (1988) 'Towards a Cartography of Taste 1935–1962', *Hiding in the Light: On Images and Things*, London: Routledge, pp. 45–76.

Heffer, Simon (2011) 'Terence Rattigan Sounded the Deep Blue Sea of English Feeling', *Daily Telegraph*, 19 March, <http://www.telegraph.co.uk/comment/columnists/simonheffer/8392230/Terence-Rattigan-sounded-the-deep-blue-sea-of-English-feeling.html>, accessed 10 July 2011.

Hefner, Hugh (1953) Editorial, *Playboy*, Vol. 1, No. 1, p. 3.

Hennessy, Peter (2006) *Having It So Good: Britain in the Fifties*, London: Allen Lane.

Heppenstall, Rayner (1956) 'Decade Talk', *New Statesman and Nation*, 14 April, pp. 377–8.

Heron, Liz (1985) 'Introduction', *Truth, Dare or Promise: Girls Growing Up in the Fifties*, ed. Liz Heron, London: Virago, pp. 1–9.

Hewison, Robert (1981) *In Anger: Culture in the Cold War 1945–60*, London: Weidenfeld & Nicolson.

—(1995) *Culture and Consensus: England, Art and Politics Since 1940*, London: Methuen.

Hewitt, John (1987) [1947] 'Regionalism: The Last Chance', *Ancestral Voices: The Selected Prose of John Hewitt*, ed. Tom Clyde, Belfast: Blackstaff, pp. 122–5.

—(1991) *The Collected Poems of John Hewitt*, ed. Frank Ormsby, Belfast: Blackstaff.

Higson, A. (1984) 'Space, Place and Spectacle, *Screen*, No. 4/5, pp. 2–21.

Hill, John (1986) 'The British "Social Problem" Film: "Violent Playground" and "Sapphire"', *Screen*, Vol. 26, No. 1, pp. 34–48.

Hiro, Dilip (1973) *Black British, White British*, Harmondsworth: Penguin.

Hoggart, Richard (1958) [1957] *The Uses of Literacy: Aspects of Working-class Life with Special Reference to Publications and Entertainments*, Harmondsworth: Penguin.

—(1996) *A Sort of Clowning*, Oxford: Oxford University Press.

—(2005) *Promises to Keep: Thoughts in Old Age*, London: Continuum.

Holderness, Graham (1989) 'Reading "Deceptions" – A Dramatic Conversation', *Critical Survey*, Vol. 1, No. 2, pp. 122–9.

Holiday Camp (1947), film, dir. Ken Annakin, UK: Gainsborough Pictures.

Hope-Wallace, Philip (1958) '"The Sport of My Mad Mother": Prize-Winning Play', *Manchester Guardian*, 27 February, p. 7.

Hopkins, Bill (1957) *The Divine and the Decay*, London: MacGibbon & Kee.

Horn, Adrian (2009) *Juke Box Britain: Americanisation and Youth Culture, 1945–60*, Manchester: Manchester University Press.

Houlbrook, M. and Chris Waters (2006) '*The Heart in Exile*: Detachment and Desire in 1950s London', *History Workshop Journal*, No. 62, pp. 142–65.

Hughes, Ted (1968) [1957] *The Hawk in the Rain*, London: Faber & Faber.

—(1971) 'Ted Hughes and *Crow*', interview with Egbert Fass, *London Magazine*, January, pp. 10–1.

—(1989) *Selected Poems 1957–1981*, London: Faber & Faber.

Huk, Romana (2005) *Stevie Smith: Between the Lines*, Houndmills: Palgrave Macmillan.

Humble, Nicola (2001) *The Feminine Middlebrow Novel 1920s to 1950s*, Oxford: Oxford University Press.

Hynes, Joseph (1988) *The Art of the Real: Muriel Spark's Novels*, London: Associated University Presses.

Innes, Christopher (2000) 'Terence Rattigan: The Voice of the 1950s', *British Theatre in the 1950s*, ed. Dominic Shellard, Sheffield: Sheffield Academic Press, pp. 53–63.

Ionesco, Eugène (1958a) *The Lesson: A Comic Drama*, trans. Donald Watson, London: Samuel French.

—(1958b) 'The Playwright's Role: A Reply to Kenneth Tynan', *Observer*, 29 June, p. 14.

Jameson, Storm (1950) *The Writer's Situation and Other Essays*, London: Macmillan.

—(1970) *Journey from the North II*, London: Collins & Harvill.

Jansson, Tove (1950) *Finn Family Moomintroll*, trans. Elizabeth Portch, London: Ernest Benn.

Jardine, Lisa (1992) 'Saxon Violence', *Guardian*, 8 December, p. A4.

Jarrell, Randall (1973) [1955] 'The Age of Criticism', *Poetry and the Age*, London: Faber & Faber, pp. 71–92.

Jellicoe, Ann (1958) 'The Sport of My Mad Mother' anonymous review, *The Times*, 26 February, p. 3.

—(1964) [1958] *The Sport of My Mad Mother*, London: Faber & Faber.

Jenkins, Robin (1980) [1955] *The Cone-Gatherers*, Harmondsworth: Penguin.

John, Errol (1985) [1958] *Moon on a Rainbow Shawl*, London: Faber & Faber.

Johnson, Paul (1958) 'Sex, Snobbery and Sadism', *New Statesman*, 5 April, pp. 430–2.

Johnston, Arnold (1978) 'Miscasting of Pincher Martin', *William Golding: Some Critical Considerations*, ed. Jack I. Biles and Robert O. Evans, Lexington: University Press of Kentucky, pp. 103–16.

Jolivette, Catherine (2009) *Landscape, Art and Identity in 1950s Britain*, Farnham: Ashgate.

Jones, David (1952) *The Anathemata: Fragments of an Attempted Writing*, London: Faber & Faber.

Kay, Jackie (1997) 'Non-Stop Party', *Children of the Revolution: Communist Childhood in Cold War Britain*, ed. Phil Cohen, London: Lawrence & Wishart, pp. 32–42.

Kemp, Peter (1974) *Muriel Spark*, London: Paul Elek.

Kermode, Frank (1977) 'The House of Fiction', *Partisan Review*, Spring 1963, repr. *The Novel Today: Contemporary Writers on Modern Fiction*, ed. Malcolm Bradbury, London: Fontana, pp. 111–35.

King, Bruce (1987) *Modern Indian Poetry in English*, Delhi: Oxford University Press.

—(2003) *V. S. Naipaul*, Houndmills: Palgrave Macmillan.

—(2004) *The Internationalization of English Literature*, Oxford: Oxford University Press.

Kinghorn, Alexander Manson (1953) 'Wha'll Pent Trulie Scotland's Heid? An Essay on the Lallans Tradition', *Studies in English*, Vol. XXXII, pp. 133–47.

Kinkead-Weekes, Mark and Ian Gregor (1985) [1967] *William Golding: A Critical Study*, London: Faber & Faber.

Kinsey, A. C., Wardell B. Pomeroy and Clyde E. Martin (1948) *Sexual Behaviour in the Human Male*, Philadelphia: W. B. Saunders.

Kneale, Nigel (1954) *The Quatermass Experiment*, TV, UK: BBC Television.

—(1955) *Quatermass II*, TV, UK: BBC Television.

—(1959) *Quatermass and the Pit*, TV, UK: BBC Television.

—(1996) *The Quatermass Memoirs*, radio, UK: BBC Radio 3, March.

Krips, Valerie (2000) *The Presence of the Past: Memory, Heritage, and Childhood in Postwar Britain*, New York: Garland.

Kynaston, David (2009) *Family Britain: 1951–1957 (Tales of a New Jerusalem)*, London: Bloomsbury.

Lacey, Stephen (1995) *British Realist Theatre: The New Wave in its Context 1956–1965*, London: Routledge.

Laing, Stuart (1983a) 'Novels and the Novel', *Society and Literature 1945–70*, ed. Alan Sinfield, London: Methuen, pp. 235–59.

—(1983b) 'The Production of Literature', *Society and Literature 1945–1970*, ed. Alan Sinfield, London: Methuen, pp. 121–71.

Lalla, Barbara (2007) 'Signifying Nothing: Writing About Not Writing in *The Mystic Masseur*', *Anthurium: A Caribbean Studies Journal*, Vol. 5, Issue 2 (Fall), no pagination, <http://anthurium.miami.edu/volume_5/issue_2/lalla-signifying.html>, accessed 14 September 2011.

Lambert, Gavin (1956) 'Free Cinema', *Sight and Sound* (Spring), pp. 173–7; <http://www.bfi.org.uk/features/freecinema/archive/lambert-freecinema.pdf>, accessed 16 August 2010, no pagination.

Lamming, George (1994) [1954] *The Emigrants*, Ann Arbor, MI: University of Michigan Press.
—(1995) [1960] *The Pleasures of Exile*, Ann Arbor, MI: University of Michigan Press.
Larkin, Philip (1946) *Jill*, London: Fortune.
—(1947) *A Girl in Winter*, London: Faber & Faber.
—(1990) *Collected Poems*, London: Faber & Faber.
—(2002) *Trouble at Willow Gables and Other Fiction 1943–1953*, London: Faber & Faber.
—(2010) *Letters to Monica*, ed. Anthony Thwaite, London: Faber & Faber.
Laurie, Peter (1965) *The Teenage Revolution*, London: Anthony Blond.
Lawrence, D. H. (1913) *Sons and Lovers*, London: Duckworth.
Leader, Zachary (2000) *The Letters of Kingsley Amis*, London: Harper Collins.
—(2006) *The Life of Kingsley Amis*, London: Jonathan Cape.
Leavis, F. R. (1953) 'The Responsible Critic: or The Function of Criticism at Any Time', *Scrutiny*, Vol. XIX, No. 3 (Spring), pp. 162–83.
—(1955) *D. H. Lawrence: Novelist*, London: Chatto & Windus.
—(1962) [1953] *The Common Pursuit*, Harmondsworth: Penguin.
—(1963) 'A Retrospect', *Scrutiny*, No. XX, pp. 1–24.
—(1972) 'Two Cultures? The Significance of Lord Snow', *Nor Shall My Sword: Discourses on Pluralism, Compassion and Social Hope*, London: Chatto & Windus, pp. 41–74.
Leavis F. R. and Denys Thompson (1950) [1933] *Culture and Environment: The Training of Critical Awareness*, London: Chatto & Windus.
Lee, Laurie (1984) [1959] *Cider With Rosie*, London: Century.
Lessing, Doris (1957) 'The Small Personal Voice', *Declaration*, ed. Tom Maschler, London: MacGibbon & Kee, pp. 11–27.
—(1968) [1959] *Each His Own Wilderness*, *Three Plays*, Harmondsworth: Penguin, pp. 85–167.
—(1972) [1950] *The Grass is Singing*, London: Michael Joseph.
—(1982) [1952] *Martha Quest*, London: Granada.
Levin, Bernard (1955) 'ITV Makes its Bow', *Manchester Guardian*, 23 September, pp. 1, 6.
Lewis, Peter (1978) *The Fifties*, London: Heinemann.
Lewis, Saunders (1962) 'Tynged yr Iaith' (The Fate of the Language), BBC Annual Lecture, first broadcast 13 February.
Lindgren, Astrid (1954) *Pippi Longstocking*, trans. Edna Hurup, London: Oxford University Press.
Loader, W. R. (1957) *Through a Dark Wood*, London: Jonathan Cape.
Lodge, David (1977) *The Modes of Modern Writing: Metaphor, Metonymy and the Typology of Literature*, London: Routledge.
The Loneliness of the Long Distance Runner (1962), film, dir. Tony Richardson, UK: Woodfall Film Productions.
Lucky Jim (1957), film, dir. John Boulting, UK: Charter Film Productions.
Lycett, Andrew (2003) *Dylan Thomas: A New Life*, London: Phoenix.
Lyons, F. S. L. (1973) *Ireland Since the Famine*, London: Fontana.
Macaulay, Mary (1957) *The Art of Marriage*, Harmondsworth: Penguin.
MacInnes, Colin (1961a) [1958] 'Pop Songs and Teenagers', *England, Half English*, London: MacGibbon & Kee, pp. 45–59.

—(1961b) [1957] 'Young England, Half English: The Pied Piper from Bermondsey', *England, Half English*, London: MacGibbon & Kee, pp. 11–16.

—(1980) [1960] *Mr Love and Justice*, London: Allison & Busby.

—(1984a) [1959] *Absolute Beginners*, London: Allison & Busby.

—(1984b) [1957] *City of Spades*, London: Allison & Busby.

Mackenzie, Compton (1959) [1956] *Thin Ice*, Harmondsworth: Penguin.

MacNeice, Louis (1957) 'Lost Generations?': Review of *Poetry Now*, ed. G. S. Fraser, and *Mavericks*, ed. Howard Sergeant and Dannie Abse, *The London Magazine*, No. IV (4 April), p. 55.

Macquarrie, John (1982) *Existentialism*, Harmondsworth: Penguin.

Mander, John (1961) *The Writer and Commitment*, London: Secker & Warburg.

Mankowitz, Wolf (1957) 'British Playwriting: Cause without a Rebel', *Encore*, No. iii, 5 (June–July), p. 17.

Marowitz, Charles, Tom Milne and Owen Hale, eds (1981) *New Theatre Voices of the Fifties and Sixties: Selections from Encore Magazine, 1956–1963*, London: Eyre Methuen.

Marr, Andrew (2009) *A History of Modern Britain*, London: Pan.

Marwick, Arthur (1984) '*Room at the Top*, *Saturday Night and Sunday Morning*, and the "Cultural Revolution" in Britain', *Journal of Contemporary History*, No. 19, pp. 127–51.

—(1990) *British Society Since 1945*, London: Penguin.

Maschler, Tom, ed. (1957) *Declaration*, London: MacGibbon & Kee.

Mass Observation (1949) File Report 3110A 'Little Kinsey' (April).

Mathieson, M. and M. T. Whiteside (1971) 'The Secondary Modern School in Fiction', *British Journal of Educational Studies*, Vol. 19, No. 3 (October), pp. 283–93.

McEwan, Ian (1986), 'Schoolboys', *William Golding: The Man and His Books. A Tribute on His 75th Birthday*, ed. John Carey, London: Faber & Faber, pp. 157–60.

Milne, Tom (1981) [1958] 'Art in Angel Lane', *New Theatre Voices of the Fifties and Sixties: Selections from Encore Magazine, 1956–1963*, ed. Charles Marowitz, Tom Milne and Owen Hale, London: Eyre Methuen, pp. 80–6.

Ministry of Education (1959) *Fifteen to Eighteen* (Crowther Report), London: HMSO.

—(1960) *The Youth Service in England and Wales* (Albemarle Report), London: HMSO.

Mitford, Nancy, ed. (1960) [1956] *Noblesse Oblige: An Enquiry into the Identifiable Characteristics of the English Aristocracy*, Harmondsworth: Penguin.

Moffett, Joe (2006) 'Anglo-Saxon and Welsh Origins in David Jones' *The Anathemata*', *North American Journal of Welsh Studies*, Vol. 6, No. 1 (Winter), pp. 1–18.

Monsarrat, Nicholas (1951) *The Cruel Sea*, London: Cassell.

Montgomery, John (1965) *The Fifties*, London: Allen & Unwin.

Moore, Brian (1959) [1955] *The Lonely Passion of Miss Judith Hearne*, Harmondsworth: Penguin.

Morgan, Edwin (1981) [1958] 'That Uncertain Feeling', *New Theatre Voices of the Fifties and Sixties: Selections from Encore Magazine, 1956–1963*, ed. Charles Marowitz, Tom Milne and Owen Hale, London: Eyre Methuen, pp. 52–6.

Morrison, Blake (1986) [1980] *The Movement: English Poetry and Fiction of the 1950s*, London: Methuen.

Mort, Frank (1999) 'The Commercial Domain: Advertising and the Cultural Management of Demand in Post-War Britain', *Moments of Modernity: Reconstructing Britain 1945–1964*, ed. Becky Conekin, Frank Mort and Chris Waters, London: Rivers Oram, pp. 55–75.

Mulhern, Francis (1995) 'Culture and Authority', *Critical Quarterly*, Vol. 37, No. 1, pp. 77–89.

Munro, George (undated) *Gay Landscape*, unpublished manuscript in the Mitchell Library, Glasgow.

Murdoch, Iris (1950) 'The Novelist as Metaphysician', *Listener*, No. 43, pp. 473–6.

—(1963) [1954] *Under the Net*, Harmondsworth: Penguin.

Musgrove, F. (1964) *Youth and the Social Order*, London: Routledge & Kegan Paul.

Myrdal, Alva and Viola Klein (1962) [1956] *Women's Two Roles: Home and Work*, London: Routledge & Kegan Paul.

Naipaul, V. S. (2001) [1957] *The Mystic Masseur*, London: Picador.

Nairn, Tom (1981) [1977] *The Break-Up of Britain: Crisis and Neo-Nationalism*, London: Verso.

Najarian, James (2003) 'Contributions to Almighty Truth: Stevie Smith's Seditious Romanticism', *Twentieth Century Literature*, Vol. 49, No. 4 (Winter), pp. 472–93.

Nixon, Richard and Nikita Khrushchev (1959) 'The Kitchen Debate', 24 July, transcript at <http://teachingamericanhistory.org/library/index.asp?document=176>, accessed 7 April 2011.

Norton, Mary (1995) [1952] *The Borrowers*, London: Puffin Modern Classics.

Oakes, Philip (1956) 'A New Style in Heroes', *Observer*, 1 January, p. 8.

O Dreamland (1953), film, dir. Lindsay Anderson, Sequence, included on *Free Cinema* (2007), UK: British Film Institute.

Ollard, Richard, ed. (2003) *The Diaries of A. L. Rowse*, London: Allen Lane.

On the Beach (1959), film, dir. Stanley Kramer, USA: Stanley Kramer Productions.

Orwell, George (1949) *Nineteen Eighty-Four*, London: Secker & Warburg.

—(2001) [1937] *The Road to Wigan Pier*, London: Penguin.

Osborne, John (1957a) *The Entertainer*, London: Faber & Faber.

—(1957b) 'You've Fallen for the Great Swindle', *News Chronicle*, 27 February, p. 4.

—(1989) [1957] *Look Back in Anger*, London: Faber & Faber.

—(1991) *Almost a Gentleman*, London: Faber & Faber.

—(1994) [1959] 'The Fifties', *Damn You, England*, London: Faber & Faber, pp. 191–3.

—(1996) 'Introduction', *Plays One*, London: Faber & Faber, pp. vii–xiv.

Owen, Sue (2008) *Rereading Richard Hoggart: Life, Literature, Language, Education*, Newcastle: Cambridge Scholars.

Parkin, Frank (1968) *Middle Class Radicalism: The Social Bases of the British*

Campaign for Nuclear Disarmament, Manchester: Manchester University Press.

Paul, Kathleen (1997) *Whitewashing Britain: Race and Citizenship in the Postwar Era*, Ithaca, NY: Cornell University Press.

Paul, Leslie (1951) *Angry Young Man*, London: Faber & Faber.

Paulin, Tom (1992) Letter to *Times Literary Supplement*, 6 November, p. 15.

Pearce, Philippa (2008) [1958] *Tom's Midnight Garden*, Oxford: Oxford University Press.

Pearson, John (1966) *The Life of Ian Fleming*, London: Cape.

Pepper, Dr Aloysius C. (1955) 'At the Poetry Reading', pseudonymous article, *Spectator*, 30 December, pp. 887–8.

Perrott, Roy (1958) 'Miss Murdoch Rings the Bell', *Manchester Guardian*, 4 November, p. 4.

Pettitt, Lance (2001) *December Bride*, Cork: Cork University Press.

Piette, Adam (2009) *The Literary Cold War: 1945 to Vietnam*, Edinburgh: Edinburgh University Press.

Pinter, Harold (1958) 'Puzzling Surrealism of The Birthday Party', anonymous review in *The Times*, 20 May, p. 3.

—(1959) *The Birthday Party: A Play in Three Acts*, London: Encore.

—(1960) *The Room: A Play in One Act*, London: Samuel French.

Plath, Sylvia (1965) *Ariel*, Faber & Faber.

—(1985) *Selected Poems*, Faber & Faber.

Pope, Dudley (1956) *The Battle of the River Plate*, London: William Kimber.

Potter, Stephen (1952) *One-upmanship: Being some Account of the Activities and Teaching of the Lifemanship Correspondence College of One-upness and Gameslifemastery*, London: Hart-Davis.

Priestley, J. B. (1956) *The Scandalous Affair of Mr Kettle and Mrs Moon*, London: Samuel French.

—(1957) 'Britain and the Nuclear Bombs', *New Statesman and Nation*, 2 November, pp. 554–6.

Priestley, J. B. and Jacquetta Hawkes (1955) *Journey Down a Rainbow*, London: Heinemann-Cresset.

'The Problem of Homosexuality: Report by Doctors and Clergy' (1954) *The Times*, 26 February, p. 5.

Rattigan, Terence (1950) 'Concerning the Play of Ideas', *New Statesman and Nation*, Vol. XXXIX, No. 991 (4 March), pp. 241–2.

—(1952), *The Deep Blue Sea*, London: Hamish Hamilton.

—(1953) *Collected Plays, Vols I and II*, London: Hamish Hamilton.

—(1955) *Separate Tables: Two Plays*, London: Hamish Hamilton.

—(1958) *Variation on a Theme*, London: Hamish Hamilton.

—(1999) *Plays: Two*, London: Methuen.

Ravetz, Alison (1989) 'A View from the Interior', in *A View from the Interior*, ed. Judy Attfield and Pat Kirkham, London: Women's Press, pp. 187–205.

Ray, Sheila G. (1982) *The Blyton Phenomenon: The Controversy Surrounding the World's Most Successful Children's Author*, London: André Deutsch.

Rebellato, Dan (1999) *1956 and All That: The Making of Modern British Drama*, London: Routledge.

Reid, P. H. (1952) *The Colditz Story*, London: Hodder & Stoughton.

'Religion Ousts Marxism at Oxford' (1956), *Sunday Times*, 3 June, p. 10.

Renault, Mary (2003) [1959] *The Charioteer*, London: Vintage.

Reynolds, Kimberley (1998) 'Publishing Practices and the Practicalities of Publishing', in *Children's Book Publishing in Britain Since 1945*, ed. Kimberley Reynolds and Nicholas Tucker, Aldershot: Scolar, pp. 20–41.

Richards Audrey I. (1982) [1956] *Chisungu: A Girl's Initiation Ceremony Among the Bemba of Zambia*, London: Tavistock.

Ritchie, Harry (1988) *Success Stories: Literature and the Media in England, 1950–1959*, London: Faber & Faber.

Roberts, Andrew (1995) *Eminent Churchillians*, New York: Simon & Schuster.

Robinson, Peter (2009) '"Readings will grow erratic" in Philip Larkin's "Deceptions"', *Cambridge Quarterly*, Vol. 38, No. 3, pp. 277–308.

Rodden, John (1989) *The Politics of Literary Reputation: The Making and Claiming of 'St. George' Orwell*, Oxford: Oxford University Press.

Room at the Top (1959), film, dir. Jack Clayton, UK: Romulus.

Rose, E. J. B and Associates (1969) *Colour and Citizenship*, London: Oxford University Press for the Institute of Race Relations.

Rosenfield, Claire (1999) '"Men of a Smaller Growth": A Psychological Analysis of William Golding's *Lord of the Flies*', *Critical Interpretations: William Golding's Lord of the Flies*, ed. Harold Bloom, Philadelphia: Chelsea House, pp. 3–13.

Rosenthal M. L. and Sally M. Gall (1983) *The Modern Poetic Sequence: The Genius of Modern Poetry*, New York: Oxford University Press.

Ross, Alan (1954) 'Contemporary Portraits', review of *Lucky Jim*, *Times Literary Supplement*, 12 February, p. 101.

Ross, Alan S. C. (1960) [1954] 'U and Non-U: An Essay in Sociological Linguistics', *Noblesse Oblige: An Enquiry into the Identifiable Characteristics of the English Aristocracy*, ed. Nancy Mitford, Harmondsworth: Penguin, pp. 7–32.

Rossen, Janice (1989) *Philip Larkin: His Life's Work*, Iowa City: University of Iowa Press.

Rudd, David (2000) *Enid Blyton and the Mystery of Children's Literature*, Houndmills: Palgrave Macmillan.

Russell, John and Suzi Gablik (1969) *Pop Art Redefined*, London: Thames & Hudson.

Russell, R. D. and Robert Goodden (1976) 'The Lion and Unicorn Pavilion', in *A Tonic to the Nation: The Festival of Britain 1951*, ed. Mary Banham and Bevis Hillier, London: Thames & Hudson, pp. 96–101.

Sagar, Keith (1983) *The Achievement of Ted Hughes*, Manchester: Manchester University Press.

Said, Edward, W. (1986) 'Intellectuals in the Post-Colonial World', *Salmagundi*, No. 70/71, pp. 44–64.

—(1989) 'Yeats and Decolonization', *Dia Art Foundation: Discussions in Contemporary Culture. Remaking History*, No. 4, p. 11.

Salinger, J. D. (1979) [1951] *The Catcher in the Rye*, Harmondsworth: Penguin.

Sandbrook, Dominic (2005) *Never Had It So Good: A History of Britain from Suez to the Beatles*, London: Little, Brown.

—(2009) 'Why We Love History in 10–year Chapters', *Observer*, Review, 19 April, pp. 6–9.

Sapphire (1959), film, dir. Basil Dearden, UK: Artna Films.

Saturday Night and Sunday Morning (1960), film, dir. Karel Reisz, UK: Woodfall Film Productions.

Scott, George (1956) *Time and Place*, London: Staples.

Scott, J. D. (1954) 'In the Movement', *Spectator*, 1 October, p. 1.

Scott, Paul (1958) *The Alien Sky*, London: Eyre & Spottiswoode.

Selvon, Sam (2006) [1956] *The Lonely Londoners*, Harmondsworth: Penguin.

Seymour-Smith, Martin (1955) 'The Literary Situation', *Departure*, No. 3 (Spring), p. 16.

Shellard, Dominic, ed. (2000) 'Introduction', *British Theatre in the 1950s*, Sheffield: Sheffield Academic Press, pp. 11–15.

Shellard, Dominic and Steve Nicholson with Miriam Handley (2004) *The Lord Chamberlain Regrets . . . : A History of British Theatre Censorship*, London: British Library.

Shute, Nevil (1957) *On the Beach*, New York: William Morrow.

Sillitoe, Alan (1958) *Saturday Night and Sunday Morning*, London: W. H. Allen.

—(1985) [1959] 'The Loneliness of the Long-Distance Runner', *The Loneliness of the Long-Distance Runner*, London: Grafton, pp. 7–54.

—(1960) *Saturday Night and Sunday Morning*, London: Great Pan.

Sims Steward, Julie (1998) 'Ceci n'est pas un Hat: Stevie Smith and the Refashioning of Gender', *South Central Review*, Vol. 15, No. 2 (Summer), pp. 16–33.

Sinfield, Alan, ed. (1983a) *Society and Literature 1945–1970*, New York: Holmes & Meier.

—(1983b) 'The Theatre and its Audiences', *Society and Literature 1945–1970*, ed. Alan Sinfield, London: Methuen, pp. 173–97.

—(1989) *Literature, Politics and Culture in Postwar Britain*, Oxford: Basil Blackwell.

—(1994) *The Wilde Century*, London: Cassell.

Sitwell, Edith (1956) 'Tragic American Visits', review of *Dylan Thomas in America*, John Malcolm, *Sunday Times*, 22 April, p. 5.

Sked, Alan and Chris Cook (1993) *Post-War Britain: A Political History*, Harmondsworth: Penguin.

Smith, Stevie (1957) 'Light Fantastic', anonymous review of *Not Waving But Drowning*, *Times Literary Supplement*, 4 October, p. 588.

—(1985) *Stevie Smith: A Selection*, ed. Hermione Lee, London: Faber & Faber.

—(1988) *New Selected Poems of Stevie Smith*, New York: New Directions.

Snell, K. D. M. (1998) 'The Regional Novel: Themes for Interdisciplinary Research', *The Regional Novel in Britain and Ireland, 1800–1990*, ed. K. D. M. Snell, Cambridge: Cambridge University Press, pp. 1–53.

Snow, C. P. (1950) 'New Novels: A Matter for Pride', *Sunday Times*, 28 May, p. 3.

—(1954) *The New Men*, London: Macmillan.

—(1969) [1959] *The Two Cultures*, Cambridge: Cambridge University Press.

Spark, Muriel (1961) 'My Conversion', *Twentieth Century*, No. 170 (Autumn), pp. 58–63.

—(1987) [1957] *The Comforters*, London: Penguin.

Spender, Stephen (1953) 'On Literary Movements', *Encounter*, Vol. 1, No. 2 (November), pp. 66–8.

Spender, Stephen and Irving Kristol (1953) 'After the Apocalypse', *Encounter*, Vol. 1, No. 1 (October), p. 1.

Spring, Howard (1957) 'The World of L. S. Lowry', *The Saturday Book*, No. 17.

Stanley, L. (1995) *Sex Surveyed 1949–1994: From Mass Observation's 'Little Kinsey' to the National Surveys and Hite Report*, London: Taylor & Francis.

Stevenson, Randall (1987) 'Scottish Theatre 1950–1980', *The History of Scottish Literature Volume 4: Twentieth Century*, ed. Cairns Craig, Aberdeen: Aberdeen University Press, pp. 349–67.

Stoney, Barbara (1974) *Enid Blyton: A Biography*, London: Hodder & Stoughton.

Storer, Richard (2009) *F. R. Leavis*, London: Routledge.

Storey, Mark (1979) 'Why Stevie Smith Matters', *Critical Quarterly*, Vol. 21, No. 2 (Summer).

Stubbs, Patricia (1973) *Muriel Spark*, Harlow: Longman for the British Council.

Sutherland, John (2000) *Reading The Decades: Fifty Years of the Nation's Best Selling Books*, London: BBC Books.

Sylvester, David (1956) 'The Anglicisation of Outer Space', *Encounter*, Vol. VI, No. 1 (January), pp. 69–72.

Symons, Julian Gustave (1952) 'Uncommitted Talents', *Times Literary Supplement*, 29 August, p. 572.

A Taste of Honey (1961), film, dir. Tony Richardson, UK: Woodfall Film Productions.

Taylor, D. J. (2008) 'The Common Touch', *Guardian*, 1 March, Review, p. 21.

Taylor, Elizabeth (1986) [1951] *A Game of Hide and Seek*, London: Virago.

—(2001) [1957] *Angel*, London: Virago.

Taylor, John Russell (1968) [1962] *Anger and After*, Harmondsworth: Pelican.

—, ed. (1983) [1968] *Look Back in Anger: A Casebook*, London: Macmillan.

Thomas, Dylan (1952a) *Collected Poems 1934–1952*, London: J. M. Dent.

—(1952b) Anonymous review of *Collected Poems 1934–1952*, *Times Literary Supplement*, 28 November, p. 776.

—(2000) [1954] *Under Milk Wood*, London: Penguin.

Thwaite, Anthony, ed. (1993) *Selected Letters of Philip Larkin 1940–1985*, London: Faber & Faber.

Tolkien, J. R. R. (1954) *The Fellowship of the Ring: Being the First Part of The Lord of the Rings*, Oxford: George Allen & Unwin.

Tomlinson, Charles (1955) *The Necklace*, Oxford: Fantasy.

—(1957) 'The Middlebrow Muse', *Essays in Criticism*, No. 7, p. 215.

Townsend, John (1958) *The Young Devils*, London: Chatto & Windus.

Toynbee, Philip (1956) 'Unlucky Jims', review of Colin Wilson's *The Outsider*, *Observer*, 27 May, p. 14.

Tressell, Robert (1955) [1914] *The Ragged Trousered Philanthropists*, London: Lawrence & Wishart.

Tuma, Keith (1998) *Fishing By Obstinate Isles: Modern and Postmodern British Poetry and American Readers*, Evanston, IL: Northwestern University Press.

Tynan, Kathleen (1988) *The Life of Kenneth Tynan*, London: Methuen.

Tynan, Kenneth (1954a) 'Apathy', *Observer*, 31 October, p. 6.

—(1954b) 'Mixed Double', *Observer*, 26 September, p. 11.

—(1955a) 'Modern Greek', *Observer*, 13 March, p. 11.
—(1955b) 'New Writing', *Observer*, 7 August, p. 11.
—(1956) 'The Voice of the Young', *Observer*, 13 May, p. 11.
—(1957) 'The Play Competition', *Observer*, 18 August, p. 11.
—(1964) *Tynan on Theatre*, Harmondsworth: Penguin.
Wade, Stephen (2002) *In My Own Shire: Region and Belonging in British Writing, 1840–1970*, Westport: Praeger.
Wain, John (1950) 'Ambiguous Gifts', *Penguin New Writing*, Vol. 40, Harmondsworth: Penguin, pp. 116–28.
—(1955a) 'A Daniel Come to Judgement', *Spectator*, 29 July, pp. 171–2.
—(1955b) 'Leavis on Lawrence', *Spectator*, 7 October, pp. 457–9.
—(1955c) 'Moral, Grave, Sublime', *Spectator*, 9 September, pp. 339–40.
—(1956a) 'New Novels', review of *French Leave* by P. G. Wodehouse, *Observer*, 29 January, p. 9.
—(1956b) '*Reading*: The Literary Critic in the University', *The Twentieth Century*, Vol. clix, No. 948 (February), pp. 142–50.
—(1957a) 'How it Strikes a Contemporary: A Young Man who is not Angry', *The Twentieth Century*, March, pp. 227–36.
—(1957b) Letter to the *London Magazine*, Vol. 4, No. 3 (March), pp. 55–7.
—(1957c) *Preliminary Essays*, New York: St Martin's.
—(1958) 'Possible Worlds', review of *Saturday Night and Sunday Morning*, *Observer*, 12 October, p. 20.
—(1970) [1953] *Hurry on Down*, London: Secker & Warburg.
Wales, Katie (2008) '"The Anxiety of Influence": Hoggart, Liminality and Melvyn Bragg's *Crossing the Lines*', *Re-Reading Richard Hoggart*, ed. Sue Owen, Newcastle: Cambridge Scholars Press, pp. 102–17.
Wandor, Michelene (1987) *Look Back in Gender: Sexuality and the Family in Post-war British Drama*, London: Methuen.
—(2001) *Post-War British Drama: Looking Back in Gender*, London: Routledge.
Wansell, Geoffrey (1995) *Terence Rattigan*, London: HarperCollins.
Warth, Douglas (1952) 'Evil Men', *Sunday Pictorial*, 25 May, p. 6.
Waterhouse, Keith (1958) 'Our Children are Changing', *Daily Mirror*, 15 September, pp. 12–13.
—(1959) *Billy Liar*, London: Michael Joseph.
Waters, Chris (1999) 'Disorders of the Mind, Disorders of the Body Social: Peter Wildeblood and the Making of the Modern Homosexual', *Moments of Modernity: Reconstructing Britain 1945–1964*, ed. Becky Conekin, Frank Mort and Chris Waters, London: Rivers Oram, pp. 134–51.
Waugh, Evelyn (1956) 'Dr Wodehouse and Mr Wain', *Spectator*, 24 February, pp. 243–4.
—(1957) *The Ordeal of Gilbert Pinfold: A Conversation Piece*, London: Chapman & Hall.
—(1960) 'An Open Letter to the Hon[ble] Mrs Peter Rodd (Nancy Mitford) On a Very Serious Subject', *Noblesse Oblige: An Enquiry into the Identifiable Characteristics of the English Aristocracy*, ed. Nancy Mitford, Harmondsworth: Penguin, pp. 57–75.
Webster, Wendy (1998) *Imagining Home: Gender, 'Race' and National Identity, 1945–64*, London: UCL Press.

Welch, Colin (1958) 'Dear Little Noddy: A Parent's Lament', *Encounter*, Vol. 10, No. 1 (January), pp. 18–23.

Wesker, Arnold (1964) *The Wesker Trilogy*, Harmondsworth: Penguin.

—(undated) 'Why I Turned Down the CBE', <http://www.arnoldwesker.com>, accessed 2 June 2011.

Westall, Claire (2005) 'Men in the Yard and On the Street: Cricket and Calypso in *Moon on a Rainbow Shawl* and *Miguel Street*', *Anthurium: A Caribbean Studies Journal*, Vol. 3, Issue 2 (Fall) – no pagination, paragraph numbers given.

White, Cynthia L. (1977) *The Women's Periodical Press in Britain 1946–76*, London: HMSO.

Wickenden, James (1958) *Colour in Britain*, Oxford: Oxford University Press and Institute of Race Relations.

Wildeblood, Peter (1956) [1955] *Against the Law*, London: Weidenfeld & Nicolson.

Williams, Francis (1962) *The American Invasion*, London: Anthony Blond.

Williams, Raymond (1959) 'Our Debt to Dr Leavis', *Critical Quarterly*, Vol. 1, No. 3, pp. 245–7.

—(1960) 'The New British Left', *Partisan Review*, No. 27 (Spring), pp. 341–7.

—(1962) [1960] *Border Country*, London: Chatto & Windus.

—(1971) [1958] *Culture and Society 1780–1950*, Harmondsworth: Pelican.

—(1976) *Keywords: A Vocabulary of Culture and Society*, London: Fontana.

—(1989) 'Fiction and the Reading Public', review of *The Uses of Literacy*, *What I Came to Say*, London: Hutchinson, pp. 24–9.

—(1991) 'Region and Class in the Novel', *Writing in Society*, London: Verso, pp. 229–38.

Williams, Raymond and Michael Orrom (1954) *Preface to Film*, London: Film Drama.

Wilmer, Clare, ed. (1982) *The Occasions of Poetry*, New York: Farrar, Straus & Giroux.

Wilson, Angus (1954) 'The Future of the English Novel', *Listener*, 29 April, p. 746.

—(1958) [1956] *Anglo-Saxon Attitudes*, Harmondsworth: Penguin.

—(1966) [1952] *Hemlock and After*, London: Secker & Warburg.

Wilson, Colin (1957) *Religion and the Rebel*, London: Victor Gollancz.

—(1958) [1956] *The Outsider*, London: Victor Gollancz.

—(2001) 'Introduction: The Outsider Twenty Years On', *The Outsider*, London: Phoenix, pp. 1–10.

Wilson, Elizabeth (1980) *Only Halfway to Paradise: Women in Postwar Britain: 1945–1968*, London: Tavistock.

Winnicott, D. W. (1957) *The Child and His Family* and *The Child and the Outside World*, London: Tavistock.

Wolfenden Report (1957) *Report of the Committee on Homosexual Offences and Prostitution*, London: HMSO.

Woods, Gregory (1998) *A History of Gay Literature: The Male Tradition*, New Haven, CT: Yale University Press.

Wyndham, Francis (1969) 'Introduction', *Visions of London*, Colin MacInnes, London: MacGibbon & Kee, pp. vii–x.

Wyndham, John (1953) *The Kraken Wakes*, London: Michael Joseph
—(1955) *The Chrysalids*, London: Michael Joseph.
—(1973) [1951] *The Day of the Triffids*, Harmondsworth: Penguin.
Wynn Thomas, M. (1998) 'Emyr Humphreys: Regional Novelist?', *The Regional Novel in Britain and Ireland, 1800–1990*, ed. K. D. M. Snell, Cambridge: Cambridge University Press, pp. 201–20.
Young, B. A. (1986) *The Rattigan Version: Sir Terence Rattigan and the Theatre of Character*, London: Hamish Hamilton.

Index

Abrams, Mark, 33
Achebe, Chinua, *Things Fall Apart*, 133
Aldiss, Brian, 14, 213–14, 214–15, 219–20
Allsop, Kenneth, 2, 48, 180, 185, 192, 193, 200, 223
Americanisation (anxiety over), 19, 31–2, 220
Amis, Kingsley, 1, 97–8, 160, 201, 219
  Lucky Jim, 11, 42, 43–5, 177, 196, 210
Anderson, Benedict, 146, 147
Anderson, Lyndsay, 174–5, 176, 195, 196–7, 204, 206n, 209
Angry Young Man/Men
  Angry novels, 45–6, 49, 137, 152–3, 181
  Angry Young Man (Leslie Paul), 223
  Declaration, 195
  media phenomenon of, 39–40, 123, 210, 220
Arden, John, *Serjeant Musgrave's Dance*, 58
Arts Council, 56–7
Auden, W. H., 121, 147
Ayer, A. J., 10, 96, 186, 193

Barry, Gerald, 11, 15
Bates, H. E.
  The Darling Buds of May, 163–6
  A Little of What You Fancy, 166
Bateson, F. W., 190–1
Beaumont, Hugh 'Binkie', 56
Beauvoir, Simone de, 92

Beckett, Samuel, *Waiting for Godot*, 59–60, 71
Behan, Brendan, *The Quare Fellow*, 57, 196
Bell, Sam Hanna, *December Bride*, 153–5
Bergonzi, Bernard, 40
Beveridge Report, The ('Social Insurance and Allied Services'), 80
Bhabha, Homi K., 36, 47, 130
Birmingham Feminist History Group, 29, 84–5
Black, Laurence, 149–50
Blyton, Enid, 82–3
Bomb, the, 2, 6, 66, 210, 211–12, 217, 218
Bond, Michael, *A Bear Called Paddington*, 83
Bourke, Joanna, 171–2
Bowen, Elizabeth, *A World of Love*, 89–90
Bowlby, John, 81
Braine, John, 196
  Room at the Top, 41, 42, 45, 175–9, 197, 210
Braithwaite, E. R., *To Sir, With Love*, 28–30, 132
Brecht, Bertholt, 57, 58
Brians, Paul, 214, 218
Brief City (film), 12
Brittain, Vera, 80
Brook, Susan, 168, 177
Brookes, Ian, 197–8
Brown, J. Dillon, 133

Brunner, John, *The Brink*, 221–2
Burgess, Anthony, 26, 139, 218
Burgess, Guy and Donald Maclean, 3, 219

Campaign for Nuclear Disarmament (CND), 217, 218
Campbell, Andrew, 148
Campbell, Olwen W., 85
Campbell, Roy, 197, 206n
Camus, Albert, *The Outsider* [*L'Étranger*], 48
Caribbean Voices (radio programme), 134
censorship (theatre) *see* Lord Chamberlain
Chatterley trial, 225
Christie, Agatha, *The Mousetrap*, 55
Churchill, Winston, 3, 129, 211–12
Clark, S. H., 104–5
Cold War, the, 6, 77, 211–12, 216, 219, 221, 222
Cole, G. D. H., 207
Collini, Stefan, 7
Colls, Robert, 172
communism, 91, 169, 207, 210
Connor, Steven, 36, 37
Conquest, Robert, 96, 97, 99, 100, 104, 150, 200
Cooper, William (H. S. Hoff), *Scenes From Provincial Life*, 41–2
Corelli, Marie, 201
Coronation, the (1953), 3–4
Coward, Noël, 14, 56
Croft, Michael, *Spare the Rod*, 24
Crosland, Anthony, 207–10, 220, 225
Crouch, Marcus, 82

Dainotto, Roberto M., 146, 147, 151
Dalton, Hugh, 208
Davie, Donald, 102, 108, 186–7, 191, 223
Davis, John, 19, 30, 35, 36
Day, Gary, 156, 188
Dearden, Basil, 142
    Sapphire, 141–4
Declaration (essays), 40, 176, 195, 196–7, 209, 210

Delaney, Shelagh, *A Taste of Honey*, 67–8, 72, 196
Dennis, Nigel, 40
    Cards of Identity, 4, 49–50
    Two Plays and a Preface, 10, 49
Devine, George, 57, 58, 59, 60
Dickens, Monica, 80–1
Dworkin, Dennis L., 169, 173

Eden, Anthony, 5
education
    Albermarle Report (1960), 19–20
    Butler, R. A., 163
    children's literature, 82
    class divisions within, 7
    Crowther Report (1959), 23
    literary treatment of, 23–4, 28–30
    scholarships *see* Scholarship Boys
    sex education, 29
Eliot, T. S., 54, 55, 103, 104, 187, 190
Empson, William, 157, 186, 190
Encore (magazine), 58, 62
Encounter (journal), 31, 82, 163, 188, 189, 193
English Stage Company (ESC), 57, 58–9
Erikson, Erik H., 20
Essays in Criticism (journal), 189, 190
Existentialism, 48–50, 99–101
Ezekiel, Nissim, 102–3

Fabian Society, 207
Farson, Daniel, 192, 196
feminism, 80, 84–5, 86, 87, 90, 92
Festival of Britain (1951), 11–16, 157, 205
film and cinema, 9, 58, 174–5, 197, 219
Finney, Albert, 198
First Reading (radio programme), 95, 96, 189, 196
Fleming, Ian, *James Bond* series, 198, 219–20
Fraser, G. S., 195
Frayn, Michael, 11, 13–14, 15
Free Cinema, 175
Freud, Sigmund, 97
Freudianism, 22, 98, 117
Fyvel, T. R., 19, 26, 32

Garland, Rodney (Adam de Hegedus),
  The Heart in Exile, 116–17, 118,
  122, 123
Geertz, Clifford, 11
Genette, Gérard, 197
Gielgud, John, 55, 113
Gilroy, Beryl, *Black Teacher*, 130–2
Goffman, Erving, 42–3
Golding, William
  Lord of the Flies, 22–3, 30
  Pincher Martin, 50, 51
Gray, Nigel, 179
Greene, Graham
  Brighton Rock, 51
  The End of the Affair, 51, 52
Gunn, Thom, 100–1, 108, 118

Hall, Stuart, 209
Hanley, James, 201
  The Welsh Sonata, 158–9
Hargreaves, Tracy, 173–4, 177–8
Hartley, Anthony, 4, 41, 201
Hartley, L. P., *The Go-Between*,
  20–2
Head, Dominic, 165
Heaney, Seamus, 108
Hebdige, Dick, 205, 220, 221
Heffner, Hugh, 205
Hennessy, Peter, 3, 7, 166, 212
Heppenstall, Rayner, 55, 223
Hewison, Robert, 14, 224
Hewitt, John, 145, 146, 147, 153,
  166
Hillary, Edmund, 4
Hiro, Dilip, 128, 129
Hoggart, Richard, 155, 172, 173,
  188, 191
  The Uses of Literacy, 10, 42, 64,
  172–4, 176, 188, 222, 225
Hopkins, Bill, *The Divine and the
  Decay*, 48
Horizon (journal), 188, 201
Horn, Adrian, 31–2
Houlbrook, Matt, 116
Hughes, Ted, 106–8, 214
Huk, Romana, 109
Humble, Nicola, 81
Hungarian uprising (1956), 6,
  209

immigration policy, 127–9
Ionesco, Eugène, 71
  The Lesson, 59

Jardine, Lisa, 102
Jarrell, Randall, 185, 194
Jellicoe, Ann, *The Sport of My Mad
  Mother*, 24–8
Jenkins, Robin, *The Cone-Gatherers*,
  151–3
Jennings, Elizabeth, 99–100, 104
Jennings, Humphrey, 15
John, Errol, *Moon on a Rainbow
  Shawl*, 64–5, 128
Johnson, Paul, 220
Jolivette, Catherine, 15, 151, 212–13
Jones, David, *The Anathemata*, 10,
  147–9

Kay, Jackie, 91
Kemp, Peter, 52–3
Khrushchev, Nikita, 77–8, 91, 220–1
King, Bruce, 47, 102, 103, 130
Kinghorn, Alexander Manson, 150–1
Kinsey Report, the (*Sexual Behaviour in
  the Human Male*), 112, 122
Kneale, Nigel, 214
Krips, Valerie, 81, 84
Kynaston, David, 3, 43, 171, 172,
  204

Lacey, Stephen, 58, 60, 63, 71, 72
Laing, Stewart, 40, 42, 50, 56
'Lallans makars', 150
Lambert, Gavin, 175
Lamming, George
  The Emigrants, 128, 132–6, 138,
  139, 140, 181
  In the Castle of My Skin, 132
  The Pleasures of Exile, 134
Larkin, Philip, 94–5, 96–7, 98, 99, 102,
  104, 105, 108
Laurie, Peter, 32
Leader, Zachary, 98, 160
Leavis, F. R., 173, 187
  approach to context, 189–91
  Cambridge University, 187, 189, 205
  influence on the Movement, 186–7,
  202

Leavis, F. R. (*cont.*)
 opinion of C. P. Snow, 187
 'organic community', 155–6, 171
Lee, Laurie, 15
 Cider With Rosie, 155–7
Lehmann, Rosamund, *The Echoing
 Grove*, 86
Leonard, Dick, 208–9, 220
Lessing, Doris, 40, 210, 212
 Each His Own Wilderness, 65–7
 The Golden Notebook, 92
 The Grass is Singing, 90–3, 210
 Martha Quest, 210
Lewis, C. S., *The Lion, the Witch and
 the Wardrobe*, 82
Lewis, Peter, 8
Lewis, Saunders, 158
'Little Kinsey' (Mass Observation File
 Report 3110A), 112, 114
Littlewood, Joan, 57, 68
Lodge, David, 9
Logical Positivism, 10, 96
Lord Chamberlain, 59–60, 113
Lyons, F. S. L., 146

Macaulay, Mary, 95
MacDiarmid, Hugh, 150
MacInnes, Colin, 31–2
 Absolute Beginners, 32–8, 141
 City of Spades, 138–41, 142, 143
 Mr Love and Justice, 139
Mackenzie, Compton, *Thin Ice*, 118
Macmillan, Harold, 5, 7, 163
MacNeice, Louis, 150
MacQuarrie, John, 48
Mander, John, 178, 200
Marowitz, Charles, 57
Marr, Andrew, 9
Maschler, Tom, 195
Maugham, Somerset, 62
Miller, Arthur, *Death of a Salesman*, 56
Mitford, Nancy, 163, 205
Moffett, Joe, 148, 149
Monsarrat, Nicholas, *The Cruel Sea*,
 219
Montgomery, John, 1, 12, 212, 218,
 221, 224
Moore, Brian, *The Lonely Passion of
 Miss Judith Hearne*, 50–1

Morrison, Blake, 95, 96, 97, 105–6,
 186
Movement, the
 influence of F. R. Leavis on, 187, 191
 literary agenda of, 95–106, 186, 201;
  see also New Lines
 opposition to, 103–4, 107, 110–11,
  150
Munro, George, *Gay Landscape*,
 68–70, 74n
Murdoch, Iris, 48–9
 Under the Net, 49
Musgrove, Frank, 20, 176
Myrdal, Alva and Viola Klein, 79, 81,
 86

Naipaul, V. S., *The Mystic Masseur*,
 46–7
Nairn, Tom, 150, 158
Najarian, James, 111
nationalisation of industry, 150, 207,
 208
New Left, the, 10, 169, 172, 173,
 208–10, 218, 224
New Left Review (journal), 209
New Lines (anthology), 96, 97, 99,
 100, 101–2, 103–4, 106, 150,
 188
New Reasoner (journal), 209
New Wave films, 174, 196
Nixon, Richard, 77–8, 221
Norgay, Tenzing, 4
Norton, Mary, *The Borrowers*, 82

Oakes, Philip, 195
Orwell, George, 157
 Nineteen Eighty-Four, 40, 186, 214
 The Road to Wigan Pier, 179, 186
Osborne, John, 58, 196
 The Entertainer, 67
 Look Back in Anger, 1, 19, 39, 54,
  60–4, 66, 67, 113, 204

paperback books, 197–9, 200
Parkin, Frank, 217
Paul, Kathleen, 127, 128, 129, 130,
 141
Paul, Lesley, *Angry Young Man*, 223
Paulin, Tom, 102

Pearce, Philippa, *Tom's Midnight Garden*, 83–4
Penguin New Writing (journal), 186, 188
Pettitt, Lance, 153
Piette, Adam, 214
Pinter, Harold
  The Birthday Party, 71
  The Room, 71
Plath, Sylvia, 109
Playboy (magazine), 205
Potter, Stephen, 11, 43
Priestley, J. B., 7, 56, 63, 204–5, 217

Quatermass trilogy, 214

race riots (1958), 5, 9, 26, 33, 35–6, 83, 129, 130, 141
radio, 9, 46, 48–9, 95, 134, 158, 189, 196
Rattigan, Terence, 55, 60, 61
  The Deep Blue Sea, 72, 113
  Separate Tables, 56, 61, 72–3, 113–14
Rebellato, Dan, 56, 57, 60, 209
Renault, Mary, *The Charioteer*, 118–20
Richards, Audrey, 30–1
Ritchie, Harry, 9, 39, 40, 179, 180, 181, 185, 194, 195, 196, 197
Roberts, Andrew, 129
Rose, E. J. B., 129
Rosenfield, Claire, 25
Ross, Alan, 163, 181–2
Rowse, A. L., 3–4
Royal Court Theatre, London, 39, 56, 58, 59, 60, 62
Rudd, David, 83

Said, Edward, 47, 145
Salinger, J. D., *The Catcher in the Rye*, 38
Sapphire (film), 141–4
Scholarship Boys, 7, 10, 44, 49, 64, 71, 165, 167, 174, 176, 185, 191, 192
science fiction, 213–15
Scott, George, 9, 63, 204, 223–4
Scott, J. D., 97, 100, 223
Scottish nationalism, 150

Scrutiny (journal), 187, 188, 190, 205
Selvon, Sam, *The Lonely Londoners*, 129, 137–8, 140, 181
Shellard, Dominic, 55, 56, 60, 68, 225
Shute, Neville, *On The Beach*, 218
Sillitoe, Alan, 196
  'The Loneliness of the Long Distance Runner', 47–8
  Saturday Night and Sunday Morning, 179–81, 197–200
Sinfield, Alan, 48, 71, 120, 123
Sitwell, Edith, 44, 192, 201
Smith, Stevie, 108–11
Snell, K. D. M., 145
Snow, C. P., 187–8, 200–1
  The New Men, 211
Spark, Muriel, *The Comforters*, 51–3
Spender, Stephen, 188–9, 224
Stevenson, Randall, 70
Stoney, Barbara, 83
Storer, Richard, 190, 191
Storey, Mark, 109
Stubbs, Patricia, 52
Suez crisis, 5, 204, 209, 219
Sutherland, Graham, 212–13, 214
Sutherland, John, 210, 219

Taylor, D. J., 179
Taylor, Elizabeth
  Angel, 88–9
  A Game of Hide and Seek, 86–8
Taylor, John Russell, 6, 54, 55, 71, 169
television, 3, 8, 82, 164–5, 195, 196, 214
theatre censorship *see* Lord Chamberlain
Theatre Workshop, 57–8, 59, 68
Thomas, Dylan, 98, 201
  Under Milk Wood, 159–62, 167
Tolkien, J. R. R., *The Lord of the Rings*, 82
Tomlinson, Charles, 103–4, 106
Townsend, John, *The Young Devils*, 24
Toynbee, Philip, 192
Tynan, Kenneth, 19, 27, 54–5, 59, 60, 61–3, 73, 204

Universities and New Left Review (journal), 209

Wade, Stephen, 158, 159, 161, 178
Wain, John, 43, 54, 95, 96, 185–6, 196, 200, 201–5
  Hurry on Down, 43
Wandor, Micheline, 63, 64, 68, 69
Warth, Douglas, 114, 121
Waterhouse, Keith, 25–6, 33–4
  Billy Liar, 44
Waters, Chris, 114, 116
Waugh, Evelyn, 163, 203, 204–5
Webster, Wendy, 78, 127, 130
Welfare State, the, 2–3, 7
Wesker, Arnold, 63–4, 69
  Chicken Soup With Barley, 169
  I'm Talking About Jerusalem, 171
  Roots, 60, 169–71
Wickenden, James, 83
Wildeblood, Peter, 114–15, 117–18
Williams, Francis, 7–8, 31–2, 221

Williams, Raymond, 147, 157, 166–7, 171, 172, 173, 188, 189, 191
  Border Country, 167–8
  Culture and Society, 10, 155–6, 169
Wilson, Angus, 39, 58–9
  Anglo-Saxon Attitudes, 120–1
  Hemlock and After, 121–3
Wilson, Colin, 10–11, 49, 192–5, 196
Wilson, Elizabeth, 80, 85, 86, 95, 124
Wodehouse, P. G., 202–3
Wolfenden Committee and Report, 113, 115, 122, 225
Woods, Gregory, 113, 122
Wyndham, Francis, 139
Wyndham, John
  The Chrysalids, 215
  The Day of the Triffids, 215–17
  The Kraken Wakes, 215

Young, Michael, 171